PRAISE FOR

Revival Culture

In this day and age, I don't know any informed believer who would say that all is well with the Church in the United States. But what can be done to pull the Church out of its malaise? One of the most practical answers to this vital question comes from my friend Michael Brodeur. As I read *Revival Culture,* chapter after chapter I saw numerous glimmers of light that together can point us to a bright and shining future. You will love this book and be greatly encouraged as you read it!

C. PETER WAGNER
Vice President, Global Spheres, Inc.

In this groundbreaking book, Michael takes the wisdom and experience he gained from more than 30 years of ministry in one of the most challenging cities in our nation and translates it into a practical guide that will enable us to reach the lost and bring them into a culture of sustained revival. Michael, along with his co-author, Banning Liebscher, provides a unique perspective and fresh insights into the purposes of God for the coming season. I strongly recommend this book.

DR. JIM GARLOW
Senior Pastor, Skyline Church
Chairman, Renewing American Leadership

We are living in the time of the greatest harvest in the history of the Church! The center of global Christianity has shifted to the southern hemisphere. Today, 80 percent of churches in the world are non-white and non-western, and 65 percent don't have paid pastors, a building or meet on Sunday. They don't need those "wineskins" because they are growing without them. *Revival Culture* addresses some of the key issues about this worldwide phenomenon and how it will shape and develop as the harvest expands. Michael Brodeur has written a timely, insightful book for those who don't want to be left behind in what God is doing.

FLOYD MCCLUNG
All Nations, Cape Town, South Africa

Revival Culture explores some of the dynamics that can prepare us for not only the awakening we need but MUST have. This book will give you fuel to feed your faith for a bright future of Kingdom reality and add some nuts and bolts of practical understanding of what new generations of Kingdom seekers are all about. Michael and Bill Johnson serve as veterans of the Jesus Movement, and they have time-tested, godly wisdom to share for those inquisitive young disciples who dare to ask how they can prepare the ground for a new visitation of the Holy Spirit. Michael's co-author, Banning Liebscher, adds insights from today's battlefield of conflicting worldviews that oppose such a visitation and also offers answers based on God's Word. Until the awakening comes, *Revival Culture* will get us ready.

DANNY LEHMANN
Hawaii Leader, Youth With A Mission

Against all odds, Michael Brodeur pastored a church in a difficult place with many spiritual and logistical difficulties. The first time I met him I was struck not only by his love for the city of San Francisco and its people but also by his obvious hunger for more of God. Having achieved much, he still looked to the horizon for more, preparing mentally and spiritually for what was to come rather than resting in what had been done. In this book, *Revival Culture*, Michael shares what he has learned over the years about the effect an outpouring of God will have on our world and what the Church can do to prepare to reap—and process—a great harvest. I highly recommend both Michael Brodeur and this book. They are gifts from God to our generation.

RANDY BOHLENDER
Author, *Jesus Killed My Church*
Director, the Zoe Foundation

Revival Culture

Prepare for the Next Great Awakening

MICHAEL BRODEUR &
BANNING LIEBSCHER

Regal

For more information and
special offers from Regal Books, email us at
subscribe@regalbooks.com

Published by Regal
From Gospel Light
Ventura, California, U.S.A.
www.regalbooks.com
Printed in the U.S.A.

Library of Congress Cataloging-in-Publication Data
Brodeur, Michael.
Revival culture : prepare for the next great awakening / Michael Brodeur
and Banning Liebscher.
pages cm
ISBN 978-0-8307-6546-1 (trade paper)
1. Religious awakening—Christianity. 2. Revivals—History.
3. Church renewal. 4. Christianity and culture. 5. Christian life.
I. Liebscher, Banning. II. Title.
BV3770.B727 2013
262.001'7—dc23
2012040719

Rights for publishing this book outside the U.S.A. or in non-English languages
are administered by Gospel Light Worldwide, an international not-for-profit
ministry. For additional information, please visit www.glww.org, email
info@glww.org, or write to Gospel Light Worldwide, 1957 Eastman Avenue,
Ventura, CA 93003, U.S.A.

To order copies of this book and other Regal products in bulk quantities,
please contact us at 1-800-446-7735.

Contents

The Greatest Awakening

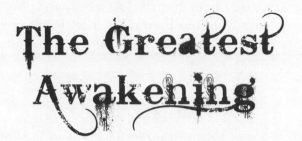

*It was the best of times, it was the worst of times, it was the age of wisdom,
it was the age of foolishness . . . it was the spring of hope, it was the winter
of despair . . . in short, the period was so far like the present.*
CHARLES DICKENS

We are living in one of the most amazing yet challenging times in
human history. During the last 100 years, there has been more tech-
nological development, medical advancements, economic increase,
cultural breakthrough and educational expansions than all of the
rest of history combined. Human discovery and development seems
to have no end in sight. At the same time, our moral and spiritual development—especially in the Western world—has remained flat at
best and, in many cases, has declined dramatically. The rise of secular humanism and the subsequent popularity of moral relativism
has given birth to a generation without a map and without a com-
pass to guide its journey into the future.

On the one hand, we are amazed by innovations such as the Internet, video cell phones, DNA mapping, genetic research and face
transplants, to name just a few. On the other hand, we are grieved by
the latest election results, statistics on teen pregnancy, abortion,
child abuse, poverty, pornography and a thousand other negative
sociological indicators. It is not hard to see that our planet is in trouble. A line in the movie *Jurassic Park* sums it up well: "Your scientists
were so preoccupied with whether or not they *could*, they didn't stop
to think about whether they *should*."

MICHAEL BRODEUR & BANNING LIEBSCHER

Yet while many are being crushed by discouragement, I find myself growing in anticipation and excitement, and this is the reason why: Every time humanity has lost its way and pursued a self-destructive path, God has been right there to intervene in the course of human events and bring about a phenomenon that has become known as "revival."

What Is Revival?

"Revival" is one of the most powerful words in the English language. Just as there is no reality more ultimate, final and irreversible than *death*, there are few things that are as miraculous as the raising of the dead. Revival is the spiritual resurrection of a person, congregation, region or nation that has lost its first love and grown cold to the passion and purpose that blazes in the heart of God. Revival is the rebirth of consecration and devotion in the lives of those who have grown complacent and have been compromised by a lifestyle that has become encumbered by the cares of this world.

Revival is the restoration of the *power* of God to the *people* of God. It leads to great awakenings and brings transformation to hungry hearts and hurting communities. Revival is the recovery of the great *purpose* of God; that His kingdom would come and His will would be done on earth as it is in heaven (see Matt. 6:10).

If you look back over the history of the Church and examine the topography of God's kingdom activity, the mountain peaks that are most memorable are those seasons in which God revived His people to transform their world. This is why from generation to generation the possibility of revival has given vision and hope to mighty men and women of God who have been unwilling to settle for a religious structure devoid of power and passion. This is also why aspiring revivalists have been willing to spend countless hours of intercession and untold days of fasting in hope "against hope" that someday spiritual revival and awakening will come.

Revival happens when the people of God awaken to the realization that Jesus is everything and this world offers nothing that can compare with the riches of complete devotion to Him. This realization brings forth repentance for wasted hours, misplaced priorities and puny passions. Revival is the personal and corporate encounter with God in which the cumulative and convicting work of the Holy Spirit reaches a fever pitch. Much like two tectonic plates in dynamic tension, the resulting earthquake shakes everything that can be shaken. During revival, the humble recognize the call of Jesus and respond to it without reservation.

The Urgent Need for Revival

Throughout the ages, scholars have studied revival to try to answer a crucial set of questions: How does revival begin? What combinations of factors are necessary to make revival happen? What is God's role in revival? What is our role? What people groups are most susceptible to revival? I would like to add some additional questions that haven't been asked often enough: Can revival be sustained beyond the few short years that have typically characterized various awakenings throughout history? What can we do to prepare for revival? What can we do to maximize the impact of revival when it happens?

This book has been written to help answer these questions and to help the Body of Christ prepare for revival.

Many prophets and prognosticators are predicting that during the next decade more than one billion souls could come to Christ. This would constitute a global harvest of souls that would dwarf any other move of God in history. In fact, in parts of Asia, Africa and Latin America, this massive harvest is already well underway. Sadly, the Western world is lagging behind and the impact of the people of God in Europe, North America and Australia has fallen dramatically. Western culture has been infected by demonic thinking and infested by forces that are opposed to God and His good purposes for this planet. We see this in the fact that many of the images and ideas carried in movies, music and media within the Western world today promote priorities and passions that enslave people to lives of futility and self-destructive behavior.

To make matters worse, we live in a world that is shrinking on a daily basis. The Technology Revolution has made it possible for people everywhere to access information at a massive rate. In addition to the many benefits that technology offers, such as computers, smart phones, the Internet, satellites, Facebook, Twitter and YouTube, they have also made it possible for harmful images and ideas to find their way to major population centers and key universities in non-Western nations as well. Young people everywhere are coming under the spell of a post-modern/post-Christian worldview. Sadly, as often happens, the enemy has seized the day and the Church is playing catch-up.

There is an urgent, growing need for a revival on a massive scale to reverse the momentum of these destructive trends and return this planet to the blessings that God originally intended. I believe we are sitting on the cusp of such a revival and that the first fruits are already visible in key centers around the world. Over the last couple of decades there has been wave, upon wave of outpourings of the Holy Spirit that have empowered many churches and believers to new levels of supernatural experience.

In fact, there are many who would call these waves of the Holy Spirit a "revival." In this sense, I would agree: When we wade into the ocean, we are "in the ocean," whether we are up to our ankles or up to our chest. In the same way, the Body of Christ in the western world is experiencing a measure of revival right now that is wonderful, even if it is only ankle deep. I am truly grateful for the measure of healing, deliverance and salvation that God has given us in this season. However, I am convinced that there is more—more healing, more freedom and more souls to be saved. No matter how wonderful our current depth of revival, it is nothing compared to the awesome fulfillment that will come when we are swimming in the deep waters of a New Great Awakening.

Let's Do the Math

Right now, there are more than 7 billion people on the face of the earth and more than 1 billion who are under the age of 20. For the first time in human history, we have the actual possibility of a billion-soul harvest. However, the generation about to come to harvest is going to be *very* different from every generation before it. The proliferation of movies, music and other forms of media have heightened the awareness level of young people—they have seen murders, sexual acts and a myriad of other images that have shaped their beliefs and behaviors.

For this reason, when revival comes, we can expect the majority of the harvest will have been influenced in this way. The question then becomes, "How do we reach this group?" And once we have reached them, "How do we help them to become wholehearted disciples of Jesus and future leaders in the Body of Christ?" In this book, I hope to present a strategy for reaching this emerging culture that is thoughtful and intelligent but also filled with supernatural power and impact. Jesus came to "seek and to save that which was lost" (Luke 19:10) and, ultimately, *a revival without souls is simply a renewal.*

Today, many leaders are talking with great excitement and anticipation about the possibility of a billion-soul harvest and a coming great awakening. However, it is troubling to me that so few people are actually doing the calculations that are needed to begin to prepare for this coming revival. Consider the following:

- It will take 10 million new pastors to care for 1 billion souls on a 1 per 100 ratio.
- This means we will need 1,000 colleges graduating 1,000 pastoral leaders per year for the next 10 years.
- One billion souls is roughly equal to 15 percent of the world's population.
- This means we need to prepare now for 15 percent of our cities to come to Jesus in the next decade.

As we consider the probability that this harvest will draw people into the Church who are mostly young, urban and post-Christian in their worldview, it doesn't take long to realize we have our work cut out for us. Furthermore, if we fail to prepare, we will be carrying on the historic pattern of the Church, which was almost never ready for the outpouring of the Holy Spirit and the great harvest of souls that followed. However, if we take the time to pray and prepare, we have the opportunity to not only change the course of human development on the earth but to also change the eternal destiny of millions of people who would have remained unreached or uncared-for after having come to Christ.

Get Ready for the Revival

This book is a preparation manual for the coming revival and the billion-soul harvest. In section 1, we will examine the current state of the world and the Church and then look at a new paradigm for retooling in light of the coming harvest. In section 2, we will focus on the obstacles and opportunities for reaching this generation and examine some of the kingdom longings in people that can provide a bridge to Jesus. In section 3, we will discuss how to cultivate revival culture in our churches and ministries.

This final section includes two powerful chapters by my co-author, Banning Liebscher, and a special contribution from Bill Johnson, which focus on the power of intergenerational ministry and how we can sustain revival in the coming generations. Banning is the director of Jesus Culture, a powerful, global ministry that began as the youth group at Bethel Church in Redding, California. Bill Johnson is the senior pastor of Bethel Church and has been used by God to bring the Body of Christ around the world into fresh understanding of the presence and power of God. I am honored to be able to lay the foundation in the first two sections of this book for the thoughts that Banning and Bill bring in the final section.

This book is not only for those with a "vision" for revival but also for those who are willing to translate their vision into reality by doing the math and taking concrete steps to prepare themselves, their friends and their faith communities for the greatest awakening humanity has ever known. It is for those who long for God's kingdom to come and His will to be done on earth as it is in heaven.

It is for those who dream of a day when the glory of God will cover the earth as the waters cover the sea. And it is for those who are possessed by a consuming vision of a victorious Church that operates in the fullness of God's presence, power and purpose and brings restoration and transformation to a fallen, broken planet.

SECTION ONE

Preparing for the Coming Harvest

*Then Jesus went about all the cities and villages, teaching in their
synagogues, preaching the gospel of the kingdom, and healing every
sickness and every disease among the people. But when He saw the multitudes,
He was moved with compassion for them, because they were weary
and scattered, like sheep having no shepherd. Then He said to His disciples,
"The harvest truly is plentiful, but the laborers are few. Therefore pray the
Lord of the harvest to send out laborers into His harvest."*

MATTHEW 9:35-38

1

The Heart of Revival

Excitement filled the air as hundreds of young people streamed into our church building in the heart of San Francisco. They came from all over the country in response to our call to commemorate the fortieth anniversary of the infamous Summer of Love and the beginning of the "Jesus Movement" revival, which is regarded by many as the last major revival that has touched Western culture. As the worship began and passionate hearts began to proclaim the beauty of Jesus, my 24-year-old daughter, Melissa, turned to me and said, "Dad, the Lord has answered your prayer."

At first, I didn't know how to take her statement. We were in the midst of a six-week prayer and outreach program called the Real Summer of Love. This outreach had already exceeded all my hopes and expectations, and I thought my daughter was saying the Lord had answered my prayer by preventing the event from becoming a complete flop.

Melissa could tell I wasn't getting it, so she said with prophetic passion, "No, Dad, this is what I mean. Twenty years ago when you were fasting and praying for revival and crying out for laborers for the harvest, God heard your cry. In response to your prayer, God moved upon moms and dads around the nation, and they came together to conceive a generation who will change the world. You thought God might not have heard you, but He did, and these young people are the answer to your prayer. It just took a while for the answer to show up."

Although I was fully aware that God did not adjust the mating habits of hundreds of couples on my behalf, my daughter's statements caused my eyes to fill with tears. God hears us when we pray, and He always answers our prayers—especially when we are praying for His kingdom to come. Even when decades go by with little or no apparent response, God is working to bring all things into alignment with His perfect will. And God's perfect will is *revival*.

This outreach in 2007 began with a handful of churches in San Francisco coming together in prayer for revival. As it grew, we put out a call to the Body of Christ around the nation to join with us as we asked God to bring a new Jesus Movement to the earth. We also created a summer internship program to help supply workers who would lead the various gatherings and ministry we were doing around the city. Hundreds of people from an amazing stadium event in Nashville known as The Call caravanned across the country to join us for this event.

We were also privileged to host dozens of leaders from three distinct generations, joining together in worship, intercession, ministry to one another and outreach to the lost. The Real Summer of Love culminated in a large gathering at the foot of the historic "Hippie Hill" in Golden Gate Park. Our speakers included Arthur Blessit, Sabine Ball and Richard Paradise—who were the older, prominent leaders in the Jesus Movement—and boomer leaders such as Ché Ahn, Lou Engle, Cindy Jacobs, Ray Hughes and Gary Goodell. We also had a number of younger leaders, including Banning Liebscher, Erica Greve, Kim Walker and Shawn Bolz.

A highlight of this outreach was an intergenerational forum to discuss the future of the Church. Each panel discussion consisted of three generations of leaders who were dreaming together about the way Christians can most effectively reach, heal, disciple, train and empower the coming generation. Many of the ideas presented in this book grew out of these powerful meetings.

Revival did not break out in San Francisco during the summer of 2007. However, like a twenty-first century Elijah, I could see the cloud the size of a man's hand, and I knew the rain of revival would soon fall upon this generation and release a spiritual harvest the likes of which the world had never seen. It is my firm conviction that the world is on the threshold of a massive global move of the Holy Spirit that will reach a billion souls for Jesus. The critical question is whether *the Church will be ready*. To this end, I am sending out a plea to the Body of Christ to prepare our hearts, lives, churches and ministries for what could be the greatest awakening in all of human history.

Hippies and Jesus Freaks

So, why did the word from my daughter touch me so deeply? Let me explain by sharing a little of my history.

Early Years in San Francisco

In December 1974, just as the flames of the Jesus Movement were beginning to die down, my relationship with God was set ablaze. I prayed to receive the Lord, which represented a 180-degree change in direction for me. I had been raised in a counter-culture household in San Francisco at the height of the Hippie Movement. My formative years were not spent in front of the television watching *Leave it to Beaver* and *Mister Ed*; instead, I was exposed to everything that characterized the 1960s and early 1970s, including sex, drugs, rock 'n' roll and New Age philosophy.

In 1960, when I was three years old, my family moved to San Francisco to escape the constraints of mid-western traditions and Roman Catholicism. By the time my parents divorced two years later, my dad had already become a beatnik artist, replete with goatee, sandals and cheap red wine. My mom, on the other hand, was drawn into the early Hippie Movement. I was shuttled back and forth between these two nonconformist households. During the infamous summer of 1967, I could be found hanging out in the Haight-Ashbury district with my best friend, who lived in the epicenter of this crazy neighborhood. I enjoyed a front row seat to a major cultural revolution that became known as "the Summer of Love."

By the time I was 10 years old, my parents had already begun to indoctrinate me into their worlds. They introduced me to marijuana when I was 11 and LSD when I was in my early teens. They taught me eastern philosophy and dabbled in the occult. From a young age, I was told that Christianity was the least evolved of all religions and was actually invented by a medieval king to control and oppress the masses. For years, that was totality of my understanding of Jesus.

Political Activism

In 1970, my mom began hanging out with a wannabe-hippie ex-convict named Ed, and we moved into a communal house in the Mission district. We hosted a revolving community of hippie freaks, including guru devotees, activists and draft-dodgers. Like I said, this was no ordinary childhood!

I became politically active at this time. I marched in rallies, protested the war and rallied for the release of various "political prisoners." I even petitioned for abortion! Some of the rallies erupted into violent altercations with the police. Once, I narrowly avoided being hit in the head by a billy club at an unpermitted protest on Market Street. In this incident, news cameras were rolling as two-dozen radicals, including me, shouted in unison, "The whole world is watching! The whole world is watching!"

During my sophomore year of high school, my mother and I left Ed. He had displayed a few major freak-outs while high on LSD and had become extremely violent toward our family and himself. My mother and I moved to Berkeley, where I attended one of the first "free" schools that was part of Berkeley High School—with the emphasis on the hippie meaning of the word "high." When I did get to class, I studied communist China, Gestalt Therapy and the evils of the U.S. prison system. For physical education, I alternated between juggling and chess. My extracurricular activities included taking drugs, exploring New Age thought, marching in more protests (People's Park was close by), and starting a rock 'n' roll band. I was the real thing.

Meeting the Jesus Freaks

One year in Berkeley was enough. The next summer, my mother, my brothers and sister and I moved to Mendocino, located about three hours northwest of San Francisco. For five months we lived in a communal campground on the Navarro River with about 80 other hippies while we looked for a house. During this season of my life, I first met my first Christians, or what we called "Jesus Freaks." I was impressed with the quality of their commitment to what they believed, but I was turned off by their narrow-mindedness and the exclusivity of their faith. I would ask questions and argue, but I never seriously considered becoming a follower of Jesus.

As a teenager, I began to hitchhike around North America. Jesus Freaks would often pick me up, and invariably they would boldly share their faith. During one trip, just before my eighteenth birthday, I had received six rides in a row from Christians, each of whom felt an urgent need to share Jesus with this poor hippie sinner. Finally, after I was dropped off in a little town called Boonville, I remember looking to heaven and saying, "God, what's up with all the Jesus Freaks? What are You trying to say?"

No sooner had I finished my little prayer than a car pulled over and the driver offered me a ride. I found myself sitting next to a little German woman dressed in a frock that made her look a bit like a nun. Her name was Sabine Ball, and she was the most notorious Jesus Person in Mendocino County. I had heard of her, but I never dreamed that I would meet her.

Sabine witnessed to me as we traveled for the next 25 miles. She did her best to convince me that Jesus was the only way to God, but I was so prejudiced against this "unenlightened" belief system called Christianity that I argued with her the whole way. I was quite proud of how brilliantly I had countered all of her arguments. I was in top form, but so was God. When Sabine let me off at the Navarro Bridge, she asked if she could pray with me. I cautiously agreed, and as she prayed I felt something inside me yield. That was the day I opened my heart to Jesus. My life soon began to change.

Encountering Christ

I had already been exploring a host of spiritual pursuits—including yoga, Tai Chi, Sufi, and Subud (which claimed to be an Islamic "Pentecostal" movement)—but all along I had found myself strangely

attracted to Jesus. I had read New Age books about Jesus, such as
the *Urantia Book*, the *Aquarian Gospel* and the *Essene Gospel of Jesus
Christ*. I knew these books were misguided and filled with false-
hood, but at the time they presented aspects of Jesus that were
more appealing to a guy like me.

A few days after my prayer with Sabine, I was sitting on my bed
doing my regular morning meditations when suddenly I saw the
silhouette of three figures. I heard a voice ask me, "Are you ready
yet?" I knew immediately what the voice was talking about. In spite
of all my supposed spirituality, I was still living for myself. I was
doing drugs, playing music and involved in immoral relationships,
and all the while I was pretending to be serious about God. After
evaluating my life, I remember replying, "No, I'm not ready . . . at
least, not yet."

Then the scene changed, and I was face to face with Jesus on
the cross. He was bloody and in excruciating pain. I had never seen
this image before, but as I stared, I heard a voice say to me, "When
you follow Me, it will be to your death." Today I know this is called
an open vision, but when it happened to me then I didn't have a
clue as to what was going on. I was simply floored. I knew it was
only a matter of time before I would die to everything other than
this amazing Man who had died for me.

Beginning Discipleship

As I look back, I believe I was truly born again when I prayed with
Sabine. However, because I had no foundation in Scripture and
no fellowship with true believers, I was left defenseless against the
internal and external forces that were using everything in their
power to keep me from following Jesus. At the same time, my attraction to Christ and my understanding of His life and mission
began to grow, and I found myself gradually beginning to step
away from sinful things and turning toward the Lord.

A year later, while hitchhiking through Montana, I met a
Blackfoot Indian named Floyd "Tinyman" Heavyrunner in the
reservation town of Browning. Tinyman was a big Indian with
long, black braids and traditional native jewelry. He made his liv-

ing building teepees for tourists and hippies. At the time he was not a follower of Jesus.

Tinyman introduced me to his grandparents, Albert and Agnes Wells, who, despite being well into their seventies at the time, invited me to live with them and learn about Jesus. This amazing couple had become Christians several decades earlier after receiving a visitation from the Lord while drinking in a bar. Dozens of people witnessed this encounter and dove under tables or ran out of the bar screaming. The Lord healed Albert that day of severe intestinal bleeding due to rot-gut liquor. He said to him, "Sober up and follow Me." Albert and Agnes told me about seven different visitations they had experienced over the years in which Jesus would come to them, teach them from Scripture, and commission them to new dimensions of ministry. This was an amazing and almost unbelievable story, even to a hippie who had seen it all. I am not sure I would have believed it, except for the fact that their lives and the fruit from their faith backed it up completely.

Albert's ministry touched thousands of people from Great Falls to Calgary, Alberta, and continued strongly for more than 40 years. By the time I met him, he was mostly retired, except for the meetings he held at his shack near Browning and the visits he would make to hospitals and homes to pray for the sick and see them healed. Albert later told me that when I showed up on his doorstep, the Lord had told him that I was His beloved son and that he was to care for me and lead me into the truth. Somehow, Albert and Agnes saw something of value in this hippie kid from San Francisco, for which I am eternally grateful. This was where my discipleship began.

These Blackfoot Indian believers were not focused on religious dogma but on the power of God to heal, deliver and save. Their continuous encounters with the supernatural world ultimately convinced me of the reality of Jesus in a way that doctrinal teaching alone could not have done. In my case, sound doctrine followed my realization of Jesus that came through witnessing His power. The apostle Paul referred to this kind of conversion when he said to the Corinthians, "My speech and my preaching were not with persuasive words of human wisdom, but in demonstration of the Spirit and of power, that your faith should not be in the wisdom of men but in the power of God" (1 Cor. 2:4-5).

These Indians were authentic believers, filled with grace and still walking in many of their cultural traditions that were not contrary to the gospel of Jesus. They were not fearful or reactionary, nor were they judgmental and controlling. They were filled with love, acceptance, mercy and joy, the likes of which I have rarely seen since that time. This part of my discipleship experience was perfect for me, as there was an absolute absence of using shame as a means of producing obedience to God.

I admit that I wasn't the average candidate for salvation, as I was raised in one of the most radical environments and had no knowledge of Jesus Christ. I would not have been attracted to a typical church of that era, nor is it likely that I would have been able to survive in that environment, for the average church of that day was antithetical to the cultural world in which I was raised. So God, in His wisdom, set me up with the perfect "church"—a motley group of Blackfoot Indians living on an impoverished reservation in the middle of nowhere. No self-respecting hippie on earth would have ever rejected a chance to live with Native Americans!

Training for Ministry
After six months of studying the Bible with Albert and Agnes and witnessing many awesome miracles, I returned to Northern California to join a Jesus People ministry. This group offered on-the-job ministry training and just happened to be planting a church in San Francisco. So after spending several months at their training center called Lighthouse Ranch near Eureka, California, I moved back to San Francisco as part of a church planting team in September 1977.

By the time I started my training as an apprentice minister, the fires of the Jesus Movement had begun to die down to glowing embers. I heard stories of the glory days of the movement during the early 1970s—friends of mine would tell me of dozens of people coming to Christ on a daily basis on Haight Street. I marveled at the stories I heard of hundreds of people being baptized each week on the beaches of Southern California, and I met others from Europe and Australia who had come to the Lord during that time and experienced similar outpourings of the Spirit.

All of these amazing stories of how God worked so powerfully in my generation filled my heart with excitement and joy, but eventually they gave birth to a deep and growing sense of holy frustration. During this season, I had witnessed to the lost at every opportunity, taking people off the streets into our discipleship house to help them grow in Christ. I had co-founded a ministry called SOS San Francisco, which mobilized hundreds of believers from dozens of churches to share their faith on the streets and parks of our city. Yet for all these efforts, I was seeing only limited fruit. I knew God was with us, yet compared to the stories of what God had been doing a few years earlier, it seemed like I had missed out.

Pursuing Revival
Although I was frustrated, I was also determined. I decided to pursue this thing called "revival" and started to do some research. I read every book on the subject that I could get my hands on and talked to anyone who had some knowledge of the subject. I started with the writings of Leonard Ravenhill, J. Edwin Orr and Winkey Pratney, and soon I was diving into books about the Great Awakenings, Charles Finney and the Azusa Street Revival in Los Angeles.

Two items from my research stood out to me. First, during the last 2,000 years there have been times and seasons in which God would move among a certain group of people in a certain region. A spiritual revolution would occur, and hearts and even cities would be transformed for Christ. However, in almost every case the revival lasted only for a short time, and the Church at large rarely received it. This troubled me. I began to fast and pray on a regular basis for an outpouring of the Spirit that would release the same harvest I had heard so much about but had only barely experienced.

The second item about revival that stood out to me was that in almost every case, the revival took the Church by surprise. In fact, one of the primary factors that influenced the limited duration of the revival was the lack of preparedness on the Church's part. This shouldn't have been a surprise to me, because the Church that existed at the time of my salvation wasn't really prepared for me, either. This lack of preparedness in the Church can be clearly seen in the events that transpired after the Jesus Movement of the 1970s.

The Origins of the Jesus Movement

During the mid-1940s, near the end of World War II, an unusual sociological phenomenon occurred that has become known as the "Baby Boom." Young men returning from the war began to settle back in to married life and conceive one of the largest and most influential generations in history. Not only was there a population surge, but the trauma of a major world war combined with the satisfaction of a conclusive victory over fascism pressed a massive "reset button" that ushered in a new period of optimism and success.

The boomers born in this Post-World War II optimism became largest, most prosperous, best-educated and most idealistic generation in American history, and their impact on Western culture was immense. As early boomers were coming of age in the 1960s, JFK was assassinated, the civil rights movement grew, and, for the first time, television coverage of the war in Vietnam brought the bloody battlefield into living rooms across the nation. The conscience of this emerging generation responded with rallies, riots and sit-ins, which increased in size and impact during the next decade.

In the midst of these amazing political, economical and cultural shifts of the 1960s, the boomers began to experiment with drugs and New Age ideas. This gave birth to a utopian quest that culminated in 1967 as the Summer of Love. Thousands of young people flocked to San Francisco and other key centers to join a new counterculture characterized by drugs, sex and rock 'n' roll. From there, the hippie movement grew into a cultural revolution that swept across the United States and Europe.

A True Countercultural Movement

Unfortunately, it didn't take long for this idealism to turn sour with the deaths of Jimi Hendrix, Janice Joplin and Jim Morrison and the introduction of hard drugs such as heroin and cocaine. The beautiful, quintessential experience of the Woodstock Festival was followed by the Hell's Angels murders at Altamont Speedway. "Peace and love" soon degenerated into various expressions of pride and selfishness. The hippie dream was shattered.

It was during this season that God answered with a true countercultural movement of His own, which soon became known as the Jesus Movement. Tens of thousands of young people began to reject the assumptions and conclusions of hippie philosophy and started to experience a spiritual hunger that could be filled only with Jesus. By the early 1970s, thousands of young people had begun to follow Jesus with a dedication that mirrored the fervor with which they had previously pursued their sin. Many of those who considered themselves hippies found true peace and love in a living relationship with the Lord Jesus Christ.

This movement captured the attention of the national media. In the summer of 1971, *TIME* magazine published an article on the Jesus People Movement that documented this amazing move of God's Spirit, and other magazines followed. By this time the movement was in full swing, and thousands were coming to Jesus all over the western world. My wife, Diane, came to the Lord in the early 1970s and was baptized on a beach called Corona Del Mar in southern California, along with hundreds of other young people. A friend who witnessed regularly on Haight Street in San Francisco told me that a "bad" night of sharing his faith was when only 10 people would come to Christ. These stories were repeated a hundredfold in Seattle, San Diego, New York and dozens of other cities around the world. There is no doubt that hundreds of thousands of young people came to Christ around the world.

The Church's Response

Unfortunately, few of the young people who were saved during that time had the same "tailor-made" discipleship experience I had. Most came to Jesus as a result of the supernatural work of the Holy Spirit, who drew them to the Father and convicted them of "sin, and of righteousness, and of judgment" (John 16:8). The work of the Spirit was then catalyzed by the witness of a radical believer, who probably made all kinds of mistakes in the process but had a faith so passionate and authentic that the contagion spread in the fertile heart prepared by God. This convergence of the Holy Spirit and a faithful witness produced a potent and saving faith, and as a result, hundreds of thousands of people were born again and filled with the Holy Spirit.

For the most part the Body of Christ, the Church, was absolutely unprepared for the new babies who were being born again around them. Figuratively speaking, these newborn believers had no crib, no changing table, no nursery and no diapers. They were dirty, they cried uncontrollably, they spit up regularly, and they left messes in their diapers several times a day. As a result, the Church often treated them as orphans or foster children rather than true sons and daughters who held in their hearts the destiny of the people of God.

In the early 1970s, only a few churches accepted these long-haired, dirty, braless hippie believers. Most didn't want them soiling their pews or even sitting on their new carpets. Too many traditional churchgoers had no comprehension or value for what God had done by saving a generation. Instead, they looked on with natural, human eyes and failed to behold the sovereign work of the Holy Spirit. Sadly, many of these new believers experienced outright rejection or conditional acceptance. "If you cut your hair and wear a suit like the rest of us," they were told, "then you can be a part of our church."

Other churches and leaders who embraced this counter-culture harvest reacted in ways that were harmful to these new believers. Some, recognizing the rebellious spirit that was on this generation, instituted a series of teachings and structures that later became known as the Shepherding or Discipleship Movement. New believers were told to submit to their elders and pastors in a way that, in many cases, was abusive and destructive. On the other hand, some groups drifted into cultic beliefs and behaviors and even into licentious practices like those of the Children of God, who used sex and drugs to lure new recruits into their group.

Although many mistakes and failures were committed in response to the Jesus Movement, there was also a strong percentage of leaders who perceived what God was doing and rose to the challenge. New kinds of churches began to emerge. Rock bands replaced organs as the sound of worship changed. New teaching styles were born as the new Christian counterculture found its voice.

Revival Culture in the Jesus Movement

The *Merriam-Webster Dictionary* defines "culture" as "the integrated pattern of human knowledge, belief, and behavior that depends upon the capacity for learning and transmitting knowledge to succeeding generations: the customary beliefs, social forms, and material traits of a racial, religious, or social group."[1] In the light of this definition, "revival culture" is an active set of values, priorities and practices that are developed and embraced to support and sustain the work of the Holy Spirit in revival.

In the Jesus Movement on the West Coast, a new kind of revival culture began to emerge. Yet this revival culture began to take on different forms in southern California as compared with their counterparts in the northern part of the state. These different expressions of revival culture can be best examined as we look at two prominent ministries of this era: Gospel Outreach and Calvary Chapel. Gospel Outreach began near Eureka, California, and emphasized true discipleship, laying down your life for Jesus, planting churches and reaching the lost. Calvary Chapel, based in Southern California, emphasized the basic teaching of the Word of God, pastoral care and friendship evangelism. The churches born out of this second group tended to be larger, more inclusive and less controlling.

Gospel Outreach

Soon after my conversion, I returned to Northern California and started looking for a place where I could be trained for ministry. I didn't want to go to Bible School because I didn't want to sit in a classroom for two years—I wanted to be out doing something for God. When I learned that Gospel Outreach was planting a church in San Francisco and they provided on-the-job ministry training, I was sold. I moved to a place called Lighthouse Ranch for six months and went through an initial training process with their ministry. Then, in the fall of 1977, I was sent to San Francisco to be part of a church-planting team and establish a Kingdom reality there in the city.

Jim and Dacie Durkin became the leaders of Gospel Outreach in the early 1970s. They operated in a fresh vision for discipleship, leadership development, and pioneering new churches around the world. Gospel Outreach took raw-recruit believers who had just come to the Lord out of dark lifestyles and brought them to a place of real submission to God's Word and the principles of His kingdom. Gospel Outreach trained them in leadership, organized them into teams, and then sent them out. The organization also built a strong culture of discipleship and personal revival that carried the ministry through two decades of significant impact.

Although Gospel Outreach believed in the supernatural, it was not a primary emphasis. Instead, their definition of revival culture had more to do with high-profile evangelism and a believer's total consecration to Jesus. As a result, most of the people who came to Jesus had radical and powerful conversions, which propelled them into a high level of commitment to Jesus and to one another. Gospel Outreach was thus able to reinforce its culture quickly and effectively, because most of its members lived in communal situations, either on ranches or farms or in communal houses in cities. This solidified their culture and made it very powerful.

Calvary Chapel

One of the most influential leaders to embrace the Jesus Movement was a Foursquare Pastor named Chuck Smith. In 1968, while pastoring a small church in Costa Mesa, Chuck was introduced to Lonnie Frisbee. Lonnie had experienced a powerful encounter with God and had given his life to Jesus. After spending some time in the San Francisco Bay area, Lonnie moved to Southern California and helped Chuck give birth to the Calvary Chapel movement. Since that time, the original Calvary Chapel in Costa Mesa has grown to a congregation of more than 9,500. The Calvary Chapel movement has 1,500 daughter churches around the world.

Calvary Chapel had a different approach to building revival culture. As I mentioned, they were open and non-controlling, and they emphasized the systematic teaching of Scripture and connection with the Holy Spirit in what they called "Afterglow Gatherings." The combination of these gatherings, amazing worship and a fierce commitment to the line-upon-line teaching of God's Word gave them a framework that lent itself to a contagious revival culture. They experienced a massive move of the Holy Spirit, and hundreds of people were baptized every weekend.

Even though the northern Jesus people often questioned the consecration level of their southern counterparts, Calvary Chapel was able to see amazing growth and impact. They were able to turn the revival of the late 1960s and mid-1970s into one of the most vibrant and powerful church movements in recent history. Calvary Chapel grew quickly, and their churches are now found all over the world. Currently, 10 of the top 25 largest churches in the United States are Calvary Chapels, and they have the highest conversion growth rate as compared to other churches and movements around the country. Although Calvary Chapel is quite different from many churches that are currently pursuing revival, they remain an undeniable source of our current move of God and have been able to sustain their unique expression of revival culture throughout the years focusing more on personal salvation and teaching rather than the supernatural gifts of the Holy Spirit.

An Army of Young People

Through these two distinct revival models, God moved in the Jesus Movement to raise up an army of young people who had dedicated their lives to Christ and were living for His kingdom. Sadly, the majority of those who *did not* come to the Lord during this period went even deeper into depravity, hedonism, false philosophy, and eastern religions. As for those who did give their lives to the Lord, by the late 1970s many were starting families, settling into jobs, and embracing suburban lifestyles in comfortable churches. These boomer believers who were born again with a dream to transform the world gradually found themselves drifting into lifestyles of mediocrity and compromise. To a great extent, the Kingdom Dream had been replaced by a worldly counterfeit called the American Dream.

During the last 30 years, the majority of boomer believers have gradually moved away from "alternative" churches and ministries and into mainstream Christianity. Most of those in current leadership roles in the Church, however, came to Christ either directly or indirectly as a result of the Jesus Movement. If we are on the cusp of a similar revival, it would be a tragedy to miss it because we failed to learn the lessons of the past! For this reason, it is crucial for us to address our lack of concern and preparedness *now* so we don't fail to prepare the Church for the huge harvest—perhaps even one billion souls—that is coming. We need to be able to recognize the signs of its approach so we do not repeat the same costly mistakes made a generation ago.

Prepare for Revival

Jesus was the first to recommend prayerful preparation for a spiritual harvest. We need to follow His admonitions and His example and prepare as well.

Jesus Prepared the Field

"Jesus went about all the cities and villages, teaching in their synagogues, preaching the gospel of the kingdom, and healing every sickness and every disease among the people" (Matt. 9:35). Jesus led His disciples in a circuit of ministry through the various towns and villages in Galilee, where He declared the gospel of the Kingdom with signs and wonders. His message was more than just a message of salvation; it was a message of God's kingdom violently breaking into the natural realm to destroy the powers of darkness and restore humanity to God's original purpose. He demonstrated this truth by healing the sick and casting out demons. In so doing, He plowed up needy hearts and prepared them to receive the gospel seed. In the same way, we need to prepare for the coming harvest by consistently recommitting ourselves to sharing the gospel of the Kingdom.

Jesus Saw the Multitudes

"But when He saw the multitudes, He was moved with compassion for them, because they were weary and scattered, like sheep having no shepherd" (v. 36). Jesus did not merely see the people through His natural eyes; He saw them through the eyes of the Spirit. He could have established their value according to their successes and failures, or through the eyes of religion as horrible and rebellious sinners, or through the eyes of judgment as reprobates beyond the scope of redemption. But instead, He saw them through eyes of compassion. He viewed them as victims of oppression, ravaged and scattered by sin. Likewise, we need to take a fresh look at the harvest and allow ourselves to be moved with compassion for the lost.

Jesus Called His Disciples to the Harvest

"Then He said to His disciples, 'The harvest truly is plentiful, but the laborers are few. Therefore pray the Lord of the harvest to send out laborers into His harvest'" (v. 37). From God's perspective, the harvest is always abundant. The Father constantly scans the horizon for the prodigal to return home, and when He sees the lost one coming, He drops everything—including protocol and decorum—and runs to embrace that child (see Luke 15:11-32). We need to be like that. We need to take responsibility for the harvest. It is not someone else's job; it is ours.

Jesus Told His Disciples to Pray for Prepared Laborers

"Therefore pray the Lord of the harvest to send out laborers into His harvest" (v. 38). It is interesting that Jesus never told us to pray for the harvest itself; rather, He tells us to pray for the laborers. What do we pray? We pray that the soil will be filled with the necessary nutrients for growth and that the seed we are planting will be appropriate to the soil and weather conditions. We pray that we will pay close attention to the prime moment for harvest. We pray that we will thresh the wheat carefully and, above all, make sure our silos are dry and prepared to carry the harvest into the future. We partner with heaven in prayer for skilled laborers to enter the harvest, and we prepare ourselves to be the answer to our own prayer.

Jesus Empowered and Instructed His Laborers

"When He had called His twelve disciples to Him, He gave them power over unclean spirits, to cast them out, and to heal all kinds of sickness and all kinds of disease. . . . These twelve Jesus sent out and commanded them, saying: 'Do not go into the way of the Gentiles, and do not enter a city of the Samaritans. But go rather to the lost sheep of the house of Israel. And as you go, preach, saying, "The kingdom of heaven is at hand." Heal the sick, cleanse the lepers, raise the dead, cast out demons. Freely you have received, freely give'" (Matt. 10:1,5-8).

Jesus empowered the 12 disciples and gave them the ability to heal the sick and cast out demons. Then He sent them forth with specific instructions about where they should go, what they should say, what they should bring, how they should respond to rejection, and how they could succeed. The disciples had to embrace this lifestyle fully so they could bring in the harvest of souls. In the same way, we must repent of complacency and compromise and embrace a lifestyle that fosters a faithful witness so we will be ready when the harvest begins.

The Harvest Is at Hand

I am convinced that a massive harvest is at hand. It will likely be the largest awakening in all of human history, and in many regions of the earth, it is already underway. It has yet to fully manifest in the Western world, but I can see a cloud the size of a man's hand on the horizon. Just as Elijah told Ahab to prepare for rain (see 1 Kings 18:44), the time of drought is over and the time of harvest is drawing near.

2

The Big One

Just a few years ago, our planet was rocked by one of the greatest natural disasters in history. For decades, two adjacent tectonic plates deep under the surface of the Pacific Ocean had been deadlocked, trying to go in opposite directions. On December 29, 2003, the stress of the impasse built to the point where it erupted just off of Sumatra, causing a violent earthquake five miles under the ocean floor. The quake displaced massive amounts of water, and the subsequent tsunami brought death and destruction to many nations and hundreds of thousands of people.

Since this cataclysmic event, there have been many earthquakes around the globe. However, none of these came near to equaling the magnitude of this devastation until 2010, when the earthquake in Haiti killed an estimated 250,000 people. Earthquakes can be one of the most destructive forces in nature—especially when we are unprepared for them.

I have lived most of my life in San Francisco, where earthquakes are fairly common. Since the larger quakes of 1906 and 1989, there have been a number of smaller tremors (in fact, there are small quakes somewhere in California virtually every day), but nothing too significant. In the Bay Area, which is built on a shelf between two shifting tectonic plates, earthquakes are inevitable. However, today scientists talk about the "Big One," and how it's not a matter of *if* this massive earthquake will hit, but a matter of *when*.

In the study of earthquakes, seismologists refer to places of "higher stress" and "lesser stress." The point where the greatest strain erupts is called the "hypocenter," a word that comes from Greek that literally means "below the center." The "epicenter," which comes from both Greek and Latin words meaning "upon or over the focal point," is the place where the projection of the eruption reaches the surface of the earth. It is at the epicenter where scientists normally register the highest reading on the Richter scale and observe the greatest impact.

There are also different kinds of earthquake faults. Some are minor lines that run like fractures under the earth. Others are major lines that indicate the actual tectonic plates of the earth, like the ones that created the Sumatra earthquake.

Just as there are geological earthquakes, there are also sociological earthquakes. History is full of examples where ideas, governments or economies collided and ground together until they released a devastating "quake." Consider Mao's overthrow of China, or the French Revolution and the bloody takeover of the Bastille, or even the American Revolution, where a mere colony accomplished an astounding victory over the feared and powerful British Empire. Intense clashes during the Civil Rights movement in the 1960s pushed through a massive cultural shift, as did the fall of the Soviet Union and the end of the Cold War in the 1980s.

Collisions between historic traditions and new perspectives, left-wing and right-wing political structures, older and younger generations, social classes, races and cultures have often given way to sociological earthquakes of massive change in relatively short periods of time. Sometimes these changes occurred for the better, and sometimes not. Yet there is more to the story. When we take a closer look, we see that the majority of social earthquakes have been accompanied or immediately followed by a wonderful work of the Holy Spirit, which we have come to call revival.

The Epicenter of Time and Eternity

Jesus lived in a time of seismic upheaval. The Roman Empire was at its zenith. The Romans had installed a puppet government in Israel, imposed severe taxes, and were keeping legions of soldiers in the land as a humiliating reminder that the once great kingdoms of David and Solomon had been reduced to servitude and submission. As the tectonic pressure between these two nations became unbearable, the people of Israel began to cry out for the Messiah who had been foretold throughout Scripture. They assumed their conquering King would save them from Rome. But God had a different plan.

Parallel to these earthly stresses, an even greater tectonic stress was growing between the invisible realm of heaven and the visible realm of earth, with each going in an opposite direction. The forces of heaven were bearing down upon the residents of a rebellious planet who stood in defiance of their loving Creator. The more God wooed, the more humankind resisted. In the "fullness of time," (Gal. 4:4), God the Son laid aside His divine prerogative, became flesh, and lived as a mere man filled with the Holy Spirit. The seismic stress between heaven and earth grew. Every healing, deliverance, and miracle that Jesus performed was an assault against the forces of evil that had usurped dominion in the visible realm.

But it wasn't until Jesus was betrayed and crucified that the "eternal earthquake" occurred. When He "who knew no sin" became "sin for us" (2 Cor. 5:21), the massive strain between heaven and earth was released in an event so significant that it pierced eternity. This is why Jesus is called "the lamb slain from the foundation of the world" (Rev. 13:8).

While the cross is the quintessential seismic moment of all time, heaven and earth remain in an ongoing friction. In fact, the history of the Church can be summed up as a series of ideological, cultural, economic, political and religious stress points that built up over a period of time and eventually produced an upheaval. I call this the "seismic theory of revival."

A Brief History of Revival Culture

I am not a historian, nor have I earned a Ph.D., but I have studied revival, history and the Bible. My theory is this: revival is the result of God's sovereign work in the invisible realm set in dynamic stress with human events in the visible realm. The prophet Isaiah spoke of this when he depicted a great clash between light and darkness and prophesied the light would prevail because the glory of the Lord has risen upon us (see Isa. 60:1-2).

This theme of the clash between God's will and human will is repeated in numerous ways throughout Scripture. As this stress between heaven and earth increases, it creates a growing hunger in the human heart for heavenly things. When cultural stability and spiritual receptivity are at their lowest points, revival is most likely to happen. We see this dynamic in the Early Church, which some actually say thrived *because* of the persecution and martyrdom they experienced. As Tertullian said, "The blood of the martyrs is the seed of the Church," and we see this same phenomenon at work during the first few centuries of the Church's existence.

The Early Church remained a revival force to be reckoned with until it began to be legitimized during the reign of the emperor Constantine in AD 312. Once Christianity was institutionalized as the state religion, the persecution no longer came from without but from within. Syncretism and corruption accomplished what 300 years of persecution could not—it began to dilute the power of true faith and pollute the Church's revival culture to a point almost beyond recognition. What followed was a millennium of darkness appropriately called the "Dark Ages."

The Protestant Reformation (1500s)
The Protestant Reformation, which officially began in 1517 when Martin Luther posted 95 theses against the Catholic Church on the door of All Saints' Church in Wittenberg, Germany, occurred in the midst of great religious persecution and political oppression. It was also a time of incredible social and cultural upheaval. The trauma of plagues and the Black Death were fresh in the people's hearts. The collective hunger for meaning and understanding had reached an apex as the arts, sciences, education and political reforms of various kinds began to emerge with increasing power. Added to this was the new technology of the printing press.

All of these comprised the ingredients of a cultural revolution. Although Luther, Zwingli and Calvin, the primary Reformation leaders, were imperfect men who even fought among themselves, they were able to stand in defiance of the power of the Roman Catholic Church and release fresh faith to the multitudes. They saw a new level of religious freedom and a true spiritual awakening.

During the next century, the Protestant movement continued to develop. Eventually it gave birth to the Puritans, who wanted a greater "purity" of worship and doctrine and believed the Church of England had not gone far enough in distancing itself from the practices of the Catholic Church. Eventually there was division and persecution, and many Puritans fled to New England to begin a new life. Although the Protestant Reformation never fully manifested as a revival in the classic sense of the term, the reforms that were sought and implemented laid the foundation for the First Great Awakening.

The First Great Awakening (1600s)
The First Great Awakening hit England and the American colonies during a period of moral decline and rising social/political unrest. Winkie Pratney, who has researched revival in depth, notes that during the late 1600s, drinking had become rampant, immorality was at an all time high, prisons were nightmares, hangings were public entertainment, and gambling was a typical pastime.[1] In addition to this social and moral decay, there were also epidemics of disease, major economic crises, and social transitions. All of these factors contributed to the spiritual hunger that gave rise to the First Great Awakening.

As with most revivals, once the tinder was placed and the wood positioned, it only took a catalytic spark to set the fire ablaze. In the case of this awakening, there were three significant sparks set by three very different leaders: John Wesley, George Whitefield and Jonathan Edwards. The First Great Awakening was largely a revival of churchgoers and had a particular impact on the youth. In my opinion, it was the Jesus Movement of the eighteenth century.

Of the three principle revivalists, Edwards was by far the most theologically prolific, and he left us a wealth of teaching on the ways of God in revival. Whitfield, on the other hand, was perhaps the truest evangelist in the group, and he led multitudes into life-changing encounters with God. Wesley was arguably the most apostolic of the three, and he was the only one who was able to build a sustained "revival culture." He developed what became known as the Methodist Movement, and throughout his lifetime he trained and mobilized hundreds of ministers to preach the gospel and establish churches throughout England and the American colonies.

John Wesley taught his followers the need for a holy lifestyle. The resulting Christlikeness they nurtured in their lives spilled over into society, catalyzing all kinds of social transformation. Wesley's life and work ultimately led to the abolishment of the slave trade, educational reform, prison reform throughout the British Empire, and the development of new regulations to protect child laborers. In a BBC survey conducted in 2002, the English voted John Wesley to be the most influential man in British history.[2] As we lead by serving and allow passion for God to influence all we do, our revival culture will affect every sphere of society in a powerful way.

The Second Great Awakening (1700s–1800s)

Less than a century later, rationalism had again gained a foothold, this time sweeping through high society and the universities. According to Pratney, several factors combined in the United States that led to an economic collapse in the 1850s, including people's greed and a focus on prosperity and getting ahead, a popular interest in the occult and the supernatural realm, immorality and a free-love philosophy, rampant corruption in the business and political worlds, and a growing national apathy, atheism, and overall indifference to God.[3] The Second Great Awakening was God's response to this social morass, and it set in motion movements that continue today.

The Second Great Awakening began in the late 1700s at camp meetings in Kentucky and continued into the mid-1800s. The revivalists of the time, such as Charles Finney and the Methodist circuit preachers, sought to correct and re-emphasize aspects of the gospel that had been neglected. They stressed a lifestyle of purity and holiness and focused on changing their communities for Christ. Finney remains one of the most effective evangelists in history, leading more than 500,000 people to salvation without the use of loud speakers or other media. He built an amazing revival culture. In fact, it is believed that 10 years after their salvation, more than 85 percent of his converts were still burning for the Lord.[4]

During this time in the mid-1800s, another compelling example of this seismic theory of revival took place in China when Hudson Taylor established the China Inland Mission. At the time, Taylor was considered a radical by many of his missionary peers, but within a generation he was being heralded as a forerunner of modern missions. In his lifetime of work in China, it is estimated that he led more than 18,000 people to the Lord and established 300 ministry bases throughout the country.[5]

During the next 50 years the Church in China grew slowly and steadily, though it was definitely hindered by the people's extreme poverty and their rising resentment against Western and Japanese imperialism. The tectonic pressure between the ruling class and the poor continued to build until civil war broke out across the land in 1927. When the communist faction finally won control over the nation in 1950, it expelled all foreign missionaries and outlawed the practice of Christianity. In the midst of this upheaval, aftershocks of the communist victory, and the subsequent Cultural Revolution, Christians were forced underground. A massive house church movement began which, during the last 50 years, is estimated to have grown from under a million people to as many as 80 million believers.[6]

The second half of the nineteenth century—which is sometimes referred to as the Third Great Awakening—saw the rise of a new wave of leaders such as D. L. Moody, George Williams (founder of the YMCA), and David Livingstone. Hudson Taylor became the premier advocate of focusing missions efforts on areas of the world that had yet to be reached with the gospel. General William Booth, founder of the Salvation Army, also rose amid the major problems of urbanization and industrialization. He brought about major reformation in the lives of many who were ravaged by poverty and drunkenness and was instrumental in reforming child labors laws in England.

The Pentecostal Awakening (Early 1900s)

The next major awakening to impact the earth was the Pentecostal Revival, which began in Southern California in 1906. In the years leading up to the events of what is called Azusa Street, God began to move around the world in amazing ways. Most notable of these movements was the Great Welsh Revival that took place in 1904. At the time, turn-of-the-century Wales was a dark land, full of violent crime, but by the time the outpouring waned it is estimated that as many as 100,000 people had given their lives to Jesus.[7]

The revival affected all areas of Welch society. Some of what had been the most lawless regions had no arrests during the revival, while in other areas entire prisons were emptied. Men stopped drinking and gambling and started taking their wages home instead. These factors, coupled with the fact that large groups of people became convicted of the need to pay back their debt (and actually started paying it all back), boosted the economy of the whole region.[8]

The Welsh Revival sparked a move of the Holy Spirit around the globe, including in India, Burma, South Africa and Argentina. Eventually, the movement inspired the revival led by William Seymour at Azusa Street in Los Angeles. What happened at Azusa Street birthed a new movement of corporate hunger for the Holy Spirit and His gifts, and Pentecostalism still bears more fruit internationally today than most other movements of the Holy Spirit in history.

The Jesus Movement (Mid-1900s)

As I have noted, the most recent "Great Awakening" was the Jesus Movement, which is a poster child for the theme of this book—the seismic theory of revival. Let's take a look at this revival from this seismic standpoint.

By the mid-1960s, the Western world had found itself in a time of major social, political and cultural upheaval. In the United States, women's rights, gay rights and rights for minorities became front-line news. The anti-Vietnam War movement—marked by the anti-draft movement, sit-ins, demonstrations and riots—picked up steam until it culminated in the shootings at Kent State in 1970.

By the early 1970s, drug use and psychedelic music had become popular. Meanwhile, civil wars tore newly independent African countries apart, communism took over China and Eastern Europe, and the Cold War between the USA and the USSR began to cast a shadow over the rest of the world.

Christianity worldwide was losing ground both to the secular state as well as to Eastern religious thought. A generational gap began to tear apart families and communities around the country as post-World War II baby boomers—the largest generation of all time—turned against the generations before them and resolved to never trust anyone over 30. The more-than-30 crowd was by and large unable to understand and embrace the longhaired, activist, hippie, pinko, commie kids.

It was in the midst of this season of upheaval that God began to move in an unprecedented way, and we believe He is about to do it again.

The Big One Is Coming

A little more than 40 years have now passed since the Summer of Love and the start of the Jesus Movement. It's only a matter of time before we experience a New Global Jesus Movement that will be far greater in scope and impact than any other move of God in history. As I mentioned, many believe this will involve more than one billion souls.

At first glance, this idea of a "billion soul harvest" may seem like an outrageous fantasy, but if we take a closer look, we can see that this magnitude of harvest is not only possible but also probable. In fact, this is really the first time in history that the world's population is large enough for a billion-soul harvest to be a reasonable expectation. In 1900 the population was around 1.6 billion, and by the mid-1960s it had only grown to 2.6 billion. During the last 40 years, it has more than doubled to almost 7 billion, and just under half of these (around 3 billion) are under the age of 25. This is a key figure because in most harvests, the vast majority (more than 75 percent) is young. Furthermore, there are a number of sociological factors that are working together to create the perfect environment for the gospel to touch billions in the coming years. We will examine these next to determine how they are indicators of coming revival.

Sociological Indicators
During the 1980s and 1990s, much of the focus of emerging culture was on personal contentment, career and consumerism. During Ronald Reagan's presidency, we enjoyed a decade of relative prosperity and safety. We also witnessed the fall of the Soviet empire and the end of the Cold War. Perhaps because cultural, economic and political pressures were at a low point in comparison with other eras, the tectonic stress was also low. However, seven months after George W. Bush assumed the presidential office in 2001, an international crisis occurred that caused the tectonic plates of culture to begin to grind again. Now we find ourselves in another unpopular and unconventional international conflict, this time with extreme Islam instead of Soviet communism.

The terrorist attacks of September 11, 2001, made this a defining day for America. The horrible attacks by militant Islamists on American soil cascaded with other world events to increase social pressure around the globe. The war on terror, global warming, homosexual and abortion "rights," the global financial recession, and issues of poverty, human trafficking and AIDS have all provided the necessary factors for a new activism. The nuclear family is coming apart at the seams because of divorce, abortion and gender confusion. And the advent of new Internet technologies provides the possibility of a social and cultural earthquake that could be greater than any other in history.

At this moment, we are in the midst of seismic stresses that rival anything that has happened in the past. The good news is that God is moving and is using all these tectonic tensions to prepare the earth for a New Great Awakening.

As is typical with every generation, the Boomers who grew up in the 1960s and 1970s eventually returned to a more traditional mindset, similar to that of their parents. All over the world, traditional, collective mentalities are clashing with a Western consumerist individualism that has been promoted through technology and media. Because traditional perspectives are being abandoned, the emerging generation is growing up in a world without clear standards or absolutes—partially the result of what sociologists have termed the "postmodern mindset." In other words, the youth of this generation are being raised in the absence of clear definitions of right and wrong. Relativism and New Age values have permeated the culture and created an environment hostile to Christian beliefs. This new worldview is more than simply a reaction to the traditional thinking of the past; it is an entirely new way of viewing truth. It has gone global and could be the greatest challenge to evangelism that the Church has ever known.

At first glance, all these sociological factors may seem negative or even hopeless, yet these pressures and tensions can also work together for God's purposes. These factors are a perfect setup for the kind of societal earthquake that can open the hearts of men and women seeking a deep, life-transforming revelation of Jesus Christ.

Spiritual Indicators

On the spiritual level, many other indicators point to the fact that we are approaching a season of Global Harvest. Never before in the history of the Church has there been such a universal focus on revival. Interest in the history of revival has been growing in various denominations and spiritual streams across the globe, and there is a worldwide increase in fasting and prayer. Houses of Prayer are springing up in hundreds of locations around the world to mobilize intercessors for revival prayer. The International House of Prayer in Kansas City, Missouri, for example, has recruited around 1,000 full-time supported prayer missionaries who have been interceding 24 hours a day for years; and Lou Engle and The Call have been gathering stadiums full of mostly young prayer warriors around the world to pray for revival and justice for the unborn.

A signs and wonders movement has also been steadily growing, which is indicative of the kind of supernatural empowerment that typically precedes a revival. A principle forerunner of this movement was John Wimber, who in 1982 led Vineyard Ministries International and provided a theological and practical bridge for mainstream Christians to understand and function in the supernatural. His legacy continues in several streams, including the Toronto Renewal, led by John and Carol Arnott; and the Bethel movement, led by Bill Johnson (who has contributed a chapter to this book). These two streams in partnership with other leaders, such as Ché Ahn, Randy Clark, Roland and Heidi Baker and the movements they represent, have become a force for revival in the nations and are laying the theological and supernatural foundations for a mighty move of God.

Prophetic Indicators

Another spiritual indicator that we are about to witness a massive global revival is found in prophecy in Scripture. Although many dispensational theologians would refute the idea of an "end-times harvest," we find many indicators in the pages of the Bible that indicate revival is coming as we approach the end of time.

The prophecy in Joel 2:28-32 (also quoted by Peter in Acts 2) represents the quintessential promise from God for His people during the last days. In this passage, God says that He will pour out His Spirit on all flesh during this period of time. When Peter cited this passage, he had no idea that the period he inaugurated would last 2,000 years. However, if the application of this Scripture was true in the first century, it is even more true today.

Another important passage found in Revelation 7:9 describes a vast multitude standing before the Throne of God from every tribe, tongue and nation that no man can number. According to the Joshua Project, there are still upward of 40 percent of the world that would be considered unreached or less-reached at the present time.[9] To bridge from this percentage to the description in Revelation 7:9 will require a massive move of God's Spirit.

Regardless of whether one believes in the pre-tribulation rapture or not, most acknowledge that hard times will be coming in increasing frequency as we approach the end times. For some, hard times are all they can see. Yet if we examine the Scripture carefully, we find that many of the prophets—including Isaiah, Jeremiah and Daniel—also foretold of a victorious Church in the last days. Jesus Himself, who gave us the Great Commission to make disciples of all nations and promised His ongoing presence to aid us in the fulfillment of this task, told us that "this gospel of the kingdom will be preached in all the world as a witness to the nations, and then the end will come" (Matt. 24:14).

Legacies of Revival

If we fast-forward through Church history, we find rich legacies of revival in every region of the globe. Somehow, during two millennia, the gospel has been preached; and, in turn, someone told it to someone who told it to someone. The message has even touched the city of San Francisco, which, some say, could be considered the "end of the earth" (Acts 1:8).

Although we have a tremendous amount of work ahead of us, it's important to understand the ongoing fulfillment of Jesus' commands and realize that He who has begun a good work will complete it (see Phil. 1:6). It's also good to note that since the time of Jesus, there have been believers who foresaw the forward motion of the gospel culminating in a massive harvest at the end of time. If we review the last hundred years, we find many significant leaders who predicted this as well. As the prophet Amos said, "Surely the Lord GOD does nothing, unless He reveals His secret to His servants the prophets" (Amos 3:7). There is a consistent unity among many leaders in the prophetic movement that revival is coming.

One hundred years ago, a revival broke out in a Los Angeles barn that has become one of the most important moves of God's Spirit in history. William Seymour, one of the main leaders of what became known as the Azusa Street Revival, prophesied in 1910 that another great spiritual outpouring would sweep the earth in 100 years. Around the same time, Charles Parham, a leader in the Pentecostal Revival, also prophesied another great move of God happening in 100 years.[10]

Thirty years after Parham and Seymour's prophecies, Smith Wigglesworth spoke of a revival coming as never before. He saw multitudes upon multitudes being saved, diseases of all kinds falling before the power of the Lord, and the dead being raised back to life. "It will be a worldwide thrust of God's power and a thrust of God's anointing," he wrote. "I will not see it, but you will."[11] Since that time, the Church has continued to be reawakened to the value of the gift of prophecy and the important role prophets have in equipping the Church for service. Prophets around the world are seeing and declaring a worldwide, massive harvest focused primarily on the younger generations.

In 1948, coinciding with the re-founding of the nation of Israel, a significant outpouring of the Holy Spirit occurred that became known as the Latter Rain revival. Erskine Holt described this period as a season in which every member knew his or her calling and was activated in ministry. The works of the Spirit were a daily occurrence, and signs, wonders and healings were commonplace. Many people came to the Lord and were filled with the Spirit. Yet after two years, the intensity of the Spirit's work seemed to subside. As the anointing was lifted, the Lord spoke through one of their prophets that this outpouring was just a foretaste of the Global Revival that would be released on the earth in the last days.

Bill Bright, the founder of Campus Crusade for Christ, was a great man of God, though no one would ever confuse him with a Pentecostal. As I have already mentioned, toward the end of his life he stated that the Lord had revealed to him there was coming a great harvest of a billion souls.[12] In 1975, Bob Jones received a similar revelation when he was given a vision of two massive lines. In one line stood the majority of humankind, wrapped up in their own gods. In "God's line" stood maybe two percent of humanity. Jones then heard the words, "I'm going to bring a billion souls unto Myself in one great wave."[13]

Other prophetic leaders, including Cindy Jacobs and Chuck Pierce, have repeated this vision and prophesied a coming harvest that will touch the earth. Paul Cain saw entire football stadiums filled with people, worshiping God on their faces and bringing their sick to get healed. He heard the words, "We have a resurrection!" Following this, he saw news anchors say on the air they had no major negative news to report—only good things. One of the points that stands out about Cain's prophecy is that the people he saw in these stadiums and auditoriums were faceless. They looked so much like Jesus that he couldn't see them as individuals.[14]

Just a couple years ago, Stacey Campbell, a prophetic leader from Canada, saw a billion-soul harvest that looked like living stones of all different kinds, sizes, ages and shapes, all fitted together in a unified container for Jesus. She said, "The harvest is so big it cannot be contained in one structure."[15]

The Scripture warns us that "we know in part and we prophesy in part" (1 Cor. 13:9). I am sure that none of these prophetic leaders would claim perfect character or absolute accuracy, yet there are so many words and visions given over the course of the decades that describe different aspects of the same thing. God *is* preparing for one last, massive, global harvest that will be led by a generation of nameless, faceless people who give all the glory to Him. The younger generation in intergenerational partnership, along with spiritual fathers and mothers, will each play a key role.

Preparing for the Big One

On October 17, 1989, the eyes of the world were glued to their TV sets for game 3 of the World Series between the Oakland Athletics and the San Francisco Giants. The game was just about to start when two opposing landmasses along the famous San Andreas Fault released decades of built-up pressure. The resulting Loma Prieta earthquake registered a 6.9 on the Richter scale. Sixty-three people were killed, thousands were injured, and millions of dollars in real estate was destroyed. Yet even though this was a major quake, it was still not the long awaited "Big One."

In the immediate aftermath of the Loma Prieta earthquake, fear gripped the population and people began to restock their pantries and invest in emergency kits. However, as usually happens, over the course of the next months the seismologists' warnings grew less frequent, and vigilance turned to apathy. In the same way, the shaking of the previous generation in our country has given way to decades of cultural passivity. Unfortunately, this same pattern of moving from preparation to passivity is repeated in many other areas of life, including the area of revival.

Many indicators point to the fact that our world is on the verge of a tremendous upheaval not at all dissimilar from the "Big One" that scientists believe will hit California. Societal and spiritual pressures are increasing around the world, and as the tectonic plates of political, economic and cultural conflict press against one another, the invisible plates between heaven and earth also increase in dynamic stress with one another. There's got to be a release, and it's coming soon. Yet the question remains: "Will the Church be ready?"

The Sleeping Giant

I have had the privilege of serving in many aspects of the church world for more than 35 years. I have done children's church, led worship, conducted outreach, led home groups, discipled people and even done janitorial work. I have also had the great honor of serving as a full-time senior pastor for more than 25 years. Today, I can say I love the Church of Jesus Christ. I love the global Church in all its ethnic beauty and manifold diversity, and I love the local church with all its strengths and weaknesses.

As I mentioned in chapter 1, in the fall of 1977 I moved to San Francisco to be part of a Gospel Outreach church planting team, where I received on-the-job ministry training. After completing six years of intensive preparation, Gospel Outreach approved me for ordination. However, before the ceremony occurred, it became evident to Diane and me that God was moving us into a different kind of ministry.

In early 1984, while on a ministry trip to the Northern California beach town of Santa Cruz, I met two men who radically impacted my life: John Wimber and Lonnie Frisbee. I had heard of these two men many times before, and I was overjoyed to finally be able to spend time with them. Wimber had been the pastor of Calvary Chapel of Yorba Linda, where the Holy Spirit had moved in an amazing way. This fresh outpouring eventually resulted in a parting of ways between Wimber and Calvary Chapel leader Chuck Smith, and Wimber went on to lead a whole new movement called the Association of Vineyard Churches. As a result of my interaction with these two men, I began to experience a level of revival culture that I had never known before.

At the end of our visit, John invited me and my wife to attend a conference in Anaheim called MC510: Signs, Wonders and Church Growth. This conference was based on a curriculum that Wimber had been teaching at Fuller Theological Seminary along with other C. Peter Wagner and Charles Kraft.

Signs, Wonders and Revival Culture

MC510 was a pivotal point in our lives, for it was during this conference that Diane and I received our first major impartation of the Holy Spirit and began to move in the power of God at a much higher level. Up to this point, we had a theology for the Holy Spirit, spoke in tongues, operated to some extent in spiritual gifts, and had even seen a few healings and miracles, but after this conference everything accelerated at warp speed.

I received prayer a number of times during the week of the MC510 conference, and at one point I was deeply touched by the Holy Spirit. I had asked for prayer during one of the ministry times, and several people had gathered around me and laid hands on me. I immediately began to feel something like a warm oil being poured over me. I trembled slightly and felt as if I were falling over. The person behind me kept me from falling, and they continued praying. When the group finally ended 10 minutes later, I was alternating between weeping and laughing as I felt the tangible love of God.

On returning home, Diane and I attended a small gathering and were asked to share about the conference. As we began to talk, something we had never experienced before began to happen. A woman in the front row slid out of her seat and began to scream and writhe on the floor. We had seen a couple of deliverances at the conference, so, when compared to everyone else in the room, we were the experts. God moved in a wonderful way, the woman was set free, and others received powerful ministry that night. Although we were still reeling from what we had experienced, Diane and I left the meeting filled with awe and wonder.

Word got out quickly that God was moving, and over the next several months we found ourselves ministering to scores of people.

One encounter we had was with a woman named Susan, who had only recently accepted the Lord. Soon after her conversion, she started to experience layers of demonic manifestation in her life. For instance, she would wake up with bite and scratch marks on her back in places where she obviously couldn't have reached herself.

A mutual friend brought Susan to us, and we prayed and commanded the demons to come out. There was a violent manifestation, but the demons didn't budge. We prayed again and commanded the demons to go, but the same thing happened. The demons manifested and spoke to us, but they refused to leave. We spent about six hours with this girl, and by the end of that time, we were *exhausted*.

Finally, Diane said, "Hey, we just need to stop and ask the Lord for more help."

So we asked the Lord for help. Suddenly, Diane saw a series of words in her mind's eye. They were written in English, but the syllables were difficult to pronounce.

"Do these words mean anything to you?" she asked Susan. As Diane "read off" what she was seeing, the girl's eyes widened. "That's my mother's maiden name in Chinese," she said.

We were just as amazed as she was. We sent the girl home and told her to go talk to her mom. We told her to ask if her mother's maiden name had any meaning to her in relationship to what she was experiencing.

A few days later, Susan came back with the story of her birth. Her mother had gotten pregnant out of wedlock, and her father had reluctantly decided to marry her because he was honor-bound to do so. When her mom started to experience the symptoms of miscarriage, she said to herself, *If I lose this baby, this man will no longer be bound to marry me.* So she went to the Temple and made a deal. She *allowed* the baby to be infested by demonic spirits in order to preserve the pregnancy and keep her fiancé.

As soon as we had this information, we were able to help Susan, and her life radically changed from that moment.

Diane and I realized that the power of God was working in our lives in a way we hadn't experienced before. Word got out that we had an anointing for revival and the "doctor bag"—that is, we knew how to "do the stuff." This began a whole new journey for us as we entered a phase of personal revival.

At this point we were hungry for more equipping, so we attended several other conferences. One was called "Wimber on Wagner." It took place during the fall of 1984, and in the conference John Wimber and C. Peter Wagner spoke on how signs and wonders work within a church growth context. We had an amazing encounter with Jesus as the Lord spoke to us that the Vineyard was our home. In those meetings, something was truly transmitted to us that was independent of our desires and abilities.

We began to pray, fast, and seek the Lord about whether we were to plant a Vineyard church. Within a matter of days, we received several clear confirmations that we should, so we ended up starting a Vineyard church with four people in our living room. During the course of the next year, we grew rapidly, trained leaders and launched five different small groups. By the time we started on Sunday mornings in the fall of 1985, we had about 80 people.

Our church continued to grow over the next few years and became one of the biggest churches San Francisco had seen in a generation. We were able to lead hundreds of people to Jesus, see hundreds of people healed, and raise up hundreds of leaders and send them out. We established a thriving school of ministry and planted more than a dozen churches and ministries around the globe. God led us into a 15-year season of extreme fruitfulness, during which time I also became an area director and, ultimately, a district overseer in northern California for the Vineyard Movement.

All this gave me a ringside seat to understand the revival culture that Wimber had fostered within the Vineyard Movement.

Vineyard Renewal and Revival Culture

I believe that when the Kingdom annals of the twenty-first century are written, John Wimber will be widely recognized as one of the most influential men of his era. *Christianity Today* agreed, selecting his seminal book *Power Evangelism* as one of the most important books that shaped evangelical Christianity from 1950 to 2000.

Wimber began as the founding member of a music group called the Righteous Brothers, which had a profound impact on popular culture during the early 1960s. But when he came to the Lord during the mid-1960s, everything changed for him.

In the early days of his faith, he was a prolific minister. By his estimates, he led more than 3,000 people to the Lord through personal evangelism and small-group ministry. He became a successful pastor, and then went on to work with an Evangelical Friends Church and help C. Peter Wagner develop the Fuller Institute of Church Growth. Obviously, Wimber was gifted in terms of understanding the mechanics and spiritual dynamics of "church."

When Wimber went to work with Calvary Chapel in the late 1970s, God began to move in a powerful way. Wimber's hunger for the presence and power of the Holy Spirit released a major wave of renewal that many have called the "Third Wave of the Holy Spirit." This term came out of the recognition that the Pentecostal Revival during the early 1900s was the first wave of the Spirit, and the Charismatic Movement of the 1960s was a second wave. Now God was moving in a third wave of outpouring and renewal.

Wimber soon withdrew from Calvary and began to work with a handful of churches founded by an amazing leader named Kenn Gulliksen. Gulliksen invited Wimber to take the lead, and the rest is history. In this way, the Vineyard movement was built with a strong foundation of *revival culture,* and Wimber became widely known as one of the greatest living experts on the "science" and "art" of church.

Wimber was one of the rare individuals who valued the presence and power of God immensely but also valued healthy structures to contain that power. He brought clarity to the Body of Christ about the need for well-defined values and priorities that form the building blocks of culture. While he was not a perfect man and did not build a perfect movement, by the grace of God he was able to empower a generation into a greater experience and understanding of worship, supernatural power and Kingdom impact than ever been before.

Wimber affected many things simultaneously. First, he affected the mainline churches (mostly Baptist, Methodist, Presbyterian, Episcopal, Nazarene and similar denominations) by giving them a fresh understanding of the Holy Spirit while, at the same time, avoiding some of the challenges traditional Pentecostal theology had created. As he bypassed some of those issues, he was able to present an entirely different theological rationale for signs and wonders in the Holy Spirit. His teachings were based on what many have called "Kingdom Theology," which was derived from an innovating and powerful way of interpreting Scripture found in the writings of George Elton Ladd. Wimber was at the very cusp of Kingdom understanding, affecting Fuller Seminary and many other seminaries around the world with his teachings.

In addition to this, Wimber was also able to bring to the Body of Christ an entirely new understanding of worship and the power of God's presence. He pioneered Vineyard Music Group, which released dozens of albums and remains on the cutting edge of Christian worship to this day. Churches around the world today still sing worship songs by David Ruis, Andy Park, Brian Doerksen and dozens of other Vineyard worship leaders.

Wimber was also able to institute large conferences that didn't merely *teach* people but actually *trained* them. People left his meetings with practical skills they could apply the very next day, and they also received a measure of *supernatural impartation* that was rare at that time. People came away prepared to pray for the sick, the wounded and the broken hearted; cast out demons; and plant churches. Wimber was able to bring a level of empowerment that had not been traditionally accepted. Eventually, Wimber came under attack from more conservative fundamentalists, especially people who believed that signs and wonders had passed away. I think the amount of criticism he received had a negative effect on the last years of his ministry. Yet by every measurement, Wimber was a game changer. The revival culture he established—though, once again, not perfect—was able to foster and carry forward a move of God that remains influential around the world to this day.

Wimber shaped my love for the Church and my understanding of the importance of revival culture. During his meetings I experienced an amazing impartation of the power and presence of God that remained for the next 15 years. In fact, it never really stopped; it just went through different ebbs and flows. And because I experienced this significant revival season in the Vineyard—and also watched as things began to change—I am more convinced than ever that God desires to empower His Church to cultivate a revival culture that will last for generations.

Revival Begins in the Church

I am committed to the Church's fruitfulness and fulfillment, so whenever I hear anyone speak negatively about the Church, I get a little defensive. If such talk weren't so damaging, it would be almost amusing to hear young leaders criticize and undermine the Church. Sometimes I wonder if they really understand the heart of Jesus toward His Bride. It is sad to see the reactionary attempts of disgruntled people to re-engineer the Church, especially when what is needed is not a new expression but a new heart.

Even so, it doesn't take 30 years of ministry to recognize that, with a few wonderful exceptions, much of the Church is broken, particularly in the Western world. The Body of Christ is injured and ailing. The Bride is in need of an extreme makeover that goes beyond the superficial remedies that many church-growth experts offer. So, at the risk of sounding like another expert, on the pages that follow I will respectfully offer my assessment of the problems, a diagnosis of the illnesses, and a brief prescription for healing. But first, we need to take a look at what Jesus intended the Church to be so we can establish a clear plumb line to revival.

Jesus' Original Intention for the Church

When God created Adam and Eve, He made them in His own image so they might discern and display His greatness and His goodness. When they sinned, it not only disrupted the personal relationship between God and two humans but also dislodged

the relationship between God and all humanity. Yet almost immediately, God set in motion a redemptive plan that culminated in
His becoming flesh to establish a new creation—a new humanity
upon the earth.

Even as the first Adam fell and lost his heavenly connection, Jesus came as a last Adam to reclaim what was lost and restore to
humanity the possibility of God's original intent: to bring forth a
people who would experience and express His glory. This restoration begins when an individual gives his or her life to Jesus and is
born again by the inner work of the Holy Spirit. Yet this work of
restoration is not complete until the person commits himself or
herself to a community of believers who covenant to join their lives
together to display God's glory.

We are individual sons and daughters of God and have been
empowered by Jesus to bring the good news of His Kingdom to
the world in word and deed. Yet as amazing as each of us is in
Christ, we were never intended to walk out our faith alone in isolation. We were created for community. As we embrace our corporate calling as an entirely new species of being, we will not only
fulfill God's original intention but also usher in God's kingdom,
which was inaugurated through Jesus' life and ministry on earth
(see 1 Pet. 2:9-10).

The Foundation of the Church

The Greek word for "church" is *ecclesia*, which means the "community of the called out ones." In ancient times, the word was used to
describe a gathering of elders at the city gates who convened to
make decisions and render judgments. Jesus was the first to use the
word in Matthew 16 in response to a question He posed about who
people said He was. Peter had risen up and declared, "You are the
Christ, the Son of the Living God" (v. 16), to which Jesus replied:

> Blessed are you, Simon Bar-Jonah, for flesh and blood has
> not revealed this to you. . . . And I also say to you that you
> are Peter [stone], and on this rock I will build My church
> [*ecclesia*], and the gates of Hades shall not prevail against

it. And I will give you the keys of the kingdom of heaven, and whatever you bind on earth will be bound in heaven (vv. 17-19).

Jesus' statement begins with a play on words that has caused scholars to debate whether He was referring to Peter as the rock or whether the revelation that Peter received was the rock. I think it is both. Peter was the premier apostle for the first decade of the church, and Scripture says that the Church is built upon the foundation of the apostles and prophets, with Jesus as the foundational cornerstone (see Eph. 2:19-20). The Church is founded upon the apostolic declaration of Jesus and His kingdom.

Now, as we consider Jesus' words, it is important to remember that what Jesus called the Church had little resemblance to the building on the corner that we call church today. Jesus' expression of church was actually more like a mobile training school that included the 12 disciples (see Luke 9:1-2), the women who ministered to Him (see Luke 8:1-2), and the 70 others who went before Jesus two by two (see Luke 10:1-2). It was more like a spiritual apprenticeship program than a community of people who needed to be fed and cared for. What Jesus built could more accurately be defined today as what we call a "missional community."

The Growth of the Church

When Jesus was betrayed, this community was still a large ministry team that served Him by managing crowds and feeding multitudes. After His death, this band of people scattered until rumors began to spread that He had risen from the dead. During the next 40 days, Jesus appeared to many of His disciples in various settings; the largest gathering was numbered at 500 (see 1 Cor. 15:3-6). Jesus commanded His disciples to wait in Jerusalem until they were filled with power from on high (see Luke 24:49), after which they would fulfill the "greater works" Jesus had earlier promised and be His witnesses (see John 14:12; Acts 1:8).

A little more than a week later, the saints were gathered together in an upper room when the Holy Spirit fell on them and filled them with power. On that day, the Church was born. Instantly, it grew from 120 to 3,000 members, and it continued to grow daily as the Lord added to them those who were being saved (see Acts 2). Throughout the period recorded in the book of Acts and the remainder of the first century, the Church increased in a powerful way until the gospel had reached the ends of the known world. In spite of all the Church's failures and fractures, it has continued to grow from heart to heart and fill the earth with the declaration and demonstration of the glory of God.

God could have chosen angels to proclaim His word. He could have spoken directly from heaven and revealed Himself to a fallen world. But instead, He chose us to proclaim His message—a frail and fault-ridden people whom He has forgiven, healed and filled with His power. We are Plan *A*, and there is no Plan *B*. God has made every provision for us to fulfill the Great Commission that Jesus gave to us, but sadly we have all too often failed to understand and appropriate it.

Waking the Sleeping Giant

In the classic tale *Gulliver's Travels* by Jonathan Swift, Gulliver is shipwrecked on a remote island and falls asleep on the shore from sheer exhaustion. When he awakes the next morning, he finds himself paralyzed from the neck down. After his initial shock, he discovers he has been bound by 100,000 tiny ropes that to him look like threads. He wants to tear away from the ropes, but there are a dozen tiny people standing on his chest, chattering to him in a tongue he can't understand.

Fear, shock and exhaustion overtake Gulliver, and he falls back into a deep sleep. A few hours later, he wakes to find that he—and his ropes—haven't moved. His mind is clearer this time, however, and he decides he isn't going to let his fate be determined by a tribe of six-inch-tall terrorists. He strains against the cords; first one arm, and then the other. He braces himself against the sand, and his body rises as the little ropes snap away. He sits up, ignoring the protests of the little guards, and swats aside a barrage of tiny arrows. Standing to his feet, he towers over his captors, who now run for cover.

Like Gulliver, the Church is a sleeping giant. It was created by Jesus to be His body, hands and heart upon the earth. But after 2,000 years of storms, the western Church has become shipwrecked on the shores of this world system. It has found itself so bound by the tiny hindrances of consumerism, complacency, compromise, cynicism and criticism that it has reached a point of paralysis and ineffectiveness.

In the remainder of this chapter, I would like to take an honest look at each of these "ropes" that bind many of our churches and many of us as believers. In so doing, my goal is to show how we can break free of them and become the Church that God intends us to be. Note that I intentionally present these five ropes in extremes, knowing that there are many exceptional churches that are wholeheartedly pursuing God's purposes and many sincere believers who are maintaining true faith and a true expression of Kingdom life on the earth.

The Rope of Consumerism

A few years ago, the Christian world was shaken by a public announcement from one of the largest and most influential churches in the United States. Bill Hybels, the pastor of Willow Creek Community Church near Chicago and the apostolic leader of a large network of churches that spans the globe, acknowledged that many of the "seeker-sensitive" priorities Willow Creek had been pursuing were not producing the hoped-for outcome. According to Hybels:

> Some of the stuff we have put millions of dollars into, thinking it would really help our people grow and develop spiritually, when the data actually came back it wasn't helping people that much. Other things that we didn't put that much money into and didn't put much staff against, is the stuff our people are crying out for. We made a mistake. . . . When people crossed the line of faith and became

Christians, we should have started telling [them] that they
have to take responsibility to become "self feeders." We
should have . . . taught people how to read their Bible between services, how to do the spiritual practices much
more aggressively on their own.[1]

In other words, if our emphasis is on generating numbers, the
seeker-sensitive model definitely works. But if our hope is to generate committed and devoted followers of Christ, it doesn't work
so well. Let me say that I have always admired Bill Hybels, but my
respect for him went way up as a result of this honest admission.
Seeker-sensitivity is not inherently wrong, but I believe consumerism is.

One of the biggest challenges in recent years has been the
tremendous pressure of the consumer or entertainment mentality
that has come into the Church. The Church is starting to be seen
as a product to be packaged and sold, and everyone is looking for
the best product at the lowest price. Unfortunately, this often involves compromising true values for the quick and easy fix.

This has been made worse by the fact that the stress of life—
especially in large metro areas—has become so strong that people
have little reserves left over for true discipleship. People have little
spare time because their careers and commutes take up much of their
lives, and they have so many entertainment options from which
to choose. In response, the Church has replaced "re-creation" with
"recreation," which never provides the rest and reflection people
need—it actually wears them down even more. As people minimize
stress by structuring their consumer lifestyles around which stores
they shop, how convenient they are, and how low the prices are,
they take this attitude into the Church as well.

When people start thinking of the Church as a consumer product, they're looking for what's cheaper, faster and most convenient.
Unfortunately, these values are not aligned with the values of the
kingdom of God, and they stand in complete contradiction to the
demands of discipleship. Jesus declared emphatically, "If anyone
desires to come after Me, let him deny himself, take up his cross,

and follow Me" (Matt. 16:24). This is a very inconvenient message in the consumer age. However, when a church runs according to consumer values and fails to effectively reach and disciple the lost, it ends up with a flock of spectators pulled from other churches who are unable to transform their worlds for Christ.

Christianity was never intended to be a spectator sport, but the consumer mentality created by the current trends in church life has not only left the average believer dependant on the system but actually demanding more. This spirit of entitlement causes disgruntled believers who perceive they are not being fed to look for better options, much as one might switch from McDonald's to Burger King.

I am not suggesting that it is always wrong to contextualize our gatherings and messages to the audience we are reaching, nor am I saying it is always wrong for someone to leave one church and go to another. I am also definitely not saying that a church should avoid seeking to meet the felt needs of its membership and community. What I am proposing is that it is essential for every leader to do everything possible to limit a consumerist attitude from forming in the church.

President John F. Kennedy famously said, "Ask not what your country can do for you—ask what you can do for your country." With deference to JFK, the Kingdom message is, "Ask not what your church can do for you, but what you can do for God's kingdom." Or, as Jesus put it, "It is more blessed to give than to receive" (Acts 20:35; see also Matt. 5:40-44). The problem is that the Church has become a business replete with buildings, budgets and bureaucracies, which often creates the impression that it is something other than an assembly of believers. These three Bs cost money, and in too many cases the vast majority of resources in the local church are spent to maintain the institution and not advance the Kingdom. Something has to change.

To break the ropes of consumerism that are holding us down, we must learn how to equip and empower the people of God to move from consumer to contributor. We must return to Christ, our first love, and realize that only His love will move us from a

place of taking to a place of giving. We must seek first God's kingdom so that everything will be added to us (see Matt. 6:33), and give
so that it will be given unto us (see Luke 6:38). Love gives us this generosity of spirit, which overcomes selfishness and self-centeredness
and returns us to a place of true Kingdom motivations.

The Rope of Complacency

Merriam-Webster's Dictionary defines complacency as "self-satisfac-
tion with an existing situation or condition without perceiving
potential dangers or deficiencies."[2] Once the Church drifts away
from sacrificial faith into consumerist demands—once it changes
from a place that empowers people to serve to a place where people demand service—it's only a matter of time before complacency
sets in. We begin indulging in self-centeredness and build a church
on the values of that self-centeredness.

Complacency causes us to stop caring about the things Jesus
cares about and become satisfied with a sub-standard status quo.
When this occurs, an inferior spiritual "ecology" is established in
our lives, where the values and priorities that determine our allocation of time, talent and treasure become fixed and difficult to reset. We stop caring about the lost and about ministering to the
poor, sick and tormented. We stop fellowshipping with others and
instead fellowship with our huge flat-screen TVs. We stop serving
others and, by attrition, end up only serving ourselves. Then we
wonder why our sense of fulfillment and spiritual enjoyment has
seemed to vanish.

Consumerism and complacency take root when we become
overcome by the cares of this world. Like the seed that fell among
thorns in Jesus' parable of the sower (see Luke 8:4-15), the seed of the
Kingdom is planted and begins to grow, but then is choked out by
the weeds and thorns that are growing up around it. In Revelation
3:15-18, Jesus rebuked the Laodicean Church for this very thing:

> I know your works, that you are neither cold nor hot. I could
> wish you were cold or hot. So then, because you are luke-

warm, and neither cold nor hot, I will vomit you out of My mouth. Because you say, "I am rich, have become wealthy, and have need of nothing"—and do not know that you are wretched, miserable, poor, blind, and naked—I counsel you to buy from Me gold refined in the fire, that you may be rich; and white garments, that you may be clothed, that the shame of your nakedness may not be revealed; and anoint your eyes with eye salve, that you may see.

A number of today's largest churches are located in some of the most unreached neighborhoods in our nation, where the crime, drug and suicide rates are the highest. In many cases, thousands of people drive from their homes in the suburbs to the church in the inner city, and then drive back after the service. Somehow, even though thousands of people carrying the power and love of the kingdom of God meet and worship each week, the adjacent neighborhood remains unchanged. This was never God's intention. It is a consequence of complacent Christianity, and if we are ever to see revival, it has to stop. If our faith isn't making a measurable impact on the community around us, we need to examine ourselves to see if we're really walking and living out the life we were meant to live.

The Body of Christ can break the ropes of complacency by cultivating kingdom passions in our hearts and realizing Jesus was "moved with compassion" (Mark 1:41) and had "zeal for [the Lord's] house" that consumed Him (John 2:17). As we touch His desires and allow His Spirit to work within us to "will and to do of His good pleasure" (Phil. 2:13), we will be able to cultivate the spiritual hunger that will drive us to "lay hold of that for which Christ has also laid hold of [us]" (Phil. 3:12).

The Rope of Compromise

A story is told by the Voice of the Martyrs about an underground gathering of believers in Eastern Europe during the height of the communist persecution of Christians. Believers were meeting in a dark cellar in the middle of a wooded area when suddenly they heard a loud knocking at the door. The door flew open, and half a dozen communist soldiers burst into the room with their machineguns in hand.

The soldiers commanded everyone to lie down on the ground, and then the lead soldier yelled, "Anyone who is not fully committed to Christ must renounce their faith and leave right now, and the rest of you must make your peace with your God." In the midst of the fearful whimpers and gasps, a few individuals raised their heads and began to look around. They slowly rose to their feet and sheepishly made their way out of the cellar. When they were gone, the lead soldier barred the door, placed his rifle against the wall, and said, "Good. My men and I are absolutely *unwilling* to worship with anyone who is not willing to die for Jesus."

This story may seem shocking to those of us who have never experienced persecution, but it illustrates in stark terms the reality of compromise. Compromise comes in many forms and is driven by many motives. For instance, there is the compromise of truth because the fear of man causes us to choose the politically correct position over God's Word. There is the compromise of lifestyle because temptation or peer pressure is more persuasive than the conviction of the Holy Spirit. And there is the compromise of ethics because sometimes the expedient choice seems like the easiest or only way.

These examples and many others are running rampant in the Western Church. In recent years, many pastors and leaders have fallen into various levels of compromise, including adultery, pornography, homosexuality, divorce, drug and alcohol abuse, exaggerations, outright lies, shady land deals . . . you name it, Christian leaders have done it! If it's in the world, it is in the Church. I know God gives mercy and grace, but when we in the Body of Christ compromise with the world, it undermines our intimacy with God, our access to His power, our authority over darkness, and our witness to the world. Like the other, compromise holds the sleeping giant captive. Doesn't Jesus deserve better than this?

I am not suggesting that God is a slave driver. If He were, He would have made our bodies to work continuously without sleep or rest. Instead, He created us to function best by being out of commission a third of every day. I love relaxation, entertainment and recreation, but even a good thing in excess can become harmful. I am not advocating legalism or duty-driven religion, but I am warning against the sense of entitlement (what the Bible calls licentiousness), which justifies excessive behavior in the name of grace. Licentiousness is actually another kind of religious spirit that feeds on pride and rebellion. When we feel entitled to indulgence, we drift into compromise.

There is a space between legalism and licentiousness that is called liberty. This is the place where holiness and grace intersect—a place where faith and works embrace and forgiveness and justice stand watch. Liberty is sometimes a razor's edge and sometimes a vast plain, but either way, it is the place where God's presence dwells. As we read in God's Word:

Where the Spirit of the Lord is, there is liberty (2 Cor. 3:17).

Stand fast therefore in the liberty by which Christ has made us free, and do not be entangled again with a yoke of bondage.... For you, brethren, have been called to liberty; only do not use liberty as an opportunity for the flesh, but through love serve one another (Gal. 5:1,13).

But he who looks into the perfect law of liberty and continues in it, and is not a forgetful hearer but a doer of the work, this one will be blessed in what he does (Jas. 1:25).

The Body of Christ can break the ropes of compromise by cultivating true holiness and by realizing that complete dedication is not a duty but a delight. Holiness is not so much a separation *from* but a consecration *to* a God whose beauty is beyond comparison and whose worth is above everything else. The only reasonable response to so great a God is to align ourselves with Him in complete integrity and love.

The Rope of Cynicism

One of the most destructive ropes binding the Body of Christ to-day is cynicism, which can be defined as an attitude that distrusts or disparages the motives of others and expresses contempt or pessimism. When we are cynical, we express contempt for accepted standards of honesty or morality and we undermine the simplicity and sincerity that binds us together. Cynicism is rampant in the youth culture of the world, and it is continuously reinforced in movies, music, on the Internet and in media. It has also bled into the Church in an alarming manner. On one level, cynicism is the jaded response to the boy who cried wolf or to the naked emperor gazing fondly at his "new clothes." It is the response of those who have seen the dark underbelly of life and have come to the conclusion that nothing is true and nothing is to be trusted.

In the periodic table of God's kingdom, there are elements of greater and lesser value. Among the top three elements are faith, hope and love (see 1 Cor. 13:13). In the same way that consumerism and complacency demonstrate a lack of love and compromise demonstrates a declining faith, so cynicism demonstrates an absence of hope. Sometimes the hopelessness attacks us at random, coming at us like a demonic spirit, but in most cases it is a product of genuine disappointment that has never been healed. Unfortunately, the Church is full of individuals who have allowed disappointment to fester into a cynical heart, and this has led to a cynical malaise that has undermined our fruitfulness in every area of Kingdom ministry.

Disappointment is somewhat unavoidable in our lives as Christians, because the basic premise of God's purpose is to bring His kingdom and His will on earth as it is in heaven (see Matt. 6:10). As Bill Johnson puts it, "Our destination is heaven, but our assignment is to bring heaven to earth," and yet this assignment is not an exact science. Not every sickness will be healed when we pray, and not every person to whom we witness will be saved. As believers, we need to learn how to process disappointment in a positive, faith-sustaining and hopeful way. This is something Bill Johnson has taught in his global ministry, and I believe this message has done more to remove the offense of unanswered prayer and increase the work of the Holy Spirit in the Western world than any other teaching.

The Body of Christ needs to renounce hopelessness and cynicism and embrace hope anew. We must learn to process disappointment and unmet expectations in a redemptive way, acknowledging the goodness of God. We need to celebrate testimonies of answered prayer and boldly rise to every challenge of faith with our eyes on the author and finisher of our faith.

The Body of Christ can break the ropes of cynicism by cultivating a spirit of hope and by realizing that love "bears all things, believes all things, hopes all things, endures all things" (1 Cor. 13:7). For as the author of Hebrews wrote, "This hope we have as an anchor of the soul, both sure and steadfast" (Heb. 6:19). Hope empowers us to maintain Kingdom optimism and reject jadedness because our hope is not in people or circumstances but in the Lord.

The Rope of Criticism

The final rope that I would like to identify is perhaps even more harmful than cynicism: the rope of criticism. One of Jesus' strongest commandments was, "Judge not, that you be not judged. For with what judgment you judge, you will be judged; and with the measure you use, it will be measured back to you" (Matt 7:1-2). Unfortunately, these have been the most challenging words for Christians to obey. Followers of Jesus have been guilty of criticizing family, friends, pastors, leaders, governmental officials, other churches, movements and denominations.

We serve the God of love, who demonstrated love to the point of dying on the cross and commanded us to love others, yet we have become known as one of the most judgmental groups on earth. In fact, a recent study by the Barna Group found that 87 percent of 16-to 29-year-olds in the United States believe Christianity is judgmental and 85 percent believe Christians are hypocritical. The study goes on to say that 91 percent of this age group—and a whopping *80 percent* of Christians the same age—believe the word "anti-homosexual" describes contemporary Christianity. Both groups say Christianity doesn't look like Jesus. The study concludes, "Half of young churchgoers said they perceive Christianity to be judgmental, hypocritical, and too political. Half said it was old fashioned and out of touch with reality."[3]

We should consider the results of the Barna survey carefully, as Jesus Himself gave the world permission to judge the Church by our love for one another (see John 13:35). He taught, "Let your light so shine before men, that they may see your good works and glorify your Father in heaven" (Matt. 5:16). When the world perceives us as judgmental, it is clear we have lost our way. Where is the light that Jesus spoke about?

If love is truly the distinguishing mark of a follower of Jesus, the world should not be perceiving Christians as judgmental, hypocritical and hateful. While there is certainly a media bias against our faith and the Church's good works are given almost no attention in the press, this alone cannot account for all the negative perception. Maybe the world is seeing something real. If loving others is the true mark of a Christian, perhaps each of us should ask ourselves this famous question: *If we were arrested for following Jesus, would there be enough evidence to convict us?*

In Scripture, there are three primary words that can be translated "to judge": *diakrino, dokimazo* and *krino.* The first two words are more accurately translated "discern." Jesus used the third word, *krino,* when He forbade us to judge. The difference between the two concepts is important. We are called to *discern* good from evil, right from wrong and clean from unclean, but we are never called to condemn.

As a pastor, I have had to lovingly confront individuals who were out of order or who were being harmful to others. In these confrontations, the key difference between condemnation and discernment was love and honor. If we believe in the individual and hold that person in high esteem in spite of the behavior, we can discern the error and fault without condemning him or her. We love the sinner, but hate the sin. Unfortunately, because so many of us are influenced by fear, anger, stress or unresolved pain from the past, our tendency is to punish, shame or control the sinner. By doing so, we misrepresent the love of Jesus.

The simple distinction between judgment and discernment is that judgment desires punishment while discernment desires correction and redemption. Judgment condemns and wants the violator to fall and fail, while discernment cares deeply for the violator and desires him or her to be restored and blessed. As Paul wrote, "Brethren, if a man is overtaken in any trespass, you who are spiritual restore such a one in a spirit of gentleness, considering yourself lest you also be tempted. Bear one another's burdens, and so fulfill the law of Christ" (Gal. 6:1-2).

The clearest way to tell the difference between discernment and judgment is in the fruit that is produced. Did the disagreement resolve itself in love or in division and strife? If there was a messy resolution, were we able to walk away with love and peace in our heart toward the other person in spite of the fact he or she was offended? The Body of Christ can break the ropes of criticism by cultivating a spirit of blessing and by realizing that anyone can be a faultfinder and identify problems. God desires us to be problem solvers who provide solutions. Jesus told us to bless those who curse us, and to do good to those who are spiteful toward us (see Luke 6:28). James also wrote that blessing and cursing should not proceed out of the same mouth (see Jas. 3:10). We are called to "overcome evil with good" (Rom. 12:21).

The Glorious Church

While these are just some of the problems that constrict the Body of Christ and keep it from rising to fullness, it does not represent the whole picture. There exist today many wonderful examples of the Glorious Church, the Called-Out-Ones, the Body and Bride of Christ, the Pillar and Ground of the Truth, the Temple of the Living God. Many indeed are demonstrating that they are the "fullness of Him who fills all in all" (Eph. 1:23) and are displaying His glory on the earth.

In spite of all the weaknesses and problems, persecution and marginalization, pollution and dilution, the Church of the Lord Jesus Christ has continued to march forward and carry the torch of revival and transformation. Today, we stand on the brink of the greatest days the Church has ever known. It is time for us to arise and shine, for our light has come and the glory of the Lord has risen upon us (see Isa. 60:1).

So let's stop hitting the snooze button and cast off the ropes that have hindered us. Let's rise up in the power of the Holy Spirit and make ourselves ready for what God is about to do in the earth. As we rise and shine, God will raise us up and enable us to tackle the challenges of the coming harvest. It's time to realign ourselves with the King of Kings to see His kingdom come on earth as it is in heaven.

Paradigm Shift

Because of my crazy upbringing, I have a soft spot in my heart for people in the counter-culture. This is why I was so excited when I was approached by a group of individuals in our church about a new ministry they were starting called Prodigal Project. The year was 1994. By this time, The Vineyard of San Francisco was approaching its apex.

As I mentioned, we had planted the church 10 years before in 1984, and by this time it had grown to be the largest church that San Francisco had seen in a generation. We were attracting hundreds of people from around the Bay, and we had about 600 adults and more than 100 kids attending services. God was moving in an amazing way, with signs, wonders and healings on a regular basis. We had one of the largest auditoriums in the city, on the corner of 7th and Harrison Street, right across from the Hall of Justice.

The leader of the Prodigal Project was a woman named Cathi Mooney who had recently joined our church. She had been a successful advertising executive, first in New York and then in California. Cathi was brilliant, creative and articulate, and she was sold out for Jesus. She had first envisioned the project when she began to spend time on Haight Street with a few friends, where she noticed a community of teenagers and young adults living on the streets and in nearby Golden Gate Park. Most of these kids were homeless, and many were trying to revive the hippie movement that had ended more than 20 years before. A number of them had dreadlocks, tattoos and piercings and were as much in need of a shower as any hippie in the sixties. We began using terms like "global nomads" and "neo-hippies" to describe these young people.

Danny Lehmann, a friend of mine from Youth With A Mission (YWAM), came to our church and spoke on evangelism. About 70 people came forward in an altar call and declared that they were called to be evangelists. Out of that group of individuals, a number joined Cathi on Haight Street and began to do regular outreaches. They quickly realized they couldn't just share the gospel but also had to demonstrate the gospel by providing for the young people in practical ways.

So, during the next year, the group sought to find the right situation into which they could bring the kids so they could feed them, clothe them and provide them with showers. When they couldn't locate a suitable facility, they realized the best alternative was to actually buy a house. Cathi, who had recently sold her business, purchased a place on Ashbury Street, half a block off of Haight. This three-story Victorian became the home for our ministry for the next seven years. We converted the garage into a kitchen and feeding center so we could care for people from the streets in a practical way. We had a little meeting room as well where we could pack in 40 to 50 people. There were also different apartments throughout the building where we could house our workers. The Prodigal Project quickly became a thriving ministry.

We soon found that many of the kids coming to San Francisco were nomads traveling through the city on their way to somewhere else. A great number, we discovered, were actually traveling on tour with the Grateful Dead or other bands such as Phish and String Cheese Incident—what are now called "jam bands." The people we were reaching were travelers, so we began to secure buses and vans so we could travel around the nation with them.

The *700 Club* found out about our ministry and sent a team to San Francisco to interview Cathi, myself and a few other people. Later, a woman who owned a beautiful bed and breakfast inn on the Eel River, just outside a little town called Leggett, saw the video segment. In the middle of the night, the Lord awakened her and impressed upon her heart that she should watch a replay of the *700 Club*. When she saw our interview, the Lord moved her to donate her land to us. She and her husband owned seven acres and

20 cabins, which slept about 40 people. After a wonderful meeting, they ended up giving this land to our church, and we established the Prodigal Project Land.

Brian Heltsley, my friend and ministry partner, moved to Leggett from Santa Cruz and launched a discipleship school that began to bring salvation and transformation to kids who were coming off the road. Many of them had been taking multiple hits of LSD, and some were even strung out on heroin and other major drugs. We turned the land into an excellent discipleship center that helped set people free and trained them to serve the Lord.

We fulfilled this ministry from 1996 until 2004, when we decided to sell the land so we could focus more on our outreach to global neo-Hippie nomads traveling in Asia, Israel and Europe. Throughout these years, we were able to bring a level of revival culture into a subculture that impacted young adults around the world.

Understanding the Great Commission

When Jesus gave the Great Commission, He commanded us to go into all the world and make disciples of all nations, teaching them to do everything He commanded (see Matt. 28:16-20). So, beginning with the apostles, somebody told somebody, who told somebody else, who told somebody else, and so the gospel moved across the earth. It spread through the centuries and across cultures, and, ultimately, ended up reaching me when I was hitchhiking through northern California at 17 years of age. That same gospel reached me again through Blackfoot Indians, who led me into a discipleship relationship that eventually brought me into full-time ministry. I cannot imagine a path to Jesus that could have been more perfect for me.

In the Gospels, whenever Jesus spoke to people, He spoke to them using the language and culture they understood. Because He lived in an agrarian society that consisted of herding cattle and farming crops, many of His parables and allegories were about sheep, seeds, planting and harvesting—the language and the symbols of the day. But what are the language and symbols of our day? How can we embrace the methods of Jesus for our generation?

There is a spiritual harvest of souls that is ripening all around us, yet it is a different crop than we have ever harvested before. If we want to reach the emerging generation with the love of God, the seed we're planting, the methods of evangelism we're employ-ing, the soil we are cultivating and the harvesting tools we are us-ing all need to be appropriate to the people we are reaching. For example, if we change from farming wheat to farming corn, we must retool our machinery so we don't destroy the harvest. Yet I submit that in the harvest of souls today we are not merely mov-ing from wheat to corn, which are similar, but from wheat to broc-coli. In other words, the people who will be coming to Christ in the coming years will be very different from those of previous gen-erations. For this reason, our ability to retool is even more urgent than before. To take the analogy further, because of the growing diversity of our communities, we are no longer dealing with a sin-gle kind of crop but with a multitude of distinct cultures and sub-cultures that each requires its own special care.

Let's look more at how Jesus' Great Commission applies to any people group that shares a common culture, both large and small, from neo-hippies on Haight Street to baristas at Starbucks to people in the gay community to a remote tribe in Brazil. This is what I call the "emerging missions movement."

Understanding the Emerging Missions Movement

In John 4:35, Jesus said to His disciples, "Behold, I say to you, lift up your eyes and look at the fields, for they are already white for harvest!" Like Jesus, I also like to use farming terms to define our need to prepare for the coming harvest. So let's start with the *soil* and the *seed*.

In Jesus' parables, the soil is the environment in which the seed is planted. It may be an individual heart, as in the parable of the sower, or it can be the world at large, as in the story of the wheat and the tares. We can also apply this metaphor to families, com-munities, workplaces, schools, neighborhoods, cities, nations, cultures and subcultures. Each of these can be represented as a kind of *soil* in which God desires to plant the Word of the Kingdom.

In the same way that farmers must select the specific seed that is right for each type of soil, so we must, as wise farmers, carefully select our specific seed in order to produce the maximum harvest of souls in a particular field. Jesus commissioned us to baptize, teach, disciple and demonstrate His power and presence among all nations—that is, among all *ethne,* or different people groups (see Matt. 28:19-20). When Jesus com*mission*ed the church, He literally gave the church a *mission*. So, missions work, in every context, is the complete task of the Church.

One of the most exciting developments that is happening in our generation is the massive mobilization of believers around the world to share their faith in power. It is a wonderful season, because a fresh authenticity in emerging Christian culture is finding its expression in a number of ways. However, as we have already discussed, those of us in the Church have historically not been good at paying attention to the soil and the way it changes over time. In fact, we tend to notice cultural shifts *after* they've happened, and by the time we've come up with programs to meet those needs, society has moved on and we're 10 years behind. Our ability to have maximum impact on the world around us depends largely on our awareness of the change and the timeliness of our response.

Aiming the Ball to Reach the Receiver

Few things are more beautiful to watch than a professional quarterback throwing the perfect pass to a talented receiver who is running with all his might. The ball sails through the air, and the receiver, without the slightest break in stride, stretches out his hands and picks the ball from the sky just as he crosses into the endzone. Even a person with no passion for sports can admire the synchronicity of such a play. The secret of this accuracy is in the quarterback's ability to anticipate the direction, speed and distance of the receiver and throw the ball to the exact point where he *will be* when the ball arrives.

Our culture is racing down the field, looking for answers to life's deepest questions. As Christians, we're called to deliver a message and pioneer churches and ministries that meet people not only where they are but also where they will be. Unfortunately, we've been aiming for where the world was a decade ago instead of aiming toward where it is going. We're similar to a quarterback who throws the ball *behind* the receiver, forcing him to break stride and come back to where he was instead of where he can take it further. It takes strategy and planning to throw the gospel where the world *will be* so it won't be outdated by the time it gets there. I believe revival is the result of a perfectly thrown pass.

God dwells in eternity and sees the whole field of history at once. When He became flesh and dwelt among us, He became the perfectly thrown pass that landed in Israel at just the right moment in time. He unleashed the Original Jesus Movement, which released the first Holy Spirit revival in history. Yet even in human form God did not violate this principle but manifested Himself as a Hebrew, with all the cultural dimensions of what it meant to be of that race. He did not come in a business suit, sporting the latest version of an iPad.

In the same way, we need to rethink our approach to the coming harvest. Effective ways of reaching youth in the 1970s during the Jesus Movement won't always click with people of this generation. For example, the baby boomer generation was strongly affected by words and ideas, which explains why gospel tracts and the Roman Road were so effective. Today's generation, however, craves genuine experiential relationships with both God and people. They want far more than just ideas and words alone—they want a tangible experience of the presence and power of God. So, we need to take these ideas and recontextualize the gospel message into a language and form that today's generation is able to understand. A shift in our mindset needs to take place.

As we anticipate what could well be the greatest single human harvest in all of history, we must remember that God is similar to a farmer who rotates His crops. He grows soybeans, but then He grows wheat, tomatoes or cotton. Every different crop has different needs, and its growth requires a different type of soil and nutrients.

Changes in the Harvest Field

So, it is clear that this coming harvest will be distinct from every other human harvest in history, because the people are different. Industrialization and the information age are influencing every region of the world. Today, Europe, Australia and North America train the majority of the world's professors, and as a result many of the cultural values and ideologies in western educational structures are filtering through to the rest of the world. While there are still regions that are either tightly controlled by cultural rules or haven't yet been exposed to technology, western culture, or education, these areas are becoming more and more rare.

Changing entertainment has also had a huge effect on the harvest field. The Internet, movies, music, television and even sports are quietly and effectively infiltrating western values and ideologies into people's thinking, shifting the worldviews of entire cultures. Kids today spend a great deal of time indoors on the computer. They communicate through instant messaging, watch movies, and play video games in place of traditional larger-group activities that are more active and involve more face-to-face collaboration. As a result, the mindsets and thought processes of this emerging generation are very different than those of their predecessors.

As a culture, our worldview has changed. The emerging generation been raised in an absence of absolutes and clear definitions of right and wrong and is consistently wounded by a barrage of victimization and sin. In the meantime, relativism and New Age values have permeated our culture and created an environment that is hostile to Christian beliefs. Christianity and Jesus are perceived to be irrelevant, outdated and narrow-minded. No one is interested in "old" thinking. This strong, almost drastic shift toward this entirely new way of viewing truth has become one of the greatest challenges to the Church.

The emerging generation is typically young, urban and uninterested in Christianity. Again, a large part of this shift is the result of how the Church has interacted with the world. This is why we need a new understanding of missions and evangelism to reach the emerging generation. To help distinguish this new approach, I want to give a perspective on the history of missions, beginning with the apostle Paul.

The Emerging Missions Movement

In Acts 13, we read of an important, catalytic event that took place in the Early Church. The Holy Spirit told certain prophets and teachers in Antioch to "separate to Me Barnabas and Saul for the work to which I have called them" (v. 2). From there, Paul and Barnabas were sent out on the first of several missionary journeys.

Paul was motivated by an incredible desire of Jesus to touch those who had been untouched and reach those who had been unreached. There were two essential elements that helped Paul reach this goal. The first was *koine*, which means the "common" Greek language. Paul was able to take the gospel and bring it immediately into the language in any city he entered. The second essential element that helped Paul spread the gospel was the *Pax Romana* and the Roman Road. The Roman government brought peace to the empire and built massive thoroughfares through the known world. As Christians went out to plant seeds of the gospel, they had easy access to centers of culture.

This was the basic form of missions up until the third or fourth century, after which time the Church went into a relatively dark period. For about 1,000 years, there were essentially two churches: the Orthodox Church and the Catholic Church. The most life we find in the Church during the Middle Ages occurred in the monastic movements. Monks did a good deal of missionary work, but missions didn't occur at an intense level until after the Protestant Reformation during the sixteenth century.

In 1722, a group of Moravian refugees gathered in Germany on the lands of Count Nikolaus Ludwig von Zinzendorf. They set up a gathering of continuous, 24-hour prayer that lasted more than 100 years. In so doing, they started the new wave of modern missions. They began to send out missionaries all around the world.

One of the most moving stories of this era were of two Moravian men who heard about an island in the Caribbean Sea where a slave owner was so evil and corrupt that he would not allow missionaries on the land. Apparently, the man was afraid that if his slaves adopted Christianity, they wouldn't serve him as well. So these two Moravian men sold themselves into slavery, and with the money they received for their own lives, they bought passage to this island. As they were leaving the docks to spend the rest of their lives serving the poor in that place, one of them raised his hand in salute to his weeping relatives and friends and said, "May the Lamb that was slain receive the reward of His sufferings."

A few decades later, we find a wave of missionaries like J. Hudson Taylor, C. T. Studd, David Livingston and other men and women who left the comfort of their homes to reach out to foreign lands. Up until this time, the standard philosophy of missions was to import Western European culture along with the gospel. So, when a missionary brought the gospel to an unreached people group, the group had to let go of their own culture and adopt the missionary's manner and style of dress, speech and customs. But with the new wave of missions, this idea began to change. Hudson Taylor, for example, left behind most aspects of his English culture to adopt the culture of the Chinese. He began to dress like the Chinese, grow his hair like the Chinese, work like the Chinese, and even carry water like the Chinese. He took on a Chinese lifestyle and helped introduce the Church to a new understanding of what missions is really about.

Some 1,800 years after Paul's time, the Church began to recognize three primary elements of missions, which we will focus on throughout the rest of the chapter: (1) *investigation*, (2) *incarnation*, and (3) *indigenousness leaders*. These three elements have become the framework of modern missions and are the same principles we used to reach the nomadic young people through the Prodigal Project.

Investigation

The first of these three important principles is *investigation*, or studying the target group to discover specific keys and "Kingdom longings" that God has already placed within that culture to introduce the people to His heart. The more we learn about a culture and identify its values, the more we discover that God has truly placed eternity in the hearts of man (see Eccles. 3:11).

People *yearn* for life in His kingdom, whether they are aware of what they're seeking or not. If we take the time to closely watch a group of people, we will discover clear values and desires they share as a culture that are also found in the kingdom of God. If we share the Lord through these values already inherent in their culture, they will be less likely to see Jesus as a foreign religion that is superior and contrary to their own. As a result, we will see a lot more fruit.

Kingdom Keys

One of my favorite examples of this appears in *Peace Child* by Don Richardson. *Peace Child* is the true story of how Don and his wife, Carol, went about reaching the Sawi tribe in New Guinea. After moving to this remote location, they spent many long months studying the language and culture of this unreached people group. Unfortunately, they hit a roadblock in their first attempts to share the gospel because the culture of this tribe held treachery as a virtue. When Don and Carol taught the gospel story, the Sawis saw Judas as the hero and Jesus as the chump!

The Richardsons were frustrated in their attempts until they discovered a kingdom key that had already been planted within the culture. It seems that when a war broke out between tribes, the only way they could make peace with one another was by exchanging a baby son, one from each tribe. The enemy tribe received the new baby, laid hands on him, and embraced him and the peace he symbolized. The boys' new fathers also exchanged names and called themselves by the name of their new son's birth father.[1] That concept was the window through which the gospel of a Peace Child from heaven could be introduced. Because this idea was already intrinsic in the Sawi culture, the tribes were able to understand and receive this truth, and the tribes came to the Lord.[2] In many ways, the story of the peace child is the quintessential story of modern missions.

Similar keys like this are found within every culture—we just need to uncover them. This requires going into a culture to investigate it so we can understand where it is coming from, where it will emerge, and where it will go. We look at its values: What does the culture care about? What are some of the assumptions that it has concerning the nature of the universe? What are its traditions? What are its family structures, and how do these work in relation to other structures? What governmental structures work within the culture? As missionaries and evangelists, we go through a natural investigatory process in order to understand the people we are trying to reach. Once we find the keys God has put in that culture, we are able to present His message through something the people already value and are searching for.

Kingdom Barriers
On the flip side of this, just as there are cultural keys that point back to the Lord, there are also cultural *barriers* that Satan has built to keep people from seeing or receiving truth (see 2 Cor. 4:3-4). It is almost as important and strategic to identify these cultural barriers as it is to identify the kingdom keys of God, because once we understand the work of the enemy, we can help tear down the strongholds that are influencing and controlling the people (see 2 Cor. 10:4).

As previously mentioned, one of the kingdom barriers that Don and Carol encountered with the Sawi people was the fact that betrayal and treachery were glorified in the culture. Because of the tribe's worldview, they assumed that Judas, not Jesus, was the hero in the gospel story, and as a result they weren't able to understand the gospel for what it really was. The enemy had built a spiritual and cultural framework to keep them from seeing the truth.

In 2 Corinthians 4:4-5, Paul writes that the gospel is "veiled to those who are perishing, whose minds the god of this age has blinded, who do not believe, lest the light of the gospel of the glory of Christ, who is the image of God." Spiritual investigation is basically the process of praying for a people group (either from a distance or on site), attempting to understand God's heart for them, and then determining the supernatural dynamics that relate to the group. It involves seeking to uncover how the enemy has manifested himself in a given culture in order to blind the people's minds to the truth.

Spiritual Mapping
This is what John Dawson, co-director of YWAM, called "spiritual mapping" in his groundbreaking book *Taking Our Cities for God*.[3] Spiritual mapping is the process of developing a strategic understanding of a people and a region by doing a prayer-based, historical and demographic study of the different aspects of the culture. Those who are skilled in spiritual mapping come away with a clear sense of God's redemptive purpose for a given people group. They are also able to discern the enemy's strategies and the sociological factors that keep the people from receiving the Lord.

Investigating a people group allows us to understand them better so we can partner with God more effectively as He seeks to make Himself visible among them. Once we find the keys God has put in that culture, we are able to declare His message in ways that bypass the barriers and builds bridges to their hearts.

Incarnation

The second important principle in modern missions is *incarnation*. When we incarnate ourselves into a culture, we settle among the people, build relationships with them, and allow them to test our credibility and sensitivity to their identity. We attempt to identify with them, and we give them time to see how much we genuinely care for them. In other words, we open ourselves up to them on their level.

Simply put, incarnation is what Jesus did when He became flesh and dwelt among us (see John 1:14). God had communicated to His people in many ways—through prophets, angelic visitations and other kinds of spiritual encounters—but Jesus represented something different. Through Jesus, God could truly communicate with us in the way He intended (see Heb. 1:1-4). As Paul describes it, Jesus "made Himself of no reputation, taking the form of a bond-servant, and coming in the likeness of men" (Phil. 2:7). God *wanted* to be understood, so He manifested Himself in no uncertain terms. He lived as a man filled with the Holy Spirit on the earth, and He said, "He who has seen Me has seen the Father" (John 14:9).

The process is that we *investigate* culture from both a natural and spiritual standpoint and then seek to *incarnate* within that culture—we go to people on their own terms. This doesn't mean we adopt their sinful patterns and cultural misbehaviors. Rather, we seek to *blend* into their culture and manifest ourselves among them to whatever extent we can, just as Jesus did. Christ did not come in visible glory—He came in the clothing of the ancient Hebrews and was "found in appearance as a man" (Phil. 2:8). As the author of Hebrews says, "In all things He had to be made like His brethren." That is the heart of the modern missionary: we do as Jesus did and go to the people as a part of the people. A. W. Tozer put it this way: "We are to be in the world, but not of the world" (see John 17:13-16).

Indigenous Leaders

The third important principle to consider in modern missions is developing *indigenous leaders* from among the group that is being reached. Paul did this all the time during his missionary journeys. He would establish a church, appoint elders, and then move on. We find this same practice with Jesus. When He left the earth, He left His Church in Peter's hands (see Matt. 16:13-20).

Throughout history, the indigenous leader has been the sign of a missionary's success in a region—a people group has truly been reached when those people have a church in their language and culture and the church has an indigenous leader who was born and raised among that people. In whatever culture we are trying to reach, our goal is to raise up an indigenous leader, or multiple indigenous leaders, within that culture.

When K. P. Yohannan, founder and president of Gospel for Asia, was trying to bring the gospel to his native India, he discovered it was much better to send in an indigenous missionary than a foreign one. There were two reasons for this: (1) it was much less expensive, and (2) the indigenous missionary was already familiar with the culture. Gospel for Asia is now an organization made up of indigenous Christians who, with financial support from their Western brothers and sisters, bring the good news of Jesus Christ to lost men, women and children throughout Asia. The indigenous leader is not only the time-tested fruit of successful missions but also tends to be the most prolific and beneficial.

When I look at the human element of the gospel, I am bowled over by Jesus' strategy for evangelism and changing the world. It was a unique strategy that many in modern corporate America might even consider to be backward. In establishing world missions, Jesus didn't change the world by going mass media or launching a large congregation. Instead, He chose Peter and 11 other individuals and made them His priority. He focused on *quality*. He didn't neglect His responsibility toward the masses and the *quantity* of the equation, but He ended up pouring the majority of His time, wisdom and power into a few men and women. Clearly, He considered one of His greatest assets to be His human resources.

So Jesus began an "organic missions movement." He set in motion a spiritual and generational transfer of this amazing message of the gospel. This is a system in which fathers and mothers in the Lord give birth to babies in the Lord, who then grow up to become fathers and mothers in their own right and give birth to others. Within this system, we find a phenomenal process of discipleship where everything Jesus commanded us to do is passed down from one generation to the next, and in this way the purity of the gospel is carried around the world in its fullness. Even with the current dynamics of mass media, the potency of this faith transmission remains at its greatest when it comes mouth to mouth, person to person, and heart to heart.

The New Jesus Movement

In the beginning of 2000, a couple of years after John Wimber's passing, Diane and I began to feel God was calling us in a new direction. After much prayer and counsel, we relaunched our church as Promised Land Fellowship. Within about six months, we also began a school of ministry called the Advanced Institute of Ministry (AIM). The focus of the school was to bring the gospel to emerging subcultures around the world and be a catalyst for a new harvest of souls.

As we began to pursue this vision and focus on the outward opportunities, God continued to work in my inner world to deepen my heart for the unreached and strengthen my passion for revival. During this time, I began to study different youth subcultures so I could understand what they believed and how they worked. I looked first at the group with which I was most familiar, the hippie subculture, and then explored other groups, such as the rave or dance club scene, the hip-hop world, the punk and hardcore scene, and others. I interviewed people from these various expressions and began to learn as much as I could about their values and cultures. My quest gradually broadened to also include the student culture.

We designed our school of ministry to reach and disciple a wide range of youth cultures and strategized how to pioneer ministries and churches that could bring revival culture to these people. We already had a strong relationship with kids who had come out of the neo-hippie nomadic lifestyle, so we recruited students from across the nation who were attracted to other emerging cultures and connected with people who had come out of the punk rock scene. When a few students who had come out of the dance club scene joined us, we were back to witnessing in that world.

During our first year we had about 25 students, and we were able to do ministry in a variety of spheres. We sent teams to major events such as The Rainbow Gathering and Burning Man. We regularly ministered at rave clubs, and our teams began to reach out to people in some of the bars, much like some ministries in England who witness to people in the pubs. We did an open-air ministry in the parks and hosted booths at several of San Francisco's street fairs. We did outreaches on various campuses and communities around the Bay Area and actually put on our own rave events (which I will write about a little bit later). We attracted a number of gifted students. Some of them did break dancing, others did anime and art, and others performed spoken word.

As the school continued to grow, we began to send teams to Europe and Israel to reach out to the emerging generation in these areas. My wife, Diane, and I brought our children and 10 of our students to southern Thailand, where we traveled to an island off the mainland to minister at the world-famous Full Moon Festival. This was a monthly rave on the beach that attracted more than 10,000 people, and our team ministered there to hundreds of people who were hungry for more of God.

We encountered similar ministry opportunities on the streets of Bangkok, the beaches of Goa, India, and by the lake in Pokhara, Nepal. Our teams ministered in other parts of Asia and in Latin America, bringing the presence and power of Jesus to counter-culture people throughout the earth. Tessa, one of our students, established a ministry to punk rockers called Grandma's House. She married an amazing songwriter named Nate, and they now travel much of the year doing "folk-punk" concerts in bars and in anarchist communities around the country.

On one occasion while we traveling in north India, we landed in a town called Manali, located in the foothills of the Himalayas. This was not only one of the most beautiful places on the planet but also had the unique feature of wild marijuana growing everywhere around town. It was here my friend Jesse and I attended a Passover Seder led by Hasidic Jews, with about 150 stoned Israeli youth singing and partaking of the meal. This opened up many opportunities for us to talk about Jeshua. We eventually established a coffee house in this town called The Dylan, which served caffeine and chocolate chip cookies to the stoned-out travelers.

The day after the Seder, as I was walking alone by the river, the Lord spoke clearly to me that the experiment was over and that it was time to close the school. I was so grateful for all we learned during the AIM years and the impact it will have in the coming harvest. All of these experiences showed me that the Body of Christ is in the midst of a massive transition from modern missions to what I would call "emerging missions." This new movement is the focus of this chapter.

Emerging Missions

In 1987, Ray Bakke, a professor and specialist in urban ministry, estimated that by the year 2010, approximately 75 percent of the world's population would be relocated into urban centers.[1] This prediction has held up. Today, the majority of the earth's population is now found in massive urban centers. This migration is the result of industrialization and has only increased in the information age.

Today, only 25 percent of the world's population is located in what we have traditionally called the unreached people groups.[2] For the sake of this chapter, these unreached groups are what I am calling "pre-Christian" because, as we will see in a moment, there are "post-Christian" unreached people groups as well. The pre-Christian groups are the ones normally identified in traditional missionary work. They are often isolated by geographic boundaries such as hilly terrain or dense jungle, and many have a language into which the gospel has never been translated. They have traditions and cultures that haven't been fully understood, and no missionaries have gone in, lived among them, and really incarnated in their midst. Certainly, they don't have indigenous leaders who have been raised up to carry the gospel forward.

Although there are still millions who have never heard of Jesus, the percentage of pre-Christian unreached people is shrinking every day. Missions groups such as the U.S. Center for World Missions, YWAM and Call2all are working in concert to make sure there are no unreached people groups within our generation. For the first time since Jesus' death and resurrection, that is doable, and it is happening.

A Horizontal Shift

While I enthusiastically support these efforts to reach those who have never heard the name of Jesus, I believe the greatest bulk of unreached people is no longer located "out there" somewhere in unknown isolated regions of the world. Instead, they are post-Christian unreached people groups living in global urban centers. They have migrated to find work, education and opportunities, and they are all mixed together in increasing amounts of cultural and subcultural differentiation.

The modern missions movement has primarily focused on *vertical* categories of nations, regions, cultures and languages, but as the earth becomes smaller and more homogeneous, emerging missions has become increasingly *horizontal*. The coming harvest will travel within cultures and subcultures that now span cities, states, nations and continents. A *localized* revival such as the Great Welsh Revival will be increasingly rare, while a *global* revival like the Jesus Movement, which affected an age group across a dozen nations, will be more frequent.

The reason for this is because revival is not primarily a geographical phenomenon but is rather cultural- or *ethne*-oriented. In the past, it has only appeared to be geographic because historic regions were generally occupied by a single culture. Now, as members of those isolated cultures are relocating across the globe in urban centers, they are bringing their cultures with them. Only after they have remained for a generation is their culture able to begin to blend fully with the host culture.

To help illustrate this, let me give you an analogy of pizza and spaghetti. Traditional missions can be compared to number of separate pizza pies—completely different groups of people who were isolated from one another in unattached geographic or cultural areas. The only way we could reach the people living in each "pie" was by shifting our geography and stepping out of our own "crust" into the group's "crust," or out of our own culture and into the group's culture. But now, missions work is like a bowl of spaghetti. In the emerging world, we have hundreds of "noodles" (cultures) existing side by side in the same geographic areas, touching each other, but not connected. We don't have to pack up and leave our region in order to find an unreached people group—we can find one right next door.

San Francisco is a *very* multicultural city. Some might even call it a *city* of cities. There are dozens and dozens of distinct people groups living side by side. In a single neighborhood, you might find a first-generation family from Taiwan living next to a family who just moved there from Guatemala living next to a gay couple in a flat above a punk rock band household. Each household has almost nothing in common except proximity. There are not only different *ethnicities* living side by side but also different kinds of *subcultural groups*.

A Cross-Cultural Exercise

As I previously noted, the biblical word for a people group is *ethne*. An *ethne* is any group of people who relate to one another through specific cultural realities. Starbucks can be an *ethne*; in fact, a Starbucks manager may have more in common with the Starbucks worker he just hired than he does with his next-door neighbor. The gym or a local church can be another kind of *ethne* because we find community and connection there. The person living right next door to us may be close in proximity, but he or she could be as different from us as a person living in the Serengeti.

Let's say I have a gay couple living on one side of me and an American-born Chinese couple living on the other side. The gay couple actually has more in common with a gay person living in

Paris than they do with me. The same is true with the American-born Chinese couple. They have a lot in common with me, but they have *more* in common with other American-born Chinese who have similar parents and grandparents. This is what I mean when I say emerging missions is horizontal.

The point I am making is that any time we share the gospel, chances are it will be a cross-cultural exercise. Whether we realize it or not, once the gospel reaches an individual, it is more likely to be spread through their cultural connections than through their geographical connections. For this reason, we need to shift our focus and do the hard work of understanding the Kingdom longings of the people group whom we are trying to reach. We need to "translate" the gospel into languages and symbols that they can understand. Ultimately, we need to realize that modern evangelism is "missions" and missions is modern evangelism. In a sense, these two entities are now one, because the work that goes into studying a tribe in the Amazon is the same work that needs to go into presenting the gospel to the person next door.

This perspective represents a massive shift from the traditional missions paradigm. The majority of the world is still unreached, but most of these groups are located right next door to us in groups and subcultures that have never been adequately reached by the Church. Many of them wouldn't consider themselves pre-Christian but post-Christian, because they believe they have already examined Christianity and given it a thumbs-down. They have looked at the Church and determined that our faith is inadequate and irrelevant. In their perspective, faith in Jesus doesn't translate into their worldview. This is why for us to touch the coming harvest and bring new believers into a thriving revival culture, we must seek to match the powerful message of the gospel of the Kingdom to the seeking hearts we encounter.

Recontexualizing the Gospel

It is impossible to overstate the importance of culture. I believe that God is the author of culture and that a glorious culture exists in heaven of which earthly culture is just an imperfect reflection. I believe God has embedded the need to generate culture in the human heart as a means of connecting us to one another in deeper ways. We see this in Genesis 11, where we read that the whole earth had one language. God looked upon their cultural unity and declared that nothing would be impossible to them, so He confused their languages and separated them into different language groups. This gave birth to a diversity of culture upon the earth.

Because culture is such a powerful unifying force, the devil has used it to transmit false beliefs and harmful behaviors throughout humanity. To the extent that the enemy has infiltrated culture and used it to blind people, it can be a force of evil in the world. But it is important to understand that culture in itself is a God-given gift. Thus, as we prepare to reach the people in our communities, we need to remember three are aspects of every culture: (1) that which is patently evil, (2) that which is challenging but can be bridged, and (3) that which is divinely inspired, where some aspect of Kingdom culture is expressed by a people group. The question then becomes an issue of discernment: How much of a given culture is aligned with heaven, and how much is not? Obviously, we want to reject that which is patently evil but seek to redeem that which is challenging but can be bridged.

Consider movies as an example. Movies today have found a high level of popularity in our culture. Many believers write some these off as sacrilegious or sinful, but these films can be used to help us bridge the gospel to people with whom we would not otherwise have much in common. Using this kind of thinking, we can "redeem" aspects of culture for the Kingdom. In fact, for a few years I shared the gospel by talking about *Star Wars,* because the idea of an invisible force makes a lot of sense to a person one might bump into on a San Francisco street. Using this term helped me reach into different cultures because I had a message that was already harmonious with ideas in people's minds.

A decade later, *The Matrix* rocked box offices. Granted, the violence was over the top, but the concept that humanity is living in a demonized and deceived world was spot-on. The idea that there are liberators who have broken free from the deception and who now sacrifice their lives to set others free is absolutely true. The film depicts a parable of the Kingdom that is almost point-for-point parallel to the Gospels. I used this movie all over the world to share the gospel of the Kingdom with people who otherwise would have been deaf to the message.

The burden of communication is always on the communicator and not on the communicatee. It is up to us to do the hard work of "recontextualizing" the gospel in order to minimize barriers. However, when we seek to re-present the gospel, we must make sure we never compromise it in any way. A mistake many are making these days is that in their desire to translate the gospel into a language the world can more easily understand, they are beginning to question and even deny fundamental truths that are clear in Scripture. If we do that, we'll lose the purity and potency of the gospel.

We are responsible to communicate clearly, but we must remember that we will never ultimately be able to eliminate the offense of the cross. Ultimately, the cross will always generate stress, and repentance is ultimately at the end of a tectonic stress that has built up in the minds and hearts of men and women. Generally speaking, the quality of conversion is usually related to the quality of stress that has built up beforehand. In our desire to recontextualize Christ, we need to remember that we can't free people from that stress without damaging the conversion process. The lack of tension is often why we have such shallow conversions in western culture today.

So, as Don Richardson did with the Sawi tribes, we need to present the gospel in a way that is indigenous to the culture we are trying to reach. We should do everything we can to present a message that is well thought out and clear to the people. However, we do not ever do this in a way that denies the absolute truths of God. Before I gave my life to Jesus, I was offended and irritated by those who tried to share the gospel with me. But, like a grain of sand in the oyster, the irritation caused me to mull over the truth again and again until I could no longer deny the beauty of Jesus. As a result, a pearl of great price was formed in my heart.

Characteristics of the New Jesus Movement

In light of everything we have discussed so far, where is the world heading? We know what the harvest field *used to* look like, so based on today's cultural trends, what can we anticipate for the future? I believe we can expect the coming harvest to be predominantly *young*, *urban* and *postmodern*.

The Harvest Will Be Predominantly Young
To be the most effective, we need to have a diverse and inclusive ministry with a focus on youth. Obviously, I am not saying that other generations are less important. The Lord clearly wants everyone to be saved (see 2 Pet. 3:9; 1 Tim. 2:3-4). However, those who are young have traditionally been the most responsive to the gospel, and they also make up most of the world's current population. Approximately 52 percent of the world's population is under 30 years old, and the average age of people coming to Christ is actually going down.[3] It used to be understood that as many as 9 out of 10 people accepted Jesus before they were 18. Today, almost half of Americans who make this decision do so before they turn 13, and 2 out of 3 people do so before they turn 18.[4] This is why if we fail to plan for the young, we'll fail to reap this harvest.

The Harvest Will Be Predominantly Urban
As Ray Bakke famously said, "The Bible begins in a garden but ends with a city."[5] The world is changing rapidly, and the economic, cultural and political forces are driving the masses into the megacities. Because of this global exodus from rural areas, we can be confident that the coming harvest will be mainly *urban*. This could be good news for the Church if we respond strategically. The economic necessity and political unrest causing this mass migration could well be part of God's strategy to draw people to Himself.

Although cities are often places of extreme poverty and oppression, they can also provide the concentrated spiritual hunger and pressure that precede a great move of God.

The Harvest Will Be Predominantly Post-Christian

Finally, the harvest will be primarily post-Christian and what many would call "postmodern." The postmodern mindset tends to deconstruct every culture that it encounters. It undermines traditions, questions values, creates generation gaps between parents and children, and disrupts lines of cultural transference from generation to generation. Postmodernists question the traditional categories of thought as well as structures of thinking and the whole notion of absolute truth. They tend to be drawn toward a more existential and experiential framework for validating truth.

Concerning the theological implications, this essentially means that postmodern thought undermines the idea of authority invested in parents, in God and His writings, or in a pastor or traditional leaders. Postmodernism tends to question the very foundations by which traditional evangelism has been propagated around the world. It inherently questions the idea of a book containing absolute truth, the duality of good and evil, and the supremacy of good over that evil. Some of this thinking emerged back in the 1960s and 1970s with the hippie movement. Most of those individuals drifted back into more "normal" ways of thinking, but their children are thinking entirely outside the box.

The influx of postmodernism, western cultural imperialism and relativism have permeated all the major cultural streams today so that even emerging Muslims, Hindus and Buddhists are influenced it. During a recent trip to several countries in Africa, Ron Luce of Teen Mania noted, "Africa has been invaded by our western culture, and [it] is destroying it and making it harder for people to win others to Jesus. In Uganda they told me that it has totally broken down the family unit. There is no respect for parents, and young people are acting out what they see on the media outlets."[6]

A few years ago, I was hanging out with Indian students in Delhi, and I was surprised to find they were just as hip and sinful, sarcastic and cynical as their American counterparts. In every area of the world, the tightly woven cultural fabrics of nations and people groups are unraveling and being torn apart by thinking that questions authority. The only exceptions seem to be those cultures and regions that have either rejected western media or haven't yet received the technology to experience it. Add to this the fact that around the world teachers and professors who have bought into a post-modern, post-Christian mindset are teaching the majority of students, and we can understand the challenge we are facing.

What Can We Do?

This is what we can expect the coming harvest to look like. If we merely glance at the surface, it seems the members of this emerging youth culture are driven by lust, pride, greed, rebellion and a number of other sinful things. But as we look deeper, we can begin to see that every sinful behavior is tied to a misguided attempt to satisfy an individual's unmet Kingdom longings. So, how do we respond to this predominantly young, urban, post-Christian harvest? How can we present the gospel to them in ways they will understand? I believe there are three things we need to do: (1) pray, (2) prepare, and (3) grow in our ability to walk in the supernatural power of God.

We Need to Pray
In Luke 10:1-2, we read that Jesus saw the harvest was plentiful but the workers were few, so He instructed the disciples to "pray the Lord of the harvest to send out laborers into His harvest." Later, in Acts 2, we find the 120 praying in the upper room as the power of God is poured out on them for witness. In Acts 13, the prophets and teachers are praying and fasting when the Holy Spirit tells them to send out Paul and Barnabas. Prayer is the precursor to the supernatural power of God.

When I look at Church history, I am amazed at how Jesus prepared the Early Church for revival by making them wait until they had what they needed. This implies that the years of living with

Him, participating in the miracles and power encounters, watching His death, and hanging out with Him after He rose again,
weren't enough. He told them to wait, and they did—all day long,
every day, not knowing what they were waiting for or how long
they would have to wait.

It would be irresponsible to think we are any different. Every
revival in history began with a season of intense prayer and heart
preparation among a small group of people. As we have previously
examined, even with the forewarning of prayer, most revivals of
the past hit suddenly before the Church was prepared. Often, the
smaller initial group ended up catalyzing the outpouring while
the larger Body of Christ remained oblivious and uninvolved, as in
the Welsh and Azusa Street Revivals. Peculiarly, many revivals blow
past most of the existing Church.

Prayer is one of the primary elements of revival and awakening.
It's a way in which we can help the Church come into a place of
readiness so it can steward God's work more carefully. He will set
aside special intercessors who are called specifically to pray for revival, but ultimately each of us needs to begin to pray for the coming harvest. There is a call to center ourselves in the Lord, which
will increase our ability to hear His voice, help us to apply the
Word of God in prayer, and come to a new level with Him.

In addition to prayer, we need to focus on worship. Worship is
an irreplaceable part of the vertical connection we were created to
have with God. During the past few years, there has been a growing
recognition of its value, especially as an expression of corporate
prayer, and powerful songs have been written to lead people into
places of deep encounter with the Lord. Worship and prayer movements have been coming together in what is called the Harp and
Bowl ministry, which focuses on intimacy with God as well as the
infinite power available to us in who He is. Inspired by the amazing
ministry of the International House of Prayer (IHOP) and other
similar ministries, prayer houses are popping up all over the world
with a unified goal of continuous prayer and worship year round.

Thankfully, worship is becoming emphasized as a *lifestyle* again
as opposed to merely singing a few songs on Sunday morning.

People are realizing that how much they love and trust the Lord depends largely on how much they have cultivated this lifestyle of worship and that genuine worship is much more than a single weekly encounter. A. W. Tozer once said, "If you do not worship God seven days a week, you do not worship Him on one day a week. There is no such thing known in heaven as Sunday worship."[7] The Church needs to live out of a place of awe and wonder of God in the midst of its immediate circumstances. Until we can do this, revival will be difficult, if not impossible, to sustain.

The key in all of this is to become more in tune with God and see people the way He sees them. When Jesus looked on the multitudes, as recorded in Matthew 9:35-38, He saw them as weary and scattered, like sheep without a shepherd, and He was moved with compassion. Obviously, we can look at a person's "symptoms" and be aghast: *Oh, they have a bleeding arm. They have an oozing sore. They're caked with dirt. They're lepers. They've been burned or horribly scarred.* But these are only symptoms. Instead of looking at the symptoms, we need to look at the *root causes* of the problem.

We Need to Prepare

The first step to preparing for the coming harvest must be personal. We have to begin adjusting our lifestyles to match our vision of the future. Personal preparation is all about getting close to Jesus, discovering our gifts and passions so we can serve according to our unique design, and beginning to develop toward our God-given destiny. It is also important for us to begin to simplify our lifestyles according to God's values and priorities. As we do this, it is valuable to connect with other believers in home groups or ministries that capture our heart and direct us toward the lost.

In addition to the personal preparation, we also need to begin to prepare corporately. Ministries and churches need to strategize and plan for the coming harvest of souls. In the same way a young couple will prepare a nursery the moment they know they are expecting a child, we need to prepare for the new spiritual babies that are about to be born into the Kingdom. We are pregnant with the promise of a great harvest, so it is time to get ready.

We Need to Value the Supernatural

One of the principal items that sets the emerging culture apart is its strong attraction to the supernatural. All we have to do is look at popular movies, books and television shows to see that today's youth have a great interest in the spiritual realm. Despite its potential drawbacks—such as involvement in witchcraft and the occult—this interest in the supernatural is wonderful, because God's kingdom is supernatural.

As God's people, we are called into a lifestyle that rises above impossibilities and engages the unseen realm in such a way that signs, wonders, miracles, angels and healings become normal. God says that our words have power (see Prov. 18:21), that He has given us His authority (see Luke 10:19), that the Spirit who brought Jesus back from the dead now lives in us (see Rom. 8:11), that our faith moves mountains (see Matt. 17:20), and that whatever we ask for in His name will be ours (see John 14:13). This is supernatural life at its finest.

Jesus never separated the message of the Kingdom from the power of the Kingdom. When He was ministering to Jewish believers, signs and wonders followed, and He also reasoned with them from Scripture. When the apostle Paul later went to the Gentiles, signs and wonders were non-negotiable. In order for him to truly demonstrate the reality of Jesus Christ, signs and wonders were absolutely imperative. In the same way, as we go forth in this day and age with the gospel, we must be proficient in signs and wonders. There are many competing doctrines and ideas raging in our culture, and if we hope to bring in a harvest, we cannot present it with "persuasive words of human wisdom, but in demonstration of the Spirit and of power" (1 Cor. 2:4).

Prophecy, which throughout the Bible was an active part of the supernatural life, was largely reintroduced to the Church during revival in the early twentieth century. Since that time, it has been a long, slow and bumpy road as believers have sought to embrace it and discover how to walk in it. The Church today is relearning that though there are people the Lord sets apart as prophets, we all have prophetic ability because we're all intrinsically wired to hear and know God's voice (see John 10:4).

This ability to hear God's voice is noticeably effective in reaching a generation who is interested in the supernatural realm. In this way, our culture's God-given desire for the supernatural works hand-in-hand with how we engage the harvest. We know that everything offered by psychics, mediums, astrology, mysticism and the paranormal in general is a mere counterfeit to what is available in the kingdom of God.

A New Awakening

Most of the unreached people in the emerging generation have become resigned to the idea that even if there were a God out there somewhere, He wouldn't care about them. However, the Body of Christ as a whole is discovering how to draw upon its God-given ability to hear God's voice and respond in tangible ways. We are awakening to the gifts of the Spirit and the application of those gifts in evangelism. In the next section, we will examine how we can use those gifts to overcome obstacles and bring about revival in our family, community, economy, authority and spiritual reality.

SECTION TWO

Building the
Bridges of Revival

*And Jesus came and spoke to them, saying, "All authority has been given
to Me in heaven and on earth. Go therefore and make disciples of all the nations,
baptizing them in the name of the Father and of the Son and of the Holy Spirit,
teaching them to observe all things that I have commanded you; and lo,
I am with you always, even to the end of the age." Amen.*

MATTHEW 28:18-20

Revival Culture and Family

While serving as a pastor in San Francisco, I had the privilege of connecting with people from dozens of different lifestyles. I ministered among the homeless who struggled with mental illness, young gay prostitutes who sold their dignity for next to nothing, gang members who were wanted by the law, and college students who were burdened with the pressure of paternal expectations and demands. I ministered to successful entrepreneurs, community leaders, actors, artists, ballet dancers and everyone in between. Most of these people had one thing in common: they had experienced some measure of physical or emotional orphanhood and still carried the wounds of their dysfunctional or broken families in their lives.

Culture is a binding power for humanity. It draws us together and connects us, manifesting itself among us in five different dimensions: (1) *family*, (2) *community*, (3) *economy*, (4) *authority* and (5) *spirituality*. Each of these components has a role in helping move us into the future in peace and harmony. The role of the family, which is to provide a sense of identity and security on an individual and corporate level, is the first dimension of culture that is essential for us to understand if we hope to build a bridge between the culture of this world and the culture of revival.

I am the father of seven amazing children. Through the years, I have grown in my understanding of what Scripture teaches about the beauty, power, glory and legacy of *family*. I have also grown in my understanding of the real challenges of raising a healthy family in our generation. As I noted previously, I was raised

in a broken home, which first opened my eyes to the importance of
family. As a pastor I have worked closely with hundreds of families
of all sizes and shapes. There's no denying that family is the most
important relational structure in existence.

Sadly, the world we live in is becoming increasingly fatherless and
motherless. While it is true that broken families and broken parents
have always existed, the current pressures of life in the Western world
have resulted in even those who were raised in the best of homes to
experience a lack of parental love at an unprecedented level. So, as we
begin to examine the challenges and opportunities of reaching the
coming harvest, I want to first look at the family, which represents the
foundational component of culture. With few exceptions, the people
we will be reaching in the next few years will have been shaped within
families that, to one extent or another, were broken.

In truth, many of the personal and societal problems we face in
this world can be traced to the breakdown of the family. However, in
our attempts to find solutions, too often we choose to look at the
symptoms of the problem and not the *root cause*. Uncovering the roots
enables us to bring healing and restoration, rather than recrimina-
tion and shame. Our goal is to see what Jesus saw when He looked
at the masses: sheep without a shepherd who are in need of our compassion and guidance.

As we build the culture of family into the Church, we will be able
to connect people to the Fatherhood of God and bring healing to
the orphanhood of our world. So, in this chapter, we will take a look
at what Scripture says about family.

The Culture of Heaven:
Affirmation and Love

God's value for family is revealed in both the Old and New Testa-
ments. When Jesus became flesh and dwelt among us, the distinction
between God the Father and God the Son suddenly became visible.
We see this clearly when the Father proclaimed His affirmation of Jesus at the River Jordan, saying, "This is My beloved Son, in whom I am
well pleased" (Matt. 3:17). Notice that He did not say, "This is My

beloved Servant, in whom I am well pleased." He did not call Jesus a worker, or a governor, or even a king. He called Him *His Son*, and throughout Scripture, God reveals Himself as the Father.

I used to think that "God the Father" was a convenient metaphor God used to help us relate to Him as a loving superior. But over time, I have begun to realize that my assumption was wrong. The idea of fatherhood and family did not originate on this planet but in the heart of God. He didn't use the idea of the family as a *type* or *metaphor* of love but to reveal how He *actually operates*. The "family" on earth is patterned after the family of heaven. The apostle Paul describes this family in Ephesians 3:14-19:

> I bow my knees to the Father of our Lord Jesus Christ, from whom the whole *family in heaven* and earth is named, that He would grant you, according to the riches of His glory, to be strengthened with might through His Spirit in the inner man, that Christ may dwell in your hearts through faith; that you, being rooted and grounded in love, may be able to comprehend with all the saints what is the width and length and depth and height—to know the love of Christ which passes knowledge; that you may be filled with all the fullness of God (emphasis added).

The revelation of heaven is a revelation of *family*, and the families on earth are just a dim reflection of the glorious family in heaven. God the Father has patterned family in this way so we may experience His love and the spirit of adoption (see Rom. 8:15). Truly, we were created to be the sons and daughters of God, and in Jesus Christ, we are being restored to that original relationship.

We were created for glory, to rule and reign on the earth (see Rev. 5:10), and family is a primary means God uses to accomplish this goal. We see this in the Garden of Eden when God told Adam and Eve to "be fruitful and multiply, fill the earth and subdue it" (Gen. 1:28; see also 9:1). The father and mother were commissioned to raise children in a relational environment that would impart the vision and mission of heaven to subdue and steward our planet.

Family is the source. It is the head, or foundation, of every person's identity. To the extent that family is healthy, a child will be raised with a healthy sense of identity and destiny. To the extent that family is broken, there will broken hearts and lives.

Understanding the Kingdom Longings for Family

According to God's design, there are three primary elements, or nutrients, that a healthy family structure provides for a growing child: *trust*, *love* and *hope*. God has embedded a longing for these elements in our hearts to keep us seeking true family until we find it (see Ps. 68:6). Unfortunately, when this longing goes unfulfilled, it can drive us into attitudes and actions that work against our highest good.

Trust and Security

The first element that God imparts in family is *trust*. Trust brings security, and it comes when children know they are protected and provided for. Family is meant to instill a deep sense of safety in which the members know they are secure. That understanding is fundamental to the positive formation of identity.

The moment a child is born and brought to the mother's breast, he or she has a sense of security and trust. The child knows he or she will not be abandoned or deprived. That trust is instantaneous in the child's heart and is reinforced again and again through thousands of acts of kindness that are shown to the child during the first years of his or her life. Little children who are raised in this way are able to trust implicitly, which makes Jesus' statement in Matthew 18:3 all the more meaningful: "Unless you are converted and become as little children, you will by no means enter the kingdom of heaven."

As children, we begin life with the capability of great trust. It is only through a process of instability, abuse, loss and unfulfilled promises that we learn to distrust. For this reason, our ability to trust God as our provider and protector is ultimately linked to our ability to trust our parents. When trust is violated, insecurity sets in. Insecurity speaks to our souls and tells us we are not worthy. It tells us we will be loved only if we perform well or if we follow the rules.

As we begin to believe this lie, our trust in the world around us becomes conditional, which not only affects our relationship with human authority figures but also our relationship with God. Insecurity gives rise to fears and anxieties that undermine our confidence in God and our ability to lay hold of His grace in life. The good news is that trust and security, which may have been damaged in childhood, can be restored through healing prayer and a thriving personal relationship with Jesus. It is in this type of relationship that we discover His absolute faithfulness to protect us and provide for our every need.

Love and Identity

The second element God imparts through family is unconditional *love*, which is the source of identity. In order to form a healthy identity, a child needs to know in the depths of his or her being that he or she is loved. When parents look at their infant and the infant sees the light in their eyes, it awakens something within that child, even before he or she is old enough to understand.

Our ability to give love to others is deeply affected by the degree to which we received love. Much of the selfishness and the self-centeredness in our world is rooted in the lack of love in our homes. If the foundation of love and belonging are not laid securely in our hearts as a child, we will often end up impacting the community in ways that are destructive and harmful.

Like trust and security, love and identity can be reset and restored in a loving relationship with the living God. As we learn to receive God's love into the core of our being and begin to align our beliefs with His Word, we can be transformed by the renewing of our minds (see Rom. 12:2). God knows each of us fully, and He loves us unconditionally. He also designed each of us for His glory. We belong to Him. Through the family, He is the ultimate source of our identity.

Hope and Destiny

The third element that God imparts through family is *hope*, which is the engine of destiny. Hope fuels the desire for a good future and fulfills God's purpose in this life and in the life to come. Loving parents are given the primary responsibility for supplying the vision, motivation and guidance their children need to become the people God has called them to be.

In Psalm 127:4, Solomon writes, "Like arrows in the hand of a warrior, so are the children of one's youth." Children are "arrows" of potential that sit in the quiver of the family. God calls parents to *aim* their children toward their God-given destinies, release the string, and send them into their life callings. In other words, God has designed the family to be the incubator of destiny—an environment of trust, love and hope in which an immature and imperfect child can grow into maturity and become who he or she was created to be.

For a child to form a clear sense of destiny in his or her heart, that child must be in an atmosphere that is infused with hope. Hope focuses on the gold within a child instead of the dirt that hides the treasure. Hope processes the disappointments of life in a redemptive way and helps a child move beyond embarrassment, frustration and resignation so he or she can step into courage, perseverance and prevailing faith. When hope and destiny are lacking in childhood, they can be reestablished in relationship with the Holy Spirit, who is able to work within a person to do God's good pleasure.

The Culture of Earth: Fatherlessness and Orphanhood

When these elements of trust, security, love, hope and discipline are not provided in a family, a child can grow up with a kind of "spiritual scurvy" in his or her emotional and spiritual composition. Given this, we can see why God places so much value on family. We can also get a glimpse of what the world would have been like if the first family had not sinned. If we can imagine a world in which all children are loved unconditionally from their first breath onward, we will see a picture of heaven on earth.

The Effects of Sin

God's original plan was sabotaged in the Fall, and the family became deeply damaged. Man turned against woman, and woman against man. Sons turned against parents and against one another. As a result of sin, God exiled the family from the Garden of His presence, and their alienation from God subsequently infected the generations.

In addition to the harm humanity brought upon itself in the Garden, Satan has waged ongoing spiritual attacks against the family. The enemy is fully aware of the power of family for good or ill, and throughout history he has made it his target. Some of these attacks come in the form of fiery darts, such as temptations, accusations and tormenting thoughts (see Eph. 6:16). Some of these come in the form of systemic problems that are either the direct or indirect result of the enemy's influence in society. Meanwhile, people of faith have sought to keep the family healthy and thriving, knowing it is the fountain of future generations.

This struggle has intensified, and during the last two centuries the relationship between parents and children has increasingly deteriorated. As society moved from agrarian to industrial, the pressures against the family began to heighten. Now, in the information age, we have introduced incredible amounts of technology and entertainment into the family structure. Obviously, none of these things are inherently negative, but as a culture we have been drawn away from the kind of lifestyle that once nurtured family. The relational quality time between parents and children has become strained and limited, and at least in part, the pressures of current westernized life has minimized the role of the family.

The Spirit of Orphanhood

These societal changes and pressures, along with a climbing divorce rate and a growing number of teenage pregnancies and single-parent homes, has given rise to an increasing sense of orphanhood. What many are calling the "spirit of orphanhood" is rampant in our world and is driving much of the sinfulness that is taking place in our society. This orphan spirit produces a sense of deprivation and unmet need in the victim and can compel him or her to engage in many different kinds of addictive and self-destructive behaviors to help meet these deep inner needs. These addictive behaviors, in turn, can lead to disassociate behavior, personality fracturing or sexual impurity. People with unmet Kingdom longings are also prone to making lifestyle choices that are potentially harmful to themselves and others.

Over the years, I have counseled hundreds of men bound by homosexuality. In my experience, I have found that the vast majority of these men were raised in homes with either physically or emotionally absent fathers. This kind of upbringing creates an unmet need for male affection and often leads to the sexualization of that need. As a result, many of these men experience some degree of male attraction at a young age, and many conclude they were born gay. However, I believe in most cases this is simply a result of a true Kingdom longing that has gone unfulfilled.

Fatherlessness and orphanhood affect heterosexual men and women as well. Women who come from broken families often have a powerful desire to create that perfect family they never had, which often results in young women being attracted to the wrong kind of man and getting pregnant at a young age. This has created a growing number of single-parent homes in this country in which the unresolved issues of the heart are often passed to the next generation. There are many single-parent families out there, both moms and dads, who are doing their best to supply everything their children need to be healthy in the home, but without the help of extended family or other people in their faith community stepping in to make up the lack, they will have trouble delivering the full range of nutrients their children need to eliminate the risk of spiritual orphanhood.

Understanding the Orphaned Heart

In the parable of the prodigal son (see Luke 15:11-32), Jesus gave us an amazing picture of an extravagant, loving father who brings healing to two kinds of orphanhood. In this story, the father has two sons who are unable to see the love he has for them, and they react to this perceived lack in opposite ways. The younger son demands an early inheritance and journeys to a far city, where he parties until his money runs out. When this occurs, he tries to make it on his own, but eventually he returns to the father with a repentant heart and is forgiven and restored.

The second son responds to his pain by remaining outwardly dutiful but withdrawing from the father in resentment. When the younger son returns and the older son sees his father roll out the red carpet and restore his brother's identity, authority and destiny, it sends him into a rage. He refuses to join the party and accuses his father of being unappreciative and unfair. To this, the father responds, "You are always with me, and all that I have is yours" (v. 31).

In this way, the parable provides us with two distinct pictures of orphanhood: (1) the rebellious orphan, and (2) the dutiful orphan. These two distinctions will help us understand the effects of broken families in our world.

The Rebellious Orphan

The younger son chose to react by defying and insulting his father. By demanding his inheritance, he was essentially telling his father, "You are dead to me." In his anger, this son embraced an attitude of entitlement and rebellion that provided the justification for living the lifestyle he chose to lead. It wasn't until he hit rock bottom that he saw the error of his ways and turned back to the father's love.

Rebellious sons or daughters respond to the absence of parental love with disrespect and defiance. As with the prodigal son, they are not usually driven by the pressure to perform or succeed. These individuals tend to find comfort and release in behaviors that are considered sinful such as alcohol abuse, drug abuse, other addictive behaviors and various kinds of immorality. They tend to be careless with the use of time, money and resources and neglect family and long-term relationships.

The journey for rebellious orphans back to the Father begins with a realization of the father's love and a recognition of their broken state apart from that love. They desire forgiveness for their sins and restoration from the damage they have inflicted on themselves.

The Dutiful Orphan

The older son, on the other hand, chose to react to the father by trying harder and working harder. He sacrificed his happiness and his social life in an effort to win his father's love and favor, not realizing he had these things all along. Unfortunately, the harder he tried, the more he grew to resent his father. He withdrew his heart while at the same time maintaining his outward obedience. In his anger, this son adopted an attitude of self-righteousness and hypocrisy to justify his lifestyle of empty performance. It wasn't until he encountered his father's love for his brother that he began to recognize his own need for the father's love.

This kind of orphanhood doesn't struggle as much with outward problems but with inward ones. Often, these people are performance-driven and will judge their worth on the basis of how they feel they have succeeded. They tend to live sacrificial lives, giving up immediate pleasures for long-term goals, but often forgetting why. These kinds of orphans will be diligent at work, committed at church, faithful to their families, and responsible with their resources. Sadly, their quest for excellence is actually a search for security, identity and destiny. What they are really longing for is unconditional love.

The journey for dutiful orphans back to the Father begins with the realization that they have always had the Father's affection and that everything the Father possesses has belonged to them from the beginning. They must turn from unbelief and offense, renounce the demands of performance pressure and religious duty, and step into a life of delight in the Lord. They need to humble themselves and join the party!

Salvation Solutions

The most effective message in reaching the orphaned heart is that of unconditional love and new birth in Christ. People need to realize that following Jesus is not a self-help program in which they change themselves or fix their problems—they must be born again. When Nicodemus approached Jesus and asked how he could experience this new birth, Jesus said to him, "Most assuredly, I say to you, unless one is born of water and the Spirit, he cannot enter the kingdom of God. . . . For God so loved the world that He gave His only begotten Son, that whoever believes in Him should not perish but have everlasting life" (John 3:5,16). Later, Paul wrote, "If anyone is in Christ, he is a new creation; old things have passed away; behold, all things have become new" (2 Cor. 5:17).

The concept of family will prove to be an amazing bridge as we seek to help people transition from the culture of this world to the culture of revival. There is good news for those who have been raised in broken families *and* those whose families were relatively healthy. Our message to the unreached is that they can be born again into a new life, forgiven for the sins they have committed, and empowered to forgive those who have sinned against them. They can experience the spirit of adoption in which their interactions with the Father's love become tangible and transformational. They can begin and grow in a relationship with their heavenly Father, who is absolutely perfect. He has promised to never leave them nor forsake them (see Heb. 13:5), and He will always be "the Father of lights, with whom there is no variation or shadow of turning" (Jas. 1:17).

Our message to the unreached is that they can be part of this family of newborn people who have received forgiveness and are receiving healing and freedom from the wounds of the past. They can know the Father and be part of a Kingdom family with spiritual mothers and fathers who will impart the love that was lacking in their lives. They will be able to look to the future and see the purpose of God laid out before them and be empowered to bring transformation to the world around them.

Building Revival Culture in Families

Edith Schaeffer, co-founder of L'Abri with her husband, Francis, once compared a family to a child's mobile. A mobile is a set of figures suspended by a string and dowels that moves in the breeze. Each of the figures is connected, but each is always shifting in relation to the others. This picture has a lot of meaning for a family the size of mine. We are tied together by love, blood and a rich history of living life together, but most of all we are tied together by the Lord and His overarching care for us. Through the years, we have experienced many challenges and have enjoyed many miraculous answers to prayer. By the grace of God we have managed to maintain a bit of revival culture in our family through some unusual examples of supernatural power.

The Toronto Outpouring
In my estimation, there is no greater model for exploring how to build a revival culture of family than the outpouring that began in Toronto in 1994. This move of the Holy Spirit, which has now touched millions of people around the globe, was sparked at a conference featuring speakers Randy Clark and John Arnott. God began to move in unusual ways, and now, more than 15 years later, the Toronto Church has received 3.5 million visitors and has spawned major revivals around the world.

One of the most notable works that came out of this outpouring was Iris Ministries, led by Rolland and Heidi Baker. Iris Ministries has planted more than 10,000 churches in a little over 10 years and seen phenomenal miracles. A recent *Christianity Today* cover story documented some of these miracles, which include healings of the deaf, restoration of sight to the blind, multiplication of food, and more than 100 verified raisings of the dead.[1]

Diane and I first heard about the Toronto movement in March of 1994, a few weeks after the outpouring began. Within a week, we were on a plane to Toronto with three of our pastors to experience firsthand this move of God. We had been walking in renewal for more than 10 years, but we were hungry for more.

Our first evening began with awesome worship, great teaching—and then came the ministry time. In order for us to pray for one another, we had to stack about half the chairs in the back of the room because the space was so small. The Holy Spirit began to move in a powerful way, and dozens of people began shaking and falling under the power of God. There were tears. There was laughter. There were healings and amazing miracles. Above all, there was a revelation of the Father's love that I had never before experienced in quite the same way. The Father filled His children with the spirit of adoption and touched them with playful joy. He lifted burdens and simply threw a party for His kids. We spent the better part of a week in Toronto, attending two to three meetings a day, basking and rejoicing in the presence of God.

When we returned to San Francisco, we were uncertain about the next step to take. We knew God had touched us in an unusual way, and we were confident the touch was authentic. This impartation of the Father's love and the experience of the presence and power of the Holy Spirit was not something we could keep to ourselves, so we called a few friends and started meeting that night with about a 150 people. God began to move in a powerful way, and we ended up holding meetings six nights a week for more than a year. In the process, we ministered to thousands of people and saw tremendous miracles, signs and wonders, and we witnessed *very* authentic interactions and encounters with the Holy Spirit.

At one point, an afterschool program for disadvantaged children in the Sixth Street—the sons and daughters of drug addicts and prostitutes—began bringing their kids to our gatherings almost every night. They would fall to the ground and lay there for 45 minutes to an hour, with tears streaming down their faces, glorious smiles and beautiful countenances as they had visions of heaven and encounters with the Lord. For those of you who don't know this, skid row kids don't usually act this way!

A Key to Building Revival Culture

Each night, we hosted hundreds of these hungry hearts who came from around the Bay Area to worship the Lord and encounter the Holy Spirit. We received numerous visits from key leaders in the Toronto outpouring, including Randy Clark and the Arnotts. On many of these occasions, we had more than 1,000 people in our gatherings, and there were few nights when we had less than 200 to 300 people in attendance. By the time the Spirit of God was finished at the end of the night, scores of people would be lying on the floor, soaking in God's presence and having deep encounters with Him.

During this season, I attended a number of pastors' meetings, and the Spirit of God moved in a similar way. It wasn't always easy or without controversy, but *many* pastors in our region were powerfully touched. We traveled to churches in Latin America, Vietnam and the Philippines and saw the fire that God was releasing upon us spread to others. We also saw a tremendous move of the Holy Spirit in my mentor's Bible School and orphanage in India as a result of the Toronto outpouring. We still have an amazing video of hundreds of young Indian orphans being touched by the Father's love and ministering to one another in supernatural power.

In the process of this outpouring, we learned how to build a revival culture around what God was doing in a way that would sustain the work of the Holy Spirit and channel that work to the lost and broken. I believe that the greatest key we learned for building revival culture in families was that it is all about the message of the Father's love and the importance of the family of God. For too long, believers have been perceived as an impersonal institution when, in fact, we are supposed to be the family of God. Although the Body of Christ depends on effective organization, it should never be reduced to a mere institution. Church is about *relationship*, first with God, but also with one another. It is in relationship that we begin to understand the true power of spiritual family.

Cultivating Family Values

As we seek to build a new culture of family on the earth, we need to start with our values and priorities. Our family values should be focused on relationships and qualities such as intimacy, authenticity, integrity and love, which provide us with nutrients at the heart of our new identity in Christ. We have *truly* been born again—we have a fresh start—and we need to cultivate stability and consistency in our homes so our sons and daughters can be secure in their identities. We need to fill our environment with joy, hope and positive perspectives, which communicate to our children that their futures are bright in the Lord. That is really what *family* is all about. It is a place where we can believe, a place where we can belong, and a place where we can become everything that God created us to be.

In the same way, as we think about the approaching harvest, we need to adjust our values and priorities so we will be able to provide for the spiritual infants who will soon be coming to our homes. Imagine a young couple preparing for their first child. Up to this point, they have been enjoying the benefits of marriage without the costs of parenthood. They have the freedom to live, work and play at their own discretion. But when the pregnancy test comes back positive, everything changes. They envision themselves holding their little one—the fruit of their union. They begin to plan for a third person in their household who won't always be able to keep up with them in their live-work-and-play world. They begin to budget for the baby, because cribs and changing tables are expensive. They begin to remodel the spare room into a nursery with all the trimmings. Babies change priorities.

This is the important concept we need to grasp: if the prophecies of the coming harvest are true, it means the Body of Christ is *pregnant*, and babies are about to come into the house. If we are a true family, we will want to welcome them, take care of them and love them. The Church is more than just an orphanage—we are not simply caring for those whom nobody else wants. We are truly birthing people into a spiritual family that will not only last on this side of heaven but will also endure forever in heaven. This is part of what it means to be a spiritual family: dirty diapers.

As we foster this outcome, we can counteract the brokenness and the orphanhood of our current generation and supply answers to the Kingdom longings that people are expressing in so many broken ways.

Healthy Family Expressions

Once we have addressed our values and priorities, we need to build systems and structures that will help us care for the new babies. The first thing we must do to provide a culture of family is to build an inclusive culture that will reach out to those who are seeking and invite them to join the family. Many people who give their lives to Jesus or express an interest in Him end up feeling neglected by the Church. As believers in Christ, we need to be like the people Jesus spoke about in the parables of the lost sheep (see Luke 15:4-7), the lost coin (see vv. 8-10) and the lost son (see vv. 11-32). In each case, those who lost something were committed to seeking and saving that which was lost.

The second thing we need to do to provide a culture of family for our baby believers is to build healthy "incubators" or discipleship structures. This means that once people come into the Church, we help them learn how it functions, how the heart of God works, and how to walk out their new life in Jesus. This is not merely a matter of *teaching* but also a matter of guiding them to become the people God has called them to be. Discipleship is the process of helping toddlers grow by including them in formal and informal training opportunities, both one-on-one and in small groups. There are many good programs available to support this purpose if you are limited in your ability to develop your own.

Next, we need to make sure there is a spiritual hospital for the new babies, because the people coming in are going to be injured and infected. In much the same way hospitals have a neo-natal intensive care unit that is focused on little babies who are injured or born with defects, we need to be ready with focused care for the people coming in who will be wounded or spiritually malnourished. We are going to have to supply extra nutrients, antibiotics and intensive care to kill the "diseases" they picked up before they came to Christ.

According to Malachi 4:6, in the last days God will turn the hearts of mothers and fathers to their children and the hearts of the children to their parents, which will restrain the curse of orphanhood from further damaging the earth. For too long this world has long been stricken with the curse of fatherlessness, and we see its fruit in every aspect of society. It is time to reconnect the generations in a way that releases the full nutrients of parental love and spiritual adoption. It is time for those in the Body of Christ to be empowered to bring forth a new generation of believers who have experienced the transformation that comes from being raised in the family of God.

Revival Culture and Community

As I mentioned in chapter 5, in the year 2000 we renamed our church in San Francisco "Promised Land Fellowship." We moved to new offices on Polk Street, which is famous for its nightlife and gay prostitution. We had been doing significant outreaches on this street for years, and a number of people from that area had come to know the Lord through our ministry. Around this time, Adam and Dan, two men who had a vision to reach out to the rave club scene, joined our team.

Adam had worked at a couple of major nightclubs, including one of the most notorious gay clubs in San Francisco. It was while working there that Adam met the Lord Jesus and was radically saved. After a season of training at a strong discipleship ministry, he joined our church. Dan, on the other hand, came from a more "conservative" background, and he previously had worked with YWAM and other ministries. He was a striking figure with his shaved head, futuristic clothing and five-pointed stars shaved into his beard.

These two men of God began to use our offices on the weekends as an outreach center for the people on Polk Street. When we later moved, they converted the Polk Street storefront into a rave club. They played different kinds of club music, installed art on the walls, and had different dance environments in addition to a prayer room. They called this new ministry "Love's Revenge."

For the next several years, Love's Revenge reached out into the San Francisco underground scene, the fashion world, and the various branches of the local art community. Dan and Adam hosted major concerts and participated in many art events around the city. They began to reach many people in the local world of modeling, fashion, hair and makeup. God was moving throughout the city in wonderful ways.

We decided to take things to the next level by doing some major events in well-known secular venues. The first event of this kind was called "Identity." We held it in The Cell Space, an alternative community center used by the Burning Man group for some their events. Identity was a multi-media expression of the gospel designed to reach those who would never darken the door of a church. Through Adam's connections, we recruited models, fashion designers and makeup people from both the secular and Christian worlds to help us create this event.

To capture the theme of "identity," our designers created outfits that depicted different aspects of brokenness in our culture, including lust, materialism, pride and fear. Then, in the middle of the show, we put in a transitional moment in which one of the models, who had just recently come to the Lord, experienced a massive conversion.

This model, Derrick, was well known in the fashion community for his looks and his ongoing struggle with HIV/AIDS. He was a tall, striking black man with a shaved head and an amazing physique. He entered the catwalk with seductive clothing and a haughty attitude, but as he reached the end of the walk, he mimed an encounter with God, fell to his knees, and rose with a new heart. The fashion show changed from that point on. The models now wore beautiful clothing—royal, dignified and powerful—that reflected their new identity in Christ.

In addition to the fashion show, we wrote an evangelistic leaflet about the nature of identity and distributed it to hundreds of attendees. We offered a variety of other performances, including spoken word, a drum circle, a rock band and women in kimonos serving sushi and non-alcoholic drinks. We created a live art center, environmental installations, and even had Cirque du Soleil aerial dancers spinning on massive ribbons above the crowd. Some amazing Christian DJs mixed up some powerful beats to top off the night as hundreds of people danced their hearts out. This event was so successful that the *San Francisco Chronicle* did a full-page write up on it, complete with pictures.

In the process of pioneering Love's Revenge, we discovered an amazing bridge that brought revival culture to the culture of this world: the bridge of *community*. We live in a world of disconnection, alienation and isolation. Even in big cities with populations in the hundreds of thousands, many people struggle with feelings of lone-liness. This sense of isolation causes them to gravitate to various groups, clubs and subcultures where they can feel they belong. Un-fortunately, many of these communities offer only limited connec-tion and promote lifestyles that are contrary to the Kingdom.

God created each of us to desire community and fellowship with others. To the degree we are able to understand this power of community and build strong Kingdom communities on the earth is the degree to which we will be able to foster a revival culture that reaches the lost and sustains the next generation.

The Culture of Heaven:
Community and Fellowship

Just as the value of family is trumpeted throughout Scripture, so is the value of community—and the two are interrelated. When-ever we see heaven depicted in Scripture, we see pictures of com-munity. In Luke 2:8-14, we see that on the night Jesus was born, a multitude of angels appeared to the shepherds and sang praises to God (see Luke 2:8-14). In Revelation 7:9-11, John witnesses a multitude of angels and creatures gathered around the throne of God. In Hebrews 12:1, we are told that we are "surrounded by so great a cloud of witnesses"—departed believers who have joined the heavenly community. Based on these descriptions of heaven alone, we can see that God loves community.

Jesus launched His ministry through community, and it is vis-ible in everything He did on earth. First, as we discussed in the last chapter, He started with a "family" of 12 men (see Mark 3:14-19), and then He added 70 others (see Luke 10:1). Later, in the book of

Acts, we find that the community has grown to number 120 (see Acts 1:15). According to Paul, after Jesus' resurrection 500 people saw Him at once (see 1 Cor. 15:6). Jesus started His ministry with a family and expanded it into a community because there is great power released when different kinds of people connect in relationship and fellowship.

Kingdom community took another step forward when the Holy Spirit was poured out on the 120 believers who were meeting in the upper room in Jerusalem. From that point on, the history of the Church became an experiment in bringing the community of heaven to earth. We see this principle illustrated clearly in this account of the Early Church:

> When the Day of Pentecost had fully come, *they were all with one accord in one place.* And suddenly there came a sound from heaven, as of a rushing mighty wind, and it filled the whole house where they were sitting. . . . And they were all filled with the Holy Spirit and began to speak with other tongues, as the Spirit gave them utterance (Acts 2:1-2,4, emphasis added).

As this passage reveals, a community *in unity* attracts the presence and power of God. The result of this outpouring of the Holy Spirit was a massive harvest and an even greater expression of community:

> So continuing daily with one accord in the temple, and breaking bread from house to house, they ate their food with gladness and simplicity of heart, praising God and having favor with all the people. And the Lord added to the church daily those who were being saved (vv. 46-47).

This pattern and emphasis on the importance of community is seen throughout the New Testament. Obviously, since the days of the Early Church the Body of Christ has experienced many challenges and setbacks in maintaining this emphasis, but it has also seen many wonderful expressions of true community that reflect the loving atmosphere of heaven. In truth, the fulfillment of God's purposes on earth depends on our commitment to build the kind of churches and ministries that demonstrate His kingdom community and true revival culture.

The Culture of Earth:
Disconnection and Division

In the beginning God created the family (see Gen. 2:18-23), but as families grew and multiplied, they gave way to tribal communities (see Gen. 4:16-17). As a result of the sin that entered the world after the Fall, division and disconnection existed between God and humanity, between man and woman, between brother and brother, and between the generations of people on earth.

In Genesis 1–10 we find that all that existed at the time were families and tribal groups. However, after the Great Flood things changed. The earth's population grew and multiplied on the plains of Shinar (see Gen. 11:1-9), and the people adopted one language and one culture. They were a growing community with common values and priorities in the realms of culture, economy, government and faith. They had rediscovered a certain kind of unity, but unfortunately, their values and priorities were contrary to the heart of God.

It is interesting to note that in spite of their sin, God acknowledged the power of their *unity* expressed in community. He declared, "If as one people speaking the same language they have begun to do this, then nothing they plan to do will be impossible for them" (Gen. 11:6, *NIV*). In order to disrupt their rebellion, God disrupted their unity and caused them to scatter over the face of the earth.

We can draw many lessons from this incident, but an important one is that God has given humanity more power and authority than we realize. When we come into agreement and alignment with one another, there are few things we cannot accomplish. Community can be a source of great blessing if the values and priorities of its members are in line with God's kingdom, but it can also be source of great harm if its purposes run contrary to God's heart.

When Adam and Eve broke fellowship with God, it released a legacy of division and disunity that brought rejection, alienation, loneliness and isolation to the world. As a result, generation upon generation was afflicted with fragmentation, brokenness, separation and division. All of the curses of our planet, such as racism, sexism and international wars, can be traced to this break between humanity and God.

Because most people feel disconnected in one way or another, they spend a lot of their lives trying to *reconnect* in one way or another. In an attempt to reclaim connection, they simulate community by adapting to traditions, styles and trends, or they join clubs and gyms, or they get involved in political activism, social justice issues and political parties. They may also join subcultural groups and even gangs to provide the sense of community for which they are longing.

In our current culture, most people find community in the workplace because, as adults, that is where we most easily form relationships outside our family. In fact, we tend to be more identified with our workplace communities than we are with our next-door neighbors. Many of us live in "bedroom communities," where we never actually meet our neighbors or spend time with them. We put in eight or more hours a day at work (plus an hour each way commuting), roll up the garage door, pull the car in, and we are *done*. We relate to a larger community through the TV set or the computer screen. Yet while the Internet has opened the door to an entirely new expression of community through social media, many people find it to be a poor substitute for face-to-face connection.

Understanding the Quest for Community

God has embedded the desire for community and connection deep within the human soul. Whenever we gather together, we will inevitably form some kind of community because we are responding to the way God has wired us to operate. For this reason, when people experience a breakdown of true community, they will respond in one of two ways: (1) they create an alternative community, or (2) they reject community altogether. These responses demonstrate both the longing for connection with others and the frustration and hopelessness that many feel in relationship to community.

I began this chapter with a story of our church's efforts to reach into the club scene and the rave community. I am aware that most believers are turned off by the drugs, immorality and other broken behaviors of this culture and that it is hard for many to understand why a thousand people would want to dance for hours in a crammed space to pulsating beats and laser light shows. However, if we look a little deeper, we can see an expression of community in this subculture that in some ways outshines anything the previous "rock" generation built.

As rockers, we built our expressions around stages, with an MC and our beloved stars doing the show while everyone else watched. The dance club community usually doesn't have a stage, or, if they do, it is off to the side and barely noticeable. The DJ who is mixing the beats is almost invisible. The "show" is not on the stage; it is on the floor. Everyone is a performer, and no one is a spectator. Everyone brings his or her unique dance, style and personality to the mix, and the interaction can be amazing. It is a distinct but equally valuable expression of the Kingdom longing for community.

Whether we are talking about the Church or the world, it is fascinating to see the different creative ways in which people respond to the unmet Kingdom longing for love and connection. Granted, many of their efforts end in sinful and self-destructive behaviors that we cannot affirm, but we can learn from their desire for community.

Understanding the Kingdom Longings for Community

It is important to understand the role community plays in people's lives so we can build a bridge between the culture of this world and the culture of the kingdom of God. Most people want to know they are part of something bigger than themselves, and that sense of purpose is found in their relationships with other people. Belonging is an experience of acceptance, appreciation and inclusion. However, community is about more than merely belonging. It provides three elements, or nutrients, that humans need to lead healthy lives: *individuality, connection* and *maturity*.

Individuality and Distinction

The first element that community provides is *individuality*. This may seem contradictory at first, but I am convinced we can never truly know ourselves or be true individuals apart from community. The qualities within us that are distinct and unique are most clearly seen in the contrast of community. When we are connected to others, our individuality shines, and we are able to impact those around us in greater ways.

One of the biggest reasons some people avoid community is that they fear it will *diminish* their individuality, but in truth community brings out the best in each one of us. God created each of us to be entirely unique, and there is no better place to display His handiwork than right next to other unique creations. In fact, true unity should never be confused with uniformity. The exact opposite is true: authentic community, by definition, is a unification of diverse people for the common good. This is what the definition of the word "community" means; it implies a *coming together* of things that are completely distinct and different yet join to form one unit.

Another realization of this principle is the Kingdom longing for creative expression. We are created in the image of a God who is infinitely diverse in His creative abilities, and He has wired every person to express this creativity in a different way. Some express this in arts, some in music, some in crafts, and some in ways that others might consider mundane expressions in the workplace or in the mundane areas of life. The *ART* of life is expressed in the *HEART* with which we do all things.

Connection and Affinity

The second element community provides is *connection*. We are called to connect with others in a relational way, which breaks down the issue of alienation. In Ephesians 2:19, Paul says, "Therefore, you are no longer strangers and foreigners, but fellow citizens with the saints and members of the household of God." In the Greek, this connection is called *koinonia*, which means to share life in common. We are told in Acts 2:42 that the Early Church "continued steadfastly in the apostles' doctrine and fellowship [*koinonia*], in the breaking of bread, and in prayers" (Acts 2:42). *Community* was built into the very fabric of God's purposes for His Church.

When we connect with others, we are nourished, they are nourished, and an empowering environment is created around our fellowship that affects the entire community. Jesus referred to this when He said, "If two agree on earth concerning anything that they ask, it will be done for them by My Father in heaven," and, "Where two or three are gathered together in My name, I am there in the midst of them" (Matt. 18:19-20). We need to connect with others in meaningful ways so we can receive the resources that fellowship provides.

Maturity and Promotion

The third element that flows from community is personal growth and *maturity*. None of us can become the people God created us to be apart from the challenges of community. "As iron sharpens iron, so a man sharpens the countenance of his friend" (Prov. 27:17).

We need others around us to help expose our weaknesses and call out the gold within us. Unfortunately, many of us avoid this depth of community by distancing ourselves from community commitments, while others among us create a "community persona" that allows us to be part of the group without opening our hearts to the deeper interactions that produce true growth. In my life, I have experienced many of my most painful challenges at the hands of "friends," but God used those things to shape me according to His will. Even though it was painful at the time, I can look back now and see how each challenge was worth the growth it produced in me.

Salvation Solutions

As we look at some of the challenges and weaknesses of human community, we need to remember that as followers of Jesus, we have the *answer*. We have already determined that many people live with rejection, alienation and isolation and don't understand the power of true community, which is why they gravitate toward certain kinds of subcultures and groups that promise connection but often don't deliver. For this reason, we need to match our salvation solutions to these unfulfilled needs in the world.

I remember being five years old and starting my kindergarten class on Arguello Street in San Francisco. On that first day of school, I had a sick feeling in the pit of my stomach, like I had to go to the bathroom badly. I was deathly afraid that nobody would like me or accept me. Even at that young age, I feared I would be considered the outsider and be alienated from everybody.

We don't often think about it, but the experience I just described is the feeling many people have when they visit our churches and home groups. Many people perceive the Church as being artificial and superficial—a place where people can't be real with one another. Even though at times this has been true, it is not the *truth*. The truth is that when we come together as the Body of Christ, we are "no longer strangers and foreigners, but fellow citizens with the saints and members of the household of God . . . in whom the whole building, being fitted together, grows into a holy temple in the Lord, in whom you also are being built together for a dwelling place of God in the Spirit" (Eph. 2:19,21-22).

God desires us to cultivate the values, priorities and practices of true community and develop the strategies and structures to bring heaven to earth. As we do this, we send a message to the unreached that they don't have to be alone—that everyone can be part of a global community with a local connection. The Church is a place of dynamic unity that celebrates each person's diversity. It is a place where real, fulfilling, supportive relationships can be built that will continue into eternity. The community of Christ is the place where everyone can be loved and challenged to grow into the person God has called him or her to be.

Building Revival Culture in Communities

As previously mentioned, throughout the centuries the Church has experienced its share of disunity and division, and in so doing we have compromised our ability to set a good example for the world around us. In his first letter to the Corinthians, Paul spends 11 chapters counseling and exhorting the Church about the dangers of this disunity and division. The Corinthians had been undermining their experience of Kingdom community by fighting over which leaders they should follow, how they should correct sin in the church, how men and women should relate to one another, and a number of other issues. But in chapter 12, Paul shares with them the secret of maintaining unity in the midst of a diversity in perspectives and priorities:

> But now indeed there are many members, yet one body. And the eye cannot say to the hand, "I have no need of you"; nor again the head to the feet, "I have no need of you." No, much rather, those members of the body which seem to be weaker are necessary. And those members of the body which we think to be less honorable, on these we bestow greater honor; and our unpresentable parts have greater modesty, but our presentable parts have no need. But God composed the body, having given greater honor to that part which lacks it, that there should be no schism in the body, but that the members should have the same care for one another. And if one member suffers, all the members suffer with it; or if one member is honored, all the members rejoice with it (1 Cor. 12:20-26).

Paul goes on a few verses later to tell the believers about a "more excellent way" (v. 31)—what we know today as the famous chapter on love. He explains that love "believes all things, hopes all things, endures all things" and never fails (1 Cor. 13:7-8). God is love (see 1 John 4:8), and love is at the heart of community. He desires to bring the experience of heavenly community to earth, using the community of believers as His primary vehicle. He has placed this responsibility in our hands, and He will give us the grace and power to get it done.

Cultivating Community Values

In order to generate this kind of love and connection in our congregations, we first need to turn away from attitudes of fear, judgment and comparison that cause us to withdraw from those who don't seem to fit in. We need to reject gossip, slander and critical attitudes that create disunity and division in the Church and turn to the values that support unity and connection. As the apostle Paul encourages us:

> Let love be without hypocrisy. Abhor what is evil. Cling to what is good. Be kindly affectionate to one another with brotherly love, in honor giving preference to one another; not lagging in diligence, fervent in spirit, serving the Lord; rejoicing in hope, patient in tribulation, continuing steadfastly in prayer; distributing to the needs of the saints, given to hospitality. Bless those who persecute you; bless and do not curse. Rejoice with those who rejoice, and weep with those who weep. Be of the same mind toward one another. Do not set your mind on high things, but associate with the humble. Do not be wise in your own opinion. Repay no one evil for evil. Have regard for good things in the sight of all men. If it is possible, as much as depends on you, live peaceably with all men (Rom. 12:9-18).

Love is the fountain from which all community flows, so we need to teach it, model it and create opportunities for it to be practiced among believers and among the unreached. We must examine how we spend our time, energy and money and make loving others our *priority*. As we do so and adjust our attitudes to match, we will find that the water table of love will begin to rise in our churches and organizations. When this occurs, it will ultimately spill over into our neighborhoods and workplaces. This is the Church of which Jesus spoke when He said, "By this all will know that you are My disciples, if you have love for one another" (John 13:35).

Healthy Community Expressions

A few years ago, a friend and I began to dream about what a Kingdom community would look like if it were built on the Kingdom values of the rave club scene. As I stated previously, in a rave gathering everyone is the show, which certainly reflects a Kingdom value in that we are all called to be ministers, priests and kings. But there is more. The average dance club has several different rooms with different kinds of music playing in each room. One has house music, one has drum and base, another has two-step, and another might have dub-step. Each room also has its own décor and other features, such as art installations, a bar or a circus act on stilts.

This is very different from the "rock generation" in which I was raised, where we build churches to match our version of community. We have big stages, celebrity worship bands, charismatic speakers and clever media, and the majority of our gatherings are filled with spectators. But what would a church built by the rave generation look like? Would it have different rooms offering different experiences for participants? Perhaps one room would offer worship, another teaching, another healing prayer, and yet another a place for discussion to take place. The believers would move from room to room as the Spirit led and participate in each environment according to their needs. On one Sunday they may only do worship and prayer ministry; on another Sunday, they may do only teaching and discussion. Is it possible this would more appropriately reflect what Paul says when he writes, "Each of you has a psalm, has a teaching, has a tongue, has a revelation, has an interpretation" (1 Cor. 14:26)?

I am not suggesting we abandon traditional models of church, but to the extent that the current congregational expressions hinder the activation of every member and the establishment of true community, perhaps we need to ask the Lord to expand our vision.

One model that Peter Wagner suggests as the ideal structure of a local church includes three sizes of groups: (1) large group *celebrations*, (2) mid-sized *congregations*, and (3) small group *cells*.

Each of these groups fosters a different dimension of community. The large group celebration provides vision, momentum and resources. This gathering also serves as a place where the senior ministers can equip the Body of Christ and impart direction and movement to the church. There is something that happens in this gathering that cannot be matched in the other two, which is why I believe house churches, by themselves, are an incomplete expression of the Church.

The mid-sized congregational gathering encourages mission and connection. These groups can range in size from 30 to 80 people, and they are usually organized around a point of common interest or focused mission, such as an arts community or a singles ministry. They can also take the form of an adult Sunday School class or an outreach or healing ministry. These groups allow everyone to know everyone's name and provide a wide range of relational options at the same time.

The small group cells facilitate activation and intimacy. The size of this group, between 5 and 20 members, creates the possibility for everyone to participate in discussion and ministry to one another. Small groups are the ideal incubator to help people discover and develop their spiritual gifts and build lasting friendships. Each of these expressions of community serves a different purpose and provides different nutrients to the life of a believer, and I recommend that every person seek to be part of these kinds of gathering on a consistent basis.

In order to cultivate and sustain a lasting revival culture, it is necessary for us to reposition our hearts and redesign our gatherings to create the environment where community and connection thrive. It is time for God's people to generate a Kingdom community that values individuals, helps them grow, and unites them into a dynamic unity that will attract the lost and transform the world.

Revival Culture and the Economy

In 2003, a friend invited Diane and I to attend the Burning Man Festival, an expansive counter-culture gathering in northern Nevada. We had heard many reports of the spiritual darkness of this gathering, but because of our passion to understand and reach emerging culture, we decided to check it out. What we found was some of the best and worst of humanity being expressed in the same place at the same time.

Burning Man began in San Francisco in 1986 but soon grew so large that it was forced to relocate. Although their headquarters remain in San Francisco, in 1990 they moved the event to a salt-flat desert location in Nevada, and every year since then, the event has continued to bring people together from around the world for a week of hedonism and human expression. The gatherings now number about 50,000 people.

Burning Man is one of the biggest funders of the arts in California and prides itself in the creative expressions it sponsors. Around the world, many people revere it as an ultimate expression of human creativity and "freedom." It is an amazing and extreme display of the beauty of humanity, yet it is also filled with immorality and some of the darkest aspects of humanity. Attendees are invited to express themselves in any way they want as long as they do not harm others, which includes nudity, sexual displays, drugs and other "victimless" behaviors. Diane and I encountered this firsthand when we took a bike tour and found ourselves in a traffic jam with 5,000 topless women riding past us.

The week-long event culminates with the burning of an 80-foot wooden effigy (the "Burning Man") as a thousand fire dancers swing torches and tens of thousands of people rave through the night. This event has now become a global movement, and Burning Man communities are starting up in key cities around the world. The organization holds regular events to express its values and practices.

Similar to the raves we discussed in the last chapter, an important rule at Burning Man is that everyone is encouraged to be a participator and not just a spectator. In this, Burning Man has hit upon a Kingdom priority, for in the economy of heaven every person has something to contribute. You and I have giftings and resources the community needs, and, likewise, the community has giftings and resources that you and I individually need. None of us were created to be spectators only—everyone needs to participate because everyone has something valuable to give.

Culture and Economy

The Burning Man community is known for the unique way in which it relates to money and resources. Its members have built what they call a "gift economy" and sell few things because they believe commercialization is one of the defects of modern society. According to the organizers, "gifting" is the act of giving something (material or otherwise) to another person without any expectation of receiving something in return.

An important component of culture is *economy*, which I define as the way we manage and exchange the wide range of resources God has given us. When I use the word "economy", I want to make it clear I am not talking primarily about money. Money is important, but it is only an *exchange unit* that reflects the value of our time, energy and talent. In the same way we were created for family and community, we were also created to build a world through the power of cooperation and contribution. In other words, we were created for *synergy*.

The word "synergy" comes from the Greek word *synergos*, which means "working together," and is defined as the whole being greater than the sum of its parts. It is the cooperative, co-laboring partnership in which different members of a community contribute their time, energy, money and talents toward a common purpose. Synergy, or contribution, in a community produces an outcome that is greater than the sum of each of these resources added separately.

The Culture of Heaven: Contribution and Synergy

When God created humanity, He gave us a job to do, and He gave us the resources with which to do it. In Genesis 1–3, we see God commanding us to be fruitful and multiply—to fill the earth and subdue it. He gave us authority over the resources of the planet and commanded us to steward those resources on His behalf.

God dwells in a realm of unlimited resources. He is eternal and dwells in eternity, so He has unlimited time. He is Omnipotent and is the source of all energy, so His energy is limitless. He is the Creator who made all things out of nothing, so He has unlimited material resources. In fact, the reason economy is such an important aspect of human culture is that it originated in heaven and is part of God's design for creation. It may be difficult to imagine an economy of unlimited resources because, in our world, the balance of provision is maintained by competition, but in heaven there is no need to compete for resources because heaven is a realm of absolute abundance.

Picture a *Monopoly* game in reverse, where the winner is not determined by how much he or she can take from the other players but rather by how much that person can give away. The balance of resources is maintained by giving, not by taking, and the winner is the one who has given all for the blessing of others. Yet that person is constantly receiving the gifts of others as well, so the game never fully reaches a conclusion. I believe this is a glimpse into the economy of heaven. Unfortunately, because of sin, the earth is a very different place than what God originally intended.

Economy and the Fall
When God created Adam and Eve, He placed them in a garden with unlimited resources and set only one limitation: they were not to

eat of the Tree of the Knowledge of Good and Evil. You know the rest of the story—they ate of the tree anyway, God confronted them, and He pronounced the curse they had brought upon themselves. One of the most significant consequences of their sin was the limitation of resource:

> Cursed is the ground for your sake; in toil you shall eat of it all the days of your life. Both thorns and thistles it shall bring forth for you, and you shall eat the herb of the field. In the sweat of your face you shall eat bread (Gen. 3:17-19).

In one moment, the nature of humanity's relationship with the world went from one of abundance to one of limitation. From that point on, humans would have to labor and toil to survive and manage their resources carefully to sustain their lives. We now have limited time, limited energy and limited abilities to accomplish all we need to do. These limitations require the use of strategy and stewardship to bring the best results.

The Evolution of Economy

As humanity began to multiply on the earth, there was a subsequent multiplication of talents and abilities, and people gradually began to specialize into various professions and occupations. The Bible makes reference to this in Genesis 4:20-22:

> And Adah bore Jabal. He was the father of those who dwell in tents and have livestock. His brother's name was Jubal. He was the father of all those who play the harp and flute. And as for Zillah, she also bore Tubal-Cain, an instructor of every craftsman in bronze and iron.

A little later in Genesis 11:3-4, we find one of the first recorded examples of cooperation and trade:

> Then they said to one another, "Come, let us make bricks and bake them thoroughly." They had brick for stone, and

they had asphalt for mortar. And they said, "Come, let us build ourselves a city, and a tower whose top is in the heavens; let us make a name for ourselves, lest we be scattered abroad over the face of the whole earth."

The people of Babel began to realize their need for one another on an economic level. If they were going to build a city and a tower, they needed everyone to contribute their time, energy and talents to complete the task. That is the power of economy.

It is easy to imagine how the evolution of economy began to progress from that time forward throughout the world. The people of Babel soon discovered that one person made mortar better than another, while another person made bricks better. Perhaps one person happened to live on a piece of land that had a superior mud, so he traded his mud for the bricks and the mortar. A fourth person, who had no interest in making bricks and mortar, started growing vegetables and trading them for the materials to build his own house.

At this point a system of barter begins to form, where each person trades his or her gifts and abilities for another person's gifts and abilities, thereby creating a primitive form of economy. Eventually, money emerges as a unit of exchange for a person's time, energy, talents and resources. At first this unit of exchange was gold and silver, but over time, people begin to ascribe value to paper currency. Economy, by all accounts, had a simple beginning, but we now live within a complex structure of banks, stocks, bonds, hedge funds and taxes. The health of the economy affects everyone on the planet.

The word "economy" comes from the Greek *oikonomia,* which means "house laws," or the ways we interact with each other. If we were roommates in a house, we would share the costs of the house and the responsibilities of running a household. We would interact with each other in terms of how we use our talents, time, energy and money. As a result, we would have a certain kind of relationship, and that relationship would be an *economy.* Every community that exists in the world creates some form of economy

to manage the contributions of its various members and to sustain
the wellbeing of the group.

Each one of us is diverse, and we all have different gifts and talents. One of the key dimensions of our ability to walk together in
culture is the way we manage our resources in relationship to one
another. The *way* we spend our time, energy, talents, resources and
money with one another is an important component of culture.

In the Old Testament, God instituted the weekly Sabbath and
the tithe as a way of regularly reminding His people that He was
their provider and they could produce more wealth in six days with
His help than they could in seven days of work without Him. The
tithe is the same principle: we save more money by giving 10 percent of our income to God than we ever could if we held on to that
money for ourselves.

In the New Testament, it is interesting to note that Jesus spoke
more about economy and the wise use of money than He spoke
about heaven and hell. Clearly, this issue of economy and the use
of resources is important in God's heart.

Understanding the Kingdom Longings for Contribution

One of the most important reasons to understand the role economy plays in community is so we can build a bridge between the
culture of this world and the culture of the Kingdom. As I mentioned before, this bridge can be built when we understand the
unmet Kingdom longings of the human heart. Three specific Kingdom longings drive our quest for an economy, empower us to
manage our resources wisely, and ultimately foster the kinds of relationships we have with one another where every member is abun-
dantly blessed: *abundance*, *responsibility*, and *synergy* (which is the
result and intention of abundance and responsibility). Throughout the ages, these Kingdom longings have caused humanity to
respond in one of two ways: either people sought the Lord and
trusted in His provision, or they turned to selfishness and self-
seeking to provide for themselves.

Abundance and Generosity

The first Kingdom longing is for *abundance*. You and I were created in the image of God, and therefore He has imprinted upon us an expectation of *abundance*. This is why we are so troubled by the poverty and pain of the world. As people of conscience, when we behold the scarcity in the developing world and the waste that takes place in the western world, we are rightly grieved. When we consider that every day more than 20,000 children under five years of age die of malnutrition, bad water and preventable disease, we know humanity can do better.[1]

On a personal level, the fear of poverty is a driving force that causes us to strive for success at the expense of other important things in our lives, producing a "workaholic" lifestyle that damages our children, our families and ourselves. This striving is at the root of greed, corruption and most unethical and illegal business practices. Much of the white-collar crime in our culture is generated by a sinful response to the longing for abundance, and most petty crime—such as lying, stealing and fraud—has the same root.

The good news is that we serve a generous heavenly Father who lives in a realm of absolute abundance. As we restore our relationship with Him, He will forgive us of our sins and set us free from fear. This leads to us growing in our understanding of Him as our provider.

Responsibility and Stewardship

The second Kingdom longing in relation to economy is *responsibility*. Most of us have a love-hate relationship with this term. We recognize the need for each person to pull his or her own weight in society and community, yet most of us would rather not. God has imprinted every heart with the longing to manage our resources of time, energy, money and talents effectively and efficiently, yet most of us would admit that time and money management is a challenge.

Human responsibility, apart from God, is the cause of most of the stress and pressure in life—our performance at work, our attention to our spouses and children, and our commitments to friends and extended family. All of these can conspire to create a life of duty without joy. Many people react to this stress by falling into withdrawal, neglect, excuses and irresponsibility. Others adopt attitudes of victimization and entitlement, believing the world owes them something, and they demand that others provide for them financially and emotionally. They don't realize these responses actually rob them of the joy of fruitfulness and fulfillment.

Although God created us to bear responsibility, He never designed us to bear it alone. He always intended that we would know Him and draw on His grace as we fulfill the responsibilities of life. We need to realize God believes in us more than we believe in ourselves. He has bestowed so many blessings and resources in our lives, and He has given us the grace to manage and steward these things in a way that maximizes the blessings of those around us and magnifies Him through us.

Synergy and Contribution

The last Kingdom longing I want to focus on in relation to economy is the power of *synergy*. All of creation is interconnected in a universal "ecosystem," and the health of each part depends on the wellbeing of the other parts. God made us for community and cooperation, embedding within us the desire to contribute. Yet many of us undervalue ourselves and the blessing we can be to others, and as a result we withhold or limit our contribution to the community. We may do this out of fear or out of pride, but the result is the same: we rob the Body of Christ of the spiritual and financial resources that would have been brought had we contributed according to our capacity and God's leading.

As we get to know God more fully, we begin to understand our own significance more deeply—and the importance of our unique contribution to the community. As we offer freely to one another, the abundance of resource grows, and the dynamic power that is generated is greater by far than the impact we could have brought apart from one another.

The Culture of Earth: Poverty and Lack

I know firsthand the challenges of poverty. I was raised by a single mom, and for several years as she pursued her education, we experienced genuine need. We had no choice but to go on welfare, and we lived this way for much of my childhood. Like many welfare families, we would buy our groceries with food stamps, bring the food home, make a meal, and spend the mealtime criticizing the government for not providing more for us. We didn't understand the intrinsic responsibility God had placed upon each of us to provide for ourselves.

The Effects of Sin

Looking back, I am thankful for the provision that came through the welfare system. I am also glad we have a safety net in place for those who fall on hard times, but I am concerned that the entitlement system we have developed in our culture actually hinders people from taking responsibility for their lives and handicaps them from becoming who God created them to be.

Because we live in a world of limited resources, we struggle with fear, greed, covetousness, envy and jealousy. We do not know how to manage what we have in a way that honors God, so we end up reacting to our situation in the form of a "fight or flight" response that leads into sin. On the fight side, we respond to our longings for abundance by asserting ourselves in self-centered ways. Driven by ambition, pride and greed, we climb the ladders of success, recognition and wealth without regard to the wellbeing of others, and we even push others out of the way to get where we want to go. Some of us even resort to lying and cheating to produce a favorable outcome.

On the flight side, we withdraw from life, withhold our contribution of time, energy, resources and talent, and fearfully wall ourselves off. Fear comes in many forms—fear of pain, failure, rejection—and it is a powerful force that undermines community and individual success. The devil is obviously happy to promote either of these broken responses. He loves to inflict poverty and pain on the one hand and incite greed and materialism on the other.

He takes every advantage of the imbalances and brokenness of economic reality to cause pain and poverty throughout the earth.

Yet in spite of the enemy's actions, God is at work to cultivate the Kingdom longings of fallen humanity and create a world in which poverty of all kinds is permanently eradicated. I believe this is why the Burning Man organization is experimenting with a "gift economy"—they want to see what humanity can do when competition is eclipsed by cooperation.

Burning Man is not the only organization with this desire to find a better way to work together. In *Wikinomics*, authors Don Tapscott and Anthony D. Williams present many other examples that reveal the power and profitability of cooperation over competition. Wikipedia is one such example, as well as the open-source movement in computer programming.[2]

Understanding Poverty and Prosperity

Poverty and prosperity are two contrasting words that evoke a number of different images, but we make a mistake if we think of these words only in relationship to material things. Many kinds of poverty and prosperity have nothing to do with money or possessions. In fact, the richest people on earth are often spiritually impoverished and relationally bankrupt. On the other end of the spectrum, many people who lack material things are rich in health and enjoy what some call a "prosperous soul."

Although there are many kinds of poverty and many different causes for it, God gives us a clear set of principles to cultivate prosperity in every area of life. In his second letter to the Corinthians, Paul states:

> But this I say: He who sows sparingly will also reap sparingly, and he who sows bountifully will also reap bountifully. So let each one give as he purposes in his heart, not grudgingly or of necessity; for God loves a cheerful giver.... Now may He who supplies seed to the sower, and bread for food, supply and multiply the seed you have sown and increase the fruits of your righteousness....

> Thanks be to God for His indescribable gift! (2 Cor. 9:6-7,10,15).

In this passage, Paul uses the idea of sowing and reaping to help us understand the basic principles of economy. Each of us has a limited amount of "seed." This seed may be money, time, talents, relational ability or other material or spiritual assets. We can use the seed we have to feed ourselves, or we can use it for a future harvest. If we consume the seed, it is gone forever; however, if we *sow* the seed, it will multiply and return abundance. In other words, as we sow our talents and treasure into the soil of community, everyone prospers, including ourselves. But if we *withhold* our contribution, everyone suffers, especially ourselves.

In Matthew 25:20-23, Jesus teaches this same principle using the illustration of a business investment:

> So he who had received five talents came and brought five other talents, saying, "Lord, you delivered to me five talents; look, I have gained five more talents besides them." His lord said to him, "Well done, good and faithful servant; you were faithful over a few things, I will make you ruler over many things. Enter into the joy of your lord." He also who had received two talents came and said, "Lord, you delivered to me two talents; look, I have gained two more talents besides them." His lord said to him, "Well done, good and faithful servant; you have been faithful over a few things, I will make you ruler over many things. Enter into the joy of your lord."

As the parable continues, Jesus explains that a third servant did not invest his master's money wisely but instead buried it in the ground. So the master rebuked him, took his talent away, and gave it to the servant who had 10 talents. Kingdom community depends on all members recognizing their interdependence and contributing resources to bring prosperity to everyone—in body, soul and spirit.

Salvation Solutions

As we seek to reach the unreached and build a bridge in this area, we first need to recognize the mistakes the Church has made throughout the ages in relationship to resources. With a few exceptions, the Church has not been seen as a community that provides for the poor materially and spiritually. Rather, the world has generally perceived the Church to be self-serving and overly preoccupied with its buildings and budgets. That is not who we are supposed to be.

God intended the Church to be a people who have received the ultimate gift of eternal life and have been invited to be part of a heavenly economy founded on abundance and generosity.[3] As we get in touch with the inheritance God gave us and begin to share it with the hungry, we will have no difficulty reaching the coming harvest and inviting them into a thriving revival culture.

Our message to the unreached is that God is an extravagant Father and a generous provider. He is the source of all our resources and can empower us in ways we never imagined. He created time, and He can redeem and multiply it. He gives us talents that exceed human ability and resources that allow us to care for our needs and share into the needs of others. Ultimately, He is the source of everything, and if we seek first the kingdom of God, "all these things" will be added to us (Matt. 6:33).

God is inviting us to build a revival culture in which there is *more* than enough. As we recognize our interdependence with one another and build an economy based on abundance instead of scarcity, giving instead of taking, and contributing instead of competing, we will take a step toward fulfilling Jesus' prayer that God's kingdom will come and His will be done "on earth as it is in heaven" (Matt. 6:10).

Building the Revival Culture of Synergy

Creating any sort of culture begins in the foundation of our values and priorities. For this reason, the first step in establishing a revival culture of synergy is to embrace Kingdom values that foster collaboration and reject worldly values that foster dissent and disunity. For too long, believers have failed to embrace God as their source and have been driven by fear and insecurity to provide for themselves. This attitude always produces striving, manipulation and a sense of competition instead of collaboration. However, as we reject fear and striving, we are set free to cultivate the values that are consistent with God's kingdom, including *honor, responsibility* and *generosity*.

Honor

The first value that fosters synergy in the Body of Christ is *honor*. In Ephesians 4, Paul writes, "I, therefore, the prisoner of the Lord, beseech you to walk worthy of the calling with which you were called, with all lowliness and gentleness, with longsuffering, bearing with one another in love, endeavoring to keep the unity of the Spirit in the bond of peace. . . . To each one of us grace was given according to the measure of Christ's gift" (vv. 1-3,7).

Notice Paul begins this passage by calling each of us to "walk worthy" and humble ourselves in relationship to one another. This attitude of honor allows us to value our contributions while honoring those who have also made contributions. As we honor each other and walk in unity, we begin to recognize God is working in our brothers and sisters according to the measure of Christ's gifts within them. Honor draws out these gifts and puts them on display so everyone can benefit and be blessed. As Paul writes, "The whole body, joined and knit together by what every joint supplies, according to the effective working by which every part does its share, causes growth of the body for the edifying of itself in love" (Eph. 4:16).

Responsibility

The second value that fosters synergy is *responsibility*. As followers of Jesus, we are assigned the task of fulfilling His Great Commission. He has given us a set of resources to do our part, and we have a responsibility to contribute to the community as we are able. The apostle Paul makes this clear in Galatians 6:7-10: "Do not be deceived, God is not mocked; for whatever a man sows, that he will also reap. For he who sows to his flesh will of the flesh reap corruption, but he who sows to the Spirit will of the Spirit reap everlasting life. And let us not grow weary while doing good, for in due season we shall reap if we do not lose heart. Therefore, as we have opportunity, let us do good to all, especially to those who are of the household of faith."

Generosity

We will not be able to build a revival culture of synergy until we embrace the value of *generosity*. Generosity begins with a deep trust in God's provision and protection. As we cultivate a generous heart, we will not only give more but also forgive more. In this respect, it is not enough for us merely to fulfill a duty of obedience; we must also learn to walk in "the grace of our Lord Jesus Christ, that though He was rich, yet for your sakes He became poor, that you through His poverty might become rich" (2 Cor. 8:9).

Healthy Economic Structures

It doesn't matter whether our resources include money, time, spiritual gifts or any other thing—God desires to create a synergy between believers that multiplies our small offering of five loaves and a couple of fish into something capable of feeding *multitudes*. To do this, I believe the Lord wants us to promote *stewardship*, facilitate *servanthood*, and encourage participation in *small groups*.

Stewardship

"*Stewardship*" is defined as the wise management of resources. It includes how we make and manage money, how we schedule and spend our time, and how we invest our talents and spiritual gifts. Every church and ministry needs to teach and model good stewardship and provide ongoing opportunities for members to grow in this ability. In addition to its other benefits, this practice will be essential as we help new believers lay a good foundation in their lives.

Servanthood

Servanthood is the entry point for all ministry. In fact, the word "ministry" means "service." I am convinced we can never become whom God has called us to be if we do not commit to regular expressions of service to others—especially those types of service that do not seem to have a visible reward. We need to create many different kinds of opportunities through which people can contribute to others financially and practically. As we do this, we will experience the synergy of collaboration and help build a Kingdom economy in the community.

Small groups

Small groups continue to be one of the best vehicles for fostering the kind of participation and partnerships that will produce a culture of generosity. When the people of God come together on a regular basis to worship, pray, study Scripture and share a meal, the result is a quality of fellowship that will eventually spill over and bless the whole world. In Acts 4, we read that the early believers "were of one heart and one soul; neither did anyone say that any of the things he possessed was his own, but they had all things in common. . . . Nor was there anyone among them who lacked; for all who were possessors of lands or houses sold them, and brought the proceeds of the things that were sold, and laid them at the apostles' feet; and they distributed to each as anyone had need" (vv. 32,34-35). We need to foster this same attitude in our churches.

In every sphere of culture, God wants us to bring heaven to earth. As we contribute our resources and collaborate to build true revival culture, we will demonstrate His love throughout the world in a powerful way. That is the result of Kingdom economy—an incredible *synergy* is released as God displays His abundance through our lives.

Revival Culture and Government

In 1979, while I was working with the Gospel Outreach San Francisco church plant, I suggested we have a picnic in Golden Gate Park for all the churches in the city. I met with a dozen pastors and leaders to put it together, one of whom was a man named Larry Rosenbaum. Larry worked with a ministry called Shiloh. He said, "Sure, I'll do the picnic—as long as you come out with me the next week and preach the gospel on the streets of San Francisco." At the time, sharing the gospel out on the streets was not my favorite method of evangelism. However, if it meant getting Larry's ministry involved in the picnic, I thought I might as well go ahead and agree.

The all-church picnic ended up being a great success. Two weeks later, I joined Larry and about 80 other picnic-goers to share the love of Jesus on the streets of our city. From those small beginnings, we launched a ministry called SOS San Francisco. Within a year, our SOS leadership team had grown to a dozen individuals. About half of them were pastors of churches around the region, and the rest were leaders of different kinds of outreach ministries.

By this time, the Jesus Movement had mostly died down, and we weren't seeing the same level of openness to the gospel that we had seen early on. But we were all very passionate about the Lord, and we were determined to revive the fire of former years. We figured the best way to bring revival was by mobilizing as many people as possible to pray, worship and share the gospel.

We put out a call to the whole nation so we could see this vision become a reality. I met with Jack Hayford in Los Angeles, and then I traveled to Texas to invite David Wilkerson, Keith Green and several other leaders in the Lindale area to come out and be a part what we were doing. I also met with leaders from Washington for Jesus and Jesus People USA in Chicago. When the outreach took place, more than 300 adults showed up for a 10-day period, and on the weekends we were joined by another 400 to 500 people. We launched our first major outreach in 1980 at First Covenant Church, which happened to be where I met my wife, Diane, who had come from southern California to be a part of the event.

During the next several years, we created a revival culture based on passionate prayer, prophetic worship and powerful preaching. We provided an opportunity for more than 40 churches to go out onto the streets on a weekly basis. Then, once a year, we hosted the 10-day outreach, and believers from all over the nation joined those of us from around the Bay Area to do ministry in the city. After 32 years, SOS Ministries is still changing lives on the streets of San Francisco.

During those early years, we often encountered strong opposition from some of the local gay organizations. One of these was a city-funded organization called A Community United Against Violence that opposed the gospel. Although we had several in-depth dialogues with leaders from this group, they continued to organize counterdemonstrations against us. They mistakenly perceived us as anti-gay religious conservatives who wanted to take away their rights.

On one occasion during the summer of 1981, we gathered more than 500 believers in Union Square to worship Jesus and share the gospel. During this event, more than 2,000 people showed up to oppose us. There was a wide variety of demonstrators, including lesbians, homosexuals, witches, union members, activists, communists and many others. As we started our worship, the square began to fill with hundreds of protesters blowing whistles, screaming, tearing up Bibles and throwing bags of urine. Needless to say, we began to get a little afraid.

Somebody called the police, and about 200 officers in full riot gear came and surrounded the square. They stood there with their helmets, Plexi-glass shields and drawn Billy clubs, just waiting for the violence to break out. In the midst of all this, one of our leaders received a word of wisdom that the worship team needed to start singing "O the Blood of Jesus." So he walked up to the stage and told the worship leader, who began singing, "O the blood of Jesus, it washes white as snow . . ." over and over again.

After several minutes, the police captain, who was overseeing the riot patrol, came up to us and said, "I don't know what's in that song, but as soon as you started singing it the whole atmosphere changed. Don't stop singing that song." We continued declaring the power of the blood of Jesus for more than an hour, and God moved in a powerful way. We shared the gospel freely, prayed for salvation and healing, and witnessed incredible encounters with the people in the square. By the end of the gathering, many of those who had opposed us had come to us in tears, saying, "We misjudged you. You aren't the people we thought you were. We see nothing but love in you."

Shortly after this event, A Community United Against Violence fell into a season of disunity and was never able to organize this kind of opposition again. We believe this happened as a direct result of God's breakthrough in that situation. The gospel went forth powerfully that day, and we learned new things about the value of worship.

During the next five years, we started doing outreaches like this all the time, and we had amazing encounters and breakthroughs. We were able to lead many people to the Lord and see countless miracles on the streets. We also began to learn the importance of spiritual authority in relationship to human authority on the earth.

Jesus is the King of Kings, and Psalm 22:3 tells us that He is "enthroned in the praises" of His people. On that amazing day as we worshipped the Lord, He established His authority in our midst in a new way, and we were able to witness clear results in the authority structures of the world around us. This story serves as a launching point as we focus on the role of authority, leadership and government in the various expressions of culture in heaven and on earth.

The Culture of Heaven: Protection and Guidance

Government is an important component of culture because it provides protection and guidance as we walk together in community. As with the other components of revival culture, it is important to remember that authority and government did not originate on earth but in heaven. God is the ruler of all things and is the King of the universe. Throughout Scripture, He is seen as the Lord over all.

The Source of Authority

In Isaiah 6:1, the prophet recounts, "In the year that King Uzziah died, I saw the Lord sitting on a throne, high and lifted up, and the train of His robe filled the temple." A few chapters later, he goes on to prophesy about the coming of Christ:

> For unto us a Child is born, unto us a Son is given; and the *government* will be upon His shoulder. And His name will be called Wonderful, Counselor, Mighty God, Everlasting Father, Prince of Peace. Of *the increase of His government* and peace there will be no end, upon the throne of David and over His kingdom, to order it and establish it with judgment and justice from that time forward, even forever. The zeal of the LORD of hosts will perform this (Isa. 9:6-7, emphasis added).

Jesus is the King of kings and the Lord of lords, and His assignment was to reinstitute God's kingdom to a rebellious planet. When He began His ministry on earth, He defied the devil's false authority and began to proclaim the restoration of the kingdom of God (see Matt. 4:1-17). During His everyday life on earth, Jesus demonstrated the government of heaven on earth—He showed us mercy and gave justice. He provided a way for us to be cleansed from our sins and brought back into a right relationship with our Father. He "went about doing good and healing all those who were oppressed by the devil, for God was with Him" (Acts 10:38).

Just before Jesus ascended to heaven, He said, "All authority has been given to Me in heaven and on earth" (Matt. 28:18). On the basis of this authority, He commissioned His people to "make disciples of all the nations, baptizing them in the name of the Father and of the Son and of the Holy Spirit, teaching them to observe all things that I have commanded you" (vv. 19-20).

Delegation of Authority to Humans

All government comes from God, but He delegated government to humans when He told Adam and Eve to "fill the earth and subdue it" (Gen. 1:28). Although we forfeited our authority to the devil through sin, God never changed His mind on the matter. We are the ones He appointed to provide leadership and oversight to this world.

As we fast-forward through Scripture, we see God establishing the government of Moses, David and the kings of Israel. At the same time, we also see the emergence of the man-made governments of Egypt, Babylon, Greece and Rome. Although these systems instituted laws and policies that were contrary to God's heart, God still honored His delegated authority. He gave Joseph wisdom to save a generation in Egypt. He gave Daniel a strategy to influence the nation of Babylon. He gave Paul wisdom in relating to the Romans. In his letter to this group of believers, Paul concluded that there is no government except that which is of God (see Rom. 13), so they needed to honor that government.

Throughout history, God's strategies required His people to respect the leadership of governmental systems while maintaining primary loyalty to the kingdom of God. In this, we see that God *honors* government of all kinds, including leadership within businesses, churches and other kinds of organizations. All of these various expressions of government are important components in the work of the culture.

The Culture of Earth:
Abdication and Abuse

God created government, but that doesn't mean every government reflects His purposes. Much of the systemic pain and poverty in the world is fueled by the corruption and abuse of authority. But that is not what God intended. He intended the governments of this earth to reflect the Kingdom of heaven and release His protection, guidance and justice.

The Effects of Sin

Unfortunately, because of the fall of man, everything became infected by human sin and corruption. This includes human government, which will generally fall into one of two errors: (1) abdication or (2) abuse. When government leaders abdicate, they lose the ability to care, serve, support and bless their people. On the other hand, when leadership becomes corrupt and abusive, they end up asserting themselves in dictatorial and autocratic ways that demand more than is just from their people.

God has a plan to restore *His* kingdom, but the enemy continues to work against that plan. In fact, we can understand the importance of authority in God's kingdom simply by looking at the way the enemy has attempted to unravel it in our culture. He has a focused assault on the value of authority.

A few years ago, I dreamed I was given permission to look through the enemy's filing cabinet. I found myself in a type of Sam-Spade-black-and-white office with old-fashioned furniture. I opened one of the drawers in the filing cabinet and discovered a file labeled "San Francisco." As I opened it, I suddenly was standing outdoors looking at the sky. Emblazoned across the clouds were the words, "My purpose for San Francisco is the corruption of authority."

Through this particular dream, God gave me a key insight into how the enemy was blinding the people of the city to the gospel (see 2 Cor. 4). The devil doesn't want people to understand Jesus in the light of His beauty, power and glory, so he uses accusation and distortion to blind them to the gospel. One of his principle strategies for doing this is by encouraging corruption in leaders and breeding rebellion in the hearts of those who are being led. If the enemy can keep leaders and followers at war with one another, he can frustrate culture and constrict the Church in such a way that it is unable to move forward in releasing God's government on the earth.

In 2011, I visited the Occupy Movement in San Francisco, where I spent several hours talking to the staff and participants in an attempt to determine the Kingdom longings that were driving their cause. Most of the people I talked with were driven by a deep longing for a just economy and government—one that defended the rights of the poor and limited the power of those who used authority and wealth to abuse others. Although I don't agree with their application, I couldn't disagree with their purpose.

The Occupy Movement reminds me of the story I told at the beginning of this chapter. The organization that led the Union Square protest against our outreach believed we represented an oppressive authority, so they stood against us until they realized we were not the people they were told we were. I understand their initial response to us, because the same motivation led me to participate in dozens of similar protests in my earlier years. Our demonstrations were often misguided, but the Kingdom longing in our hearts was a desire for freedom and justice. In the same way, if we want a revival culture, we need to identify the Kingdom longings of those we desire to reach.

Servant-based Leadership

In the days leading up to the 1980 presidential election, a friend of mine named Colonel Doner led one of the biggest fundraising organizations for Moral Majority. He worked closely with Jerry Falwell, the founding pastor of Thomas Road Baptist Church in Lynchburg, Virginia, who was active in conservative political causes. Doner and Falwell traveled to different campuses, churches and arenas to present their conservative beliefs and address the moral decay and fiscal irresponsibility going on in our country. Their goal was to help elect Ronald Reagan as president.

One day while holding a rally on a particular campus, the two men were opposed by a group of radical students carrying signs who began shouting them down. Bedlam broke out. Eventually, Doner and Falwell had to pack up their gear and leave. However, when they heard Mother Teresa was going to be speaking on the same campus that evening, they disguised themselves and went to the auditorium to hear her. Mother Teresa spoke out boldly against abortion and promiscuity, for traditional marriage, and about the need to serve the poor on behalf of Jesus. It was almost the exact message Falwell and Donor had brought earlier that day.

As the men looked around, they same saw some of the same people who had held signs and heckled them just a few hours before. But now, those people were sitting in rapt attention, listening to Mother Teresa's every word. Like Doner and Falwell, she presented what most would consider a socially conservative perspective, but no one heckled her. No one said a word.

As Donor witnessed this very different response, he took a step back and reflected on why he and Falwell had been heckled while Mother Teresa had been honored. The only conclusion he could reach was that he and Falwell were perceived as those who imposed their will on others, while Mother Theresa was perceived as somebody who loved and served others. Servanthood is the foundation of all true leadership, and because the Church has lost the will to serve, in many people's eyes it has lost the right to lead. Jesus put it this way:

> You know that the rulers in this world lord it over their people, and officials flaunt their authority over those under them. But among you it will be different. Whoever wants to be a leader among you must be your servant, and whoever wants to be first among you must become your slave. For even the Son of Man came not to be served but to serve others and to give his life as a ransom for many (Matt. 20:25-28, *NLT*).

In Luke 22:27, Jesus said, "I am among you as One who serves," and in John 13:16, He told His disciples, "No servant is greater than his master, nor is a messenger greater than the one who sent him."

The principle of servant leadership applies in every area of life. In politics, business, the Church and even in the home, the leader who serves well leads well.

Kingdom Longings for Authority and Leadership

Every time people gather together, some form of government will eventually emerge, because our longing for leadership is woven into our hearts. Government defines, centralizes and distributes power for the good of society, and God created it to provide *protection*, *guidance* and *justice* for human culture.

Protection

The need for *protection* is a strong Kingdom longing of the heart. Civil government is designed to protect personal and property rights, to protect communities from crime and corruption, and to protect nations from foreign attack and trade imbalances. In business, in addition to outsmarting the competition, leaders are to protect the wellbeing of their workers and the interests of the business. In a church setting, leaders are to protect individuals from spiritual attack, temptation and theological error (see Acts 20:29). Government and leadership provide protections that ensure the fulfillment of individual and community purposes. As leadership functions in the way it was intended, the community is enriched.

Guidance

Government also provides *guidance* to the community, which answers another longing of the heart. On an individual level, most people would rather be guided by close friends, family or the counsel of their own hearts, but when a larger group gathers, it is best to have some form of leadership to define the group's purpose and guide the group in fulfilling it. Leaders in organizations help determine its destination, map its journey and guide its progress by anticipating difficulties and strategizing corrective measures. Unfortunately, when leaders lead poorly, it produces a sense of betrayal and fosters a distrust of authority throughout the organization.

Justice

One of the deepest longings of the emerging generation is for *justice*, which is the right use of authority and power. When instituted through government in the form of a constitution and laws, justice is upheld through enforcement, court systems and consequence. It exists to defend personal rights and freedoms and to punish crime, abuse and oppression. It maximizes personal liberty and equality. As professor and philosopher Cornell West once said, "Justice is what love looks like in public."

Growing up in San Francisco, my parents' extreme left-wing viewpoint shaped my political perspective. My parents considered the Peace and Freedom Party too conservative for them, and from 1970 onward, I was involved in almost every anti-war rally and political protest that took place in our city. By the time I was approaching adulthood, I had a deep distrust of all authority—not because I was an anarchist but because I felt the government did not represent my longings for freedom and justice. Justice means we are all playing by the same rules and are all equally protected by the same laws. Under those laws, we care for one another and receive impartial treatment. The law preserves for us the right to life, liberty and the pursuit of happiness, but when justice is corrupted, it undermines the value and purpose of government.

Salvation Solutions

In our efforts to reach the unreached, we need to recognize that for many people, the subject of leadership and government is a barrier to the kingdom of God. So, as we close this chapter, let's look at some ideas that might help turn this barrier into a bridge.

When Jesus began His ministry, He told people to change the way they think because the "Kingdom" of heaven was at hand. This declaration might seem like a threat unless you know the One who is speaking. If a person's only experience of authority is abuse or abdication, it is understandable that he or she would be suspicious of a statement such as the one Jesus made. However, if you know Jesus, His declaration is the epitome of good news.

Our message to the seeking heart is that God is good and He is in the process of restoring His loving rule and reign to our broken planet. He has dealt a deathblow to the powers of evil that have corrupted humanity, and He is systematically eliminating the effects of evil and corruption from every heart and from every sphere of our world. Deceptive forces have fed on their sinful beliefs and behaviors and held them captive, but now they can be set free. They can escape the prison camp of darkness and join the liberation forces that are restoring all things to the way God originally intended.

We need to tell people that each of us was created to live in relationship with the King of Kings, and we will only find true fulfillment by turning from our ways, receiving His forgiveness, and committing our life to the only One who is wise enough and true enough to lead us.

Building Revival Culture in Leadership and Government

Many people in our culture have come to the conclusion that "power corrupts and absolute power corrupts absolutely." Many have also perceived the Church as being authoritarian, controlling and manipulative in a way that robs people of their individual autonomy and authority. As a result, the majority of the people we are seeking to reach will tend to be resistant to leadership and government. If we are not careful, this can present a problem because our message is about the restoration of God's kingdom on the earth, His Lordship in the life of every person, the authority of God's Word, and the realignment of our lives in Kingdom community.

Tolerance: Bridging the Political Divide

We have been called to reach this world with the love of Jesus, but we have also been called to serve as a *conscience* to culture, representing God's perspective as clearly as possible in the public square. Sometimes these two purposes can seem to work against each other. The very people we are hoping to reach can be the ones who are campaigning for a position we would consider harmful to humanity.

This problem is made worse by the fact that in the coming years, the majority of the harvest will be under 25 years of age, and people in that age group tend to be liberal or progressive in their political views as evidenced in the re-election of President Obama. On the other end of the spectrum, the evangelical and charismatic Church tends to be aligned with conservative causes, which can put us at odds with these individuals. The Church's attitude toward immorality, abortion, homosexual marriage and other current issues has caused us to push away the people we are trying to reach. How do we remain faithful to the commands of Scripture and not alienate those who need Jesus?

When Jesus was on the earth, He lived under the boot of Rome. The Romans were oppressive, abusive and immoral, yet Jesus chose to ignore a number of these political issues in order to fulfill His mission. He chose a zealot (a radical right-winger) and a tax collector (a liberal compromiser) to be on His core team. He told His followers to give to Caesar the things that belonged to Caesar (see Mark 12:17) and declared His kingdom was not of this world (see John 18:36). Yet He also commanded them to seek to bring God's kingdom to earth (see Matt. 6:33), to make disciples of all nations (see Matt. 28:19), and to "occupy till I come" (Luke 19:13, *KJV*). Clearly, between these two extremes there is a wide expanse in which each person's conscience should guide his or her attitudes and actions.

Paul declared that we should honor our government and leaders (see Rom. 13:1-7). That command means one thing in a dictatorship and something quite different in a democratic republic. In a representative government, *honor* means participation in the political process. It means we speak up for what is right and declare, to the best of our ability, God's perspective on human affairs.

So, on the one hand we are not allowed to compromise the Word of God to avoid offending others, but on the other, we must remain loving and tolerant toward those who hold other viewpoints than our own. Simply put, we need to cultivate an attitude of respect and honor for those with whom we disagree and then explain our positions in a comprehensive and caring way. Much of the political polarity in our culture has come about as a result of incomplete arguments and substituting emotional reaction for careful response. We must also put our money where our mouth is by serving the poor, caring for orphans, and demonstrating the gospel in practical ways.

Fostering Self-government

In all forms of government—whether civil government, church leadership or office politics—leadership functions best when people are allowed to govern themselves within a preset framework. As believers, when we received Jesus as our Lord and were filled with the Holy Spirit, we were given the power to govern ourselves under the oversight of the One who loves us. In the same way that we received Jesus as our Savior, we received Him as Lord and governor of our lives.

Every government has a constitution, and ours is the Word of God. His Word is a lamp to our feet and a light to our path (see Ps. 119:105). As we submit ourselves in faith and seek to obey the things God has commanded, He will equip us and empower us for every good work (see Heb. 13:21). Said another way, to the extent we align ourselves with the God of the Word and the Word of God, we will enjoy the intimacy, instruction and inspiration that come from His throne.

One of the highest values of Bethel Church is the responsibility of believers to govern themselves in Christ. Based on the premise that God did not childproof the Garden, the leaders of the church and school of ministry do not lead by rules and regulations but by relationship and responsibility. They have created an environment in which there is no punishment, and yet everyone is expected to clean up his or her own mess. This focus on personal responsibility is a necessary source of spiritual maturity in the people of God.

Spiritual Alignment

Once a person establishes responsibility and self-government in his or her life, that person is able to build a healthy relationship with those in authority. God has given leaders to guide and protect His Church, and as believers, we are called to prayerfully align ourselves with these leaders. Although this is not always an easy process, it is essential to a healthy Christian life. We all need to align our hearts and lives with the leaders whom God has called to guide us and bring our personal "mission" into "submission" to their leadership.

As a senior pastor for more than 25 years, I practiced this advice and maintained alignment with key leaders who helped guide me as a minister. Now that I am no longer serving as a senior leader, I continue to walk in alignment with the leaders of Bethel Church, my home congregation. Again and again, I have experienced the spiritual blessing and supernatural grace that flows through the channels of spiritual alignment.

Healthy Leadership Structures

There are a few things we can do in our churches and ministries to welcome those who have been hurt and disappointed in the leadership failures of the past. As we align ourselves with Jesus' style of leadership, we can increase our influence in culture with a minimal amount of offense, and we can provide the kind of guidance and protection for God's people that will keep us thriving in a culture of revival.

Jesus created the Church to be the community of the redeemed, with its own approach to family, community, economy and government. He established leadership in the Church to provide a framework that would support and empower believers as they moved forward together through life. Again, when we are rightly aligned with one another and with God-ordained leaders, grace and glory will rest upon us, and we will be able to fulfill God's purpose in our personal lives and in our lives together.

As Bill Johnson says, God's government is family. It is not a political structure administered through laws and punishments but a relational influence that works within us "to will and to do for His good pleasure" (Phil. 2:13). In seeking to establish a true revival culture on earth, we need to help people connect with Jesus and cultivate the Spirit-led self-government that will empower them to become the leaders God has called them to be.

The first step in building healthy leadership structures is to *embrace the servant leadership* example Jesus modeled for us in Scripture and assemble our culture to match. We are here to serve others and make their journey of faith as easy and pain-free as possible. We do this by providing opportunities for involvement to new believers and by offering answers to the questions they may have as they seek to follow Jesus. Every church needs to have an "enfolding" ministry that provides clear pathways for people to get involved in the church. As we lay down our lives in service to the seeking heart, we will earn the right to lead that person on his or her journey into Jesus.

Another way we lead people is by helping them *realize they are called to be leaders*. All believers are called to be leaders in one way or another. This being the case, we need to create opportunities in which we can train people to identify their leadership potential and begin functioning in ways that help others. This training can begin in discipleship groups and small groups, but it often requires some other teaching environment as well. Every community should have a leader development program that provides teaching and internship opportunities in a variety of expressions.

The community of believers should be our launching pad for impacting and influencing the world around us. As leaders in the Church, we need to teach and model to people how to interact with the world around them. We need to create opportunities to serve the poor, influence civic leaders, stand strong for justice in our communities, and speak the truth in love as we work to restrain sinful behaviors that harm the larger community. As we lay the foundation of compassion for the world around us, servant leadership will naturally follow, and the result will be a maximum amount of influence with a minimal amount of offense.

We are called to represent the leadership and government of heaven on earth. As we cultivate the leadership of Jesus in our personal lives and honor the spiritual leaders He has brought into our circles, we will be empowered to build a true revival culture on earth and fulfill Jesus' prayer, "Your Kingdom come. Your will be done on earth as it is in heaven" (Matt. 6:10).

Revival Culture and Spirituality

In 2008, I began hearing about an unusual evangelist named Todd Bentley who was leading a series of meetings in Lakeland, Florida. A new expression of revival began to break out at these meetings and was broadcast around the world through the generosity of God TV.

Several of my friends had been touched and healed in this outpouring, so I decided to go and check it out myself. Although Todd's style was different from that with which I was familiar, the power of God was definitely moving. While I was there I witnessed several healings and enjoyed many great worship times, but what struck me the most was the boldness Todd displayed. He was a brash preacher, with tattoos, piercings and a number of rough edges (which later came to light in the form of personal difficulties), and I was impressed by his intensity and tenacity. He seemed to go after God in a way that reflected the words of Jesus in Matthew 11:12: "The kingdom of heaven suffers violence, and the violent take it by force."

I figured that if Todd Bentley could go after God in this way, why couldn't our church? After returning to San Francisco and praying with our leaders, we decided to go for it. We began to gather nightly in what became known as the Golden Gate Outpouring (GGO).

We originally planned our meetings to go for 10 days straight, but God responded to our seeking in such a powerful way that we ended up going for 73 consecutive nights through the summer and for 3 nights a week thereafter for the rest of the year. During the course of 12 months, we met for 220 nights of extended meetings in which we invited God's power and presence into the city of San Francisco. Thousands of people from all over the Bay Area came and were touched, refreshed, healed and set free. Dozens of leaders from churches around the region joined us to celebrate God's presence and carry the fire to their congregations.

We saw scores of people healed of serious diseases, and at least a half dozen people had surgeries cancelled. One woman named Regina was brought back from the point of death. She was a psychologist from the East Bay and came into our meeting using a walker. It took her many painful minutes to make her way to the front to receive prayer. She had been diagnosed with several diseases, including cancer, and had been told to prepare for the worst, but she left our church after that first meeting without her walker. Several meetings later, she presented a letter from her doctor declaring her to be completely healed. She brought in her monthly supply of medicine, which filled a one-foot square box, and placed it on our stage as an offering to the Lord.

At another gathering, an Asian gang member fell to the ground in a demonic manifestation. After several minutes of ministry, he was set free. He went home and destroyed his drugs and alcohol and threw his handgun into the San Francisco Bay.

One night after a GGO meeting, Diane and I were watching God TV and were shocked to see the ticker tape on the bottom of the screen declare a prophecy of destruction over the city of San Francisco. After 30 years of ministry we were used to receiving these kinds of predictions, but seeing it spelled out on a global television station offended us deeply. Diane called the God TV office and got through to the assistant of host Wendy Alec. She questioned the wisdom of broadcasting a prophecy of this kind about a city the God TV hosts had never visited and never held up in prayer.

The leaders of God TV were responsive and gracious. They immediately took the negative prophecy off the air and sent a cam-

era crew to San Francisco to televise a prayer meeting for our city
with key leaders from around the world. This event took place during the GGO on 8-8-08 with Lou Engle, Beni Johnson, and a number of other major leaders. Thanks to God TV, people around the
world joined us that day to pray for San Francisco, and the prophetic word over our city changed from words of destruction to
those of a song by Kristene Mueller-DiMarco: "Keep hoping Saint
Francis, you'll be a free man yet."

As a result of GGO, we discovered ways in which the power of
faith and spirituality are essential components of culture. During
the year, we hosted dozens of leaders and hundreds of believers
from many different churches who were united by their love for
Jesus and their passion to see Him move in power. What made this
unity even more impressive was the fact that our meetings were
held with little structure, few formal teachings, and an open worship format in which every attendee was free to address the congregation as the Spirit led. It was not uncommon to have 10 or 12
people teaching, exhorting or prophesying on a given night.

In those 220 meetings, we had only a mere handful of awk-
ward moments. It was a small price to pay for such a powerful
demonstration of spiritual reality. GGO exemplified an important
fact: God desires to reveal His presence and power in His people.
All we need to do is give Him the opportunity.

The Culture of Heaven:
True Spirituality

As I have already noted, whenever people gather together, they will
inevitably create some form of family, community, economy and
government, because God embedded these things within us when
He made us in His image. In addition to those four elements, people who gather consistently will also generate a shared concept of
God and expression of spirituality. Some of these concepts and expressions are more accurate than others. For example, if you were
to ask a random sampling of people on the streets of San Francisco what they believe about God, most of them will respond with

what I call Star Wars Theology: God is a universal force with a "good side" and a "dark side." (George Lucas should be proud for redefining pantheism for a new generation.) Of course, if that random person were a regular member of my church, he or she would have given a more biblically accurate answer.

In every culture, certain questions have troubled the human heart: *Who am I? Why am I here? How did we get here? Is there any point to life? Is there life after death?* In an attempt to address these and other questions, every culture has developed some form of religion and some expression of spirituality. These universal questions undergird the five major world religions—Judaism, Christianity, Islam, Hinduism and Buddhism—and drive dozens of other lesser expressions of faith. All of these questions reflect a deep Kingdom longing that God placed in the heart of humans to know their Creator and be restored to relationship with the One who made them.

As I previously shared, my earliest introduction to religion was rooted in eastern philosophy and the occult. My parents had rejected Catholicism, and I had attended church only once during my childhood, when a neighbor took me to a Christmas Eve Mass. The first book on spiritual matters I read was D. T. Suzuki's *Zen Buddhism*, and I followed this with *Be Here Now* by Ram Das, *Autobiography of a Yogi* by Paramahansa Yogananda, and a hundred other books that were popular during that era. Immersed in that world, I fasted regularly, meditated religiously, and shared my misguided beliefs evangelistically. I even traveled around the nation teaching others the things I was learning.

During my teenage years, my search for God was much like a spiritual process of elimination. I saw myself like a thirsty man hiking up a mountain stream to find the purest water source. I stopped at pool after pool, only to find the waters polluted with various kinds of dirt and disease. It wasn't until I reached the headwaters where the springs of truth bubbled up from the ground that I was finally able to quench my thirst. Jesus was the answer to the longings of my heart, and as I got to know Him better over the next few years, my longing for spiritual reality was replaced by a longing to know my true destiny in Christ.

The Power of Spirituality

Spirituality is perhaps the most important component of human culture because it determines the way in which we perceive and interact with God. However, as with the other components of culture, what we call "spirituality" did not originate with us but in heaven. Our expressions of worship, prayer and encountering God through His Word and the Holy Spirit are just a dim reflection of the reality that is occurring this very moment in the heavenly realm.

Throughout Scripture, we are given many glimpses of heaven, and in every case we see an awesome celebration of the beauty, power and majesty of God. We see angels, elders and unusual creatures gathered around the throne, worshiping and praising the Lord. Some images of heaven are solemn and awesome (see Isa. 6:1-5), while others are joyous and almost playful (see Ps. 150; Zeph. 3:17). All of these pictures display images of the reality we are called to reproduce on the earth. Jesus emphasizes this calling in the Lord's Prayer, which begins with a glimpse of God's nature:

> Our Father in heaven, hallowed be Your name. *Your kingdom come. Your will be done on earth as it is in heaven.* Give us this day our daily bread. And forgive us our debts, as we forgive our debtors. And do not lead us into temptation, but deliver us from the evil one (Matt. 6:9-13, emphasis added).

As we consider the first few lines in light of the Great Commission, we find that we have a role to play in bringing heaven to earth. In other words, there is a *partnership* between the Creator and His creation in the fulfillment of spiritual purposes. We were created to fulfill a God-given destiny on earth (see Eph. 2:10). We are called to partner with Him to reach the lost and rejoice with the angels (see Luke 15:7-10). We are called to extend God's kingdom and to disciple nations (see Matt. 28:20). We were created to rule and reign with God forever (see Rev. 5:10; 22:5).

Although we don't know the exact form this will take, we know that heaven is more than just some eternal feast in the sky—there is an ongoing purpose that begins here on earth and stretches into eternity. Spirituality is not merely about knowing God and enjoying Him forever (see Rom 1:21), but also about knowing God and *partnering with Him* in His purposes. God's intention was always to have a people with whom He could partner, with Him serving as the senior partner. "Worship" and "partnership" are two words that describe the way we will relate with God forever.

This concept of spirituality and partnership is portrayed most clearly in the life and ministry of Jesus. In the Gospel of John, Jesus declared:

> Most assuredly, I say to you, the Son can do nothing of Himself, but what He sees the Father do; for whatever He does, the Son also does in like manner. For the Father loves the Son, and shows Him all things that He Himself does; and He will show Him greater works than these, that you may marvel (John 5:19-20).

This reveals the depth of spiritual intimacy Jesus experienced with His Father and shows how committed He was to moment-to-moment partnership with the Father. It also affirms that Jesus, though fully God, emptied Himself of His divine prerogative (see Phil. 2:7) and chose to live on the earth as a man filled with the Holy Spirit. It is a *demonstration* of what we can become as we learn to walk in the fullness of the Spirit that Jesus enjoyed.

Jesus modeled a life of complete alignment and deep agreement with the Father to release God's kingdom on earth. He has invited us to join with Him in His purposes, but first we need to understand who we are in Christ and who Christ is in us. We also need to know who we are *becoming* so we can bring utmost glory to God, not just here in this present world but also in the world to come. The enemy is at work to pervert true spirituality, but God is at work to redeem it and bring us into His purposes.

The Culture of Earth:
Idolatry and Religion

God created humanity to enjoy deep intimacy and profound en-counters with Him on a consistent basis. Unfortunately, everything changed when sin entered the world. Adam and Eve withdrew from God and hid themselves in shame (see Gen. 3:8). Since that time, humanity has been torn between an impulse to hide and a yearning to reconnect with God. Some of the fruit of this dichotomy is reli-gion and idolatry. Religion is man's attempt to reach God through human effort, ritual and disciplines. Idolatry comes from the need of the human heart to ascribe worth (or "worth-ship") to someone or something. There is a temporary satisfaction that comes from false religion and idolatry because religious belief and activity "scratches the itch" of spiritual longing. Yet the human spirit re-mains dormant and, ultimately, the soul is left unsatisfied.

In *The Gifts of the Jews*, Thomas Cahill notes that during the time of Abraham, the pagan religion and idolatry of the day com-pelled people to partake in horrible beliefs and practices, such as ritual infanticide and temple prostitution. When God called Abra-ham, who was born in pagan Babylon, he heard the voice of the Lord and chose to follow Him by bringing his family to an un-known land (see Gen 12:1). This was one of the unique gifts the Jews brought: the rediscovery of *the God who speaks* who is seeking people and longing to restore them to Himself.[1]

In Abraham's time, there was no Scripture and no statements of faith—there was only "the Voice." Even when God gave the writ-ten Law 500 years later, it was His initial desire to personally de-clare the Ten Commandments to the people. Yet because of fear, Israel withdrew from the voice of God and chose instead to relate to God through Moses (see Exod. 20:18-19). For the most part, the people of Israel have alternated between religion and idolatry ever since. Just a few short days after this incident, while Moses was on Mount Sinai with God, the people were down in the val-ley worshiping the golden calf (see Exod. 32). Later, when they fi-nally received the Law, they turned it into a set of unattainable rules that ended up being a barrier to personal relationship with their Creator (see Matt. 23). Yet God never stopped speaking to Israel, initially through Abraham, and then through the Law and the Prophets, and then ultimately by becoming flesh and dwelling among them. As the author of Hebrews wrote:

> God, who at various times and in various ways spoke in time past to the fathers by the prophets, has in these last days spoken to us by His Son, whom He has appointed heir of all things, through whom also He made the worlds; who being the brightness of His glory and the express image of His person, and upholding all things by the word of His power, when He had by Himself purged our sins, sat down at the right hand of the Majesty on high (Heb. 1:1-3).

Sadly, some Christians have made the same mistake the Jews did, rejecting a relationship with the living God and opting instead for a religion of rules and regulations. Having been saved by grace through faith, they seek to walk out their faith with religious structures and laws. They prefer to trust in principles above God's presence, and they end up falling into one of two errors: legalism or licentiousness. Principles are a great safety net, but God wants us to follow in the footsteps of Jesus who lived by "every word that proceeds from the mouth of God" (Matt. 4:4). This requires intimate relationship.

If we reject the true revelation of God found in Scripture, we will inevitably create a belief system based on a warped image of God. Man-made religion is humanity's best attempt to reach God, and it does not produce an accurate image of Him. We can see this in every belief system throughout the globe, even in atheism. In the end, all religion apart from a personal relationship with Jesus will become legalistic. It will be based on human effort, obedience and perhaps the hope of multiple lifetimes of reincarnation.

One night, just before I became a believer, I walked out of my house in the middle of the night. There were no streetlights, and I was looking up at the stars and thinking about my life and how difficult it was for me to become the person I really wanted to be.

I cried out to God and said, "Why didn't You make a religion that could change me from the inside out?" I didn't realize *this* is exactly what true Christianity is all about. It isn't about a set of rules or an external structure of do's and don'ts, but about an inside-out transformation. God confirmed this fact to the prophets Jeremiah and Ezekiel, stating, "I will put My law in their minds, and write it on their hearts" (Jer. 31:33), and, "I will put My Spirit within you and cause you to walk in My statutes" (Ezek. 36:27). This is the good news of Jesus Christ.

Understanding Kingdom Longings for True Spirituality

Now that we are beginning to understand the importance of faith and spirituality in community, we can begin to build a bridge between the culture of this world and the culture of the kingdom of God. The world has been hiding itself from God in various ways ever since Adam and Eve sinned, but His imprint remains in the human soul. This imprint manifests itself in Kingdom longings for God's *truth, destiny, power* and *intimacy*, which continue to drive humanity to seek for the One who is seeking it.

Truth and Reality

One of the deepest longings of the human heart is for *truth*. Jesus declared, "You shall know the truth, and the truth shall set you free" (John 8:32). However, Jesus was not speaking about just *any truth,* but it is *the truth that displaces the lie* that will set us free. The Greek word for "truth" (*aletheian*) is rooted in the concept of reality. In other words, it is not so much about truths, principles or precepts but about what actually exists. Humanity has a limited perception of what "is," and we draw conclusions on limited information that we then call "truths."

A great example of this was the long-standing assumption that the sun revolves around the earth. Every observer on the planet could verify this assumption each and every day, but it was false. It wasn't until Copernicus presented the concept of a sun-centered system in 1543 that the truth began to be known. This was more than 450 years ago, yet we still refer to dawn as the "sunrise."

We live in a world that resists the idea of objective truth and makes it into a matter of personal opinion. Each person believes his or her perspective is correct, yet even the most objective human being is still hopelessly subjective. God possesses the only absolutely perfect perspective of reality. Jesus said, "If you abide in my Word, you are My disciples indeed. And you shall know the truth, and the truth shall make you free" (John 8:31-32). He also said to the Father, "Your word is truth" (John 17:17). Only as we align ourselves with God's truth will we be able to build the kind of culture that God desires on earth.

Destiny and Direction

The question of *destiny* is one that will unlock the hearts of this emerging generation and enable them to look at Jesus in a fresh way. Each of us was created with unique gifts and callings. As Paul declares in Ephesians 2:10, "We are His workmanship, created in Christ Jesus for good works, which God prepared beforehand that we should walk in them." Paul notes in Philippians 3:12 that he lived his life to apprehend that for which he was apprehended. In other words, he lived his life in pursuit of his *destiny*.

Every one of us is entirely unique and has a God-given destiny. It is true that we all have a *general* set of things that God has asked us to do as we follow Him, but we also have a set of *specific* things to do in accordance with our personal design. God's love of diversity and specificity can be seen in people's fingerprints, the irises of their eyes, the uniqueness of their voice patterns, the signature of their DNA and so forth. Even identical twins can have very different life experiences, as well as very different opinions and viewpoints of those experiences. Every person is truly one of a kind, yet God knows each one of us intimately and loves each one of us unconditionally. His desire is to restore each of us fully to the purpose for which He made us.

The question of spirituality is essential to understanding our direction and destiny in life. God has woven into each of our hearts the understanding that we were created for a reason and that we can accomplish great things no one else can. Unless the pains and disappointments of life have taken it from us, each of us understands that we are *significant*. We have a destiny on earth and a destiny that goes beyond this planet. There is an eternal dimension of who we are.

Power and Presence

Perhaps the greatest bridge we can build to help people into the Kingdom is to effectively steward the supernatural *power* of God. As mere human beings, we are capable of great things. We can build beautiful structures, establish helpful programs, run dynamic services and use a wide range of creative media. All of these things are good, but any club or religion can replicate each of these things. The only thing that distinguishes the people of God from every other group is His presence and power.

The people of the world are longing to experience a reality that transcends the natural, which is why so many are preoccupied with psychic power and paranormal activity. Granted, Jesus rebuked His generation for demanding a sign (see Matt. 16:1-4), but at the same time He continued to give signs and empower His disciples to do the same (see Luke 10:19-20). In Luke 7:18-35, when John the Baptist sent his disciples to ask Jesus if He was the true Messiah, He did not give them a Bible study. Instead, He healed the sick, cast out demons and told them, "Go and tell John the things you have seen and heard: that the blind see, the lame walk, the lepers are cleansed, the deaf hear, the dead are raised, the poor have the gospel preached to them" (v. 22).

After Jesus rose from the dead, He did not immediately send His disciples to preach but told them to wait for power from on high, so they would accurately represent Him (see Luke 24:49; Acts 1:8). To paraphrase Bill Johnson, we owe this generation an encounter with the living God. We have been commissioned to proclaim a complete gospel of Word and power, not merely a gospel of words. That is a primary reason God gave the Holy Spirit to the Church.

Intimacy and Encounter

There is a God-given hunger in the human heart for spiritual *intimacy*, which is clearly illustrated in the story of the woman at the well as told in John 4. Jesus and His disciples were in the midst of a long journey and had stopped at Jacob's well in Samaria. The disciples went into town to get food, leaving Jesus alone.

When a woman approached the well to draw water, Jesus built a simple bridge to her with a request: He asked her for a drink of water. When the woman began to give Him a hard time about racial differences, He interrupted her with an invitation to drink of His living water so she would never thirst again. Jesus then delivered a supernatural word about her current marital status. This encounter with God's supernatural reality blew her away, and as a result much of the city was saved:

> Many of the Samaritans of that city believed in Him because of the word of the woman who testified, "He told me all that I ever did." So when the Samaritans had come to Him, they urged Him to stay with them; and He stayed there two days. And many more believed because of His own word (John 4:39-41).

This is just one of many stories in which Jesus cut through intellectual and emotional barriers to supernaturally bring the good news to the heart of a seeking soul. Later, the apostle Paul elaborated on this supernatural strategy, saying, "My speech and my preaching were not with persuasive words of human wisdom, but in demonstration of the Spirit and of power, that your faith should not be in the wisdom of men but in the power of God" (1 Cor. 2:4-5). I am excited to live in an era in which God is restoring His supernatural strategy to His people.

Salvation Solutions

As we read the Scriptures and examine history, it is evident that God has placed eternity in every person's heart. Our job is to find the *keys* of the Kingdom that will unlock the unmet longings of the heart and bring salvation solutions to our culture.

Our message to the world is that God is real. We can know Him, we can learn to hear His voice, and we can experience His presence. We can also experience forgiveness and be empowered to forgive those who have harmed us. We can be filled with God's presence and power and impact other people's lives in supernatural ways. Essentially, our message is found in the first of the Four Spiritual Laws: "God loves you and offers a wonderful plan for your life."[2]

Our message to the world is that we are significant to God and were not an afterthought. Regardless of the circumstances of our conception or birth, God treasures us. We are one of His dearest creations—we are known by Him and loved by Him. God has bestowed us with amazing gifts and qualities so we can fulfill His purpose for our lives. We can discover our God-given destiny, and we can partner with Him to bring His love to others and help transform the world around us.

Building Revival Culture in Spiritual Realities

If we want to build and sustain a healthy revival culture, we first need to clarify our values and priorities. We are called to bring heaven to earth by experiencing God's presence and power in our everyday lives, which requires us to learn to worship God powerfully, pray passionately, listen carefully and obey courageously. There has to be a shift in our hearts in which we value God's power and presence above all things.

Kingdom Values

For this priority to work in the long run, we must strengthen our value for the Word of God and sound doctrine. As our value for the supernatural grows, we also need to cultivate a commitment to risk and faith. In 1 Corinthians 14:29-32, Paul encourages us to take supernatural risks and let others discern our accuracy and anointing. If this is done in love, we create a safe environment to experiment in the Holy Spirit and even make mistakes as part of the learning process. Growing in the gifts of the Spirit requires that we encourage everyone to take risks (see Heb. 5:14).

In the Bethel movement, we have identified a number of other core values that strengthen a supernatural revival culture, such as honor, joy, hope and the prophetic. As we reinforce these values, we cultivate an environment in which God's presence and power is free to equip and empower His people.

Healthy Spiritual Expressions

God has appointed the Body of Christ to be His embassy on earth, and He calls us to equip and empower spiritual ambassadors who will represent His kingdom in every arena of human life. But in order to accomplish this, we must develop effective ways of connecting believers to the presence and power of God. This is what Jesus was talking about when He said, "I am the vine, you are the branches. He who abides in Me, and I in him, bears much fruit; for without Me you can do nothing. . . . By this is My Father glorified, that you bear much fruit and so prove to be My disciples" (John 15:5,8).

We were created for fruitfulness, and we are called to encourage fruitfulness in one another. To do this, as this passage indicates, we first need to create opportunities for people to connect with God in intimate, life-changing encounters. This can occur during our regular worship gatherings, but it might also require us to dedicate times of special focus. I encourage every believer to set aside times of personal and corporate worship in which the only goal is to learn to abide in Christ. As in a marriage relationship, true fruitfulness comes from intimacy.

Next, we also need to encourage times of corporate prayer and intercession. Jesus said, "If you abide in Me, and My words abide in you, you will ask what you desire, and it shall be done for you" (John 15:7). He also said, "No longer do I call you servants, for a servant does not know what his master is doing; but I have called you friends, for all things that I heard from My Father I have made known to you" (v. 15). The closer we draw to God, the more we are able to confer with Him and begin to partner with Him to transform the world around us.

Finally, we need to encourage believers to function fully in the power of the Holy Spirit. We do this by providing training in the gifts of the Spirit and by providing opportunities for our members to minister to one another in the power of God. This can take place at the end of a home group or regular worship service, or it can happen in special healing gatherings. In either case, these opportunities provide a "laboratory" for believers to grow in their gifts so they can begin to function in supernatural ministry.

As we close this section, I want to underscore the importance of culture in reaching the coming harvest. As we cultivate Kingdom expressions of family, community, economy, authority and spirituality, we will unleash a power of revival culture that will equip and empower us to bring the kingdom of God to earth and release the blessings of heaven in every sphere of life.

Cultivating Revival Culture

Then He spoke a parable to them: "No one puts a piece from a new garment on an old one; otherwise the new makes a tear, and also the piece that was taken out of the new does not match the old. And no one puts new wine into old wineskins; or else the new wine will burst the wineskins and be spilled, and the wineskins will be ruined. But new wine must be put into new wineskins, and both are preserved."

LUKE 5:36-38

He said to them, "But who do you say that I am?" Simon Peter answered and said, "You are the Christ, the Son of the living God." Jesus answered and said to him, "Blessed are you, Simon Bar-Jonah, for flesh and blood has not revealed this to you, but My Father who is in heaven. And I also say to you that you are Peter, and on this rock I will build My church, and the gates of Hades shall not prevail against it. And I will give you the keys of the kingdom of heaven, and whatever you bind on earth will be bound in heaven, and whatever you loose on earth will be loosed in heaven."

MATTHEW 15:15-19

The Coffee and the Cup

As I noted in chapter 1, since my earliest days I have been fascinated by the history of revival, and for a time I voraciously consumed the work of Charles Finney. One of Finney's comments changed my life. However, this comment wasn't about revival—it was about coffee.

For some reason, Finney had a dislike for the bean. He called it that "black-liquid-made-of-God-only-knows-what." In response, I decided I would abstain from it, if only to please my deceased mentor on revival. But as soon as I started my little coffee fast, it felt as if the heavens turned to brass. God's presence seemed so far away from me. I continued diligently in my fast, thinking the spiritual blockage was just a natural result of me trying to kick the caffeine habit, which had been a part of my prayer ritual for a long time.

After about two weeks of frustration, I became concerned. "God," I prayed, "what's wrong? Why does Your presence seem so far away?"

He replied in a still small voice, "What's the problem, Michael? Am I not growing you fast enough?"

I knew exactly what He meant. I was trying to help Him out in my spiritual growth process. Did I really think I could mature more quickly by trying to abstain from certain things? I immediately broke my coffee fast, and my prayer life became richer and richer from that point on.

So today, when I think about revival, I think about coffee and about coffee cups. Coffee is black gold, the energizing treasure that many people seek to start their day. Yet coffee is not useful without a cup. Whether it is a paper to-go cup or a ceramic mug, we need a vessel in which to carry the juice. In the same way, when considering revival, we have to keep in mind that revival (the *coffee*) needs the vessel of culture (the *cup*) in order to be carried. For a move of God through revival to have lasting value, it has to be brewed and carried in the correct container.

Jesus referred to this principle in Luke 5:37-38 by using an image of *wine* and *wineskins*. He said, "No one puts new wine into old wineskins; or else the new wine will burst the wineskins and be spilled, and the wineskins will be ruined. But new wine must be put into new wineskins, and both are preserved." All of us who are interested in revival are seeking the new wine of the Spirit, but if we fail to create the proper wineskin in which to hold and carry the wine, it will not produce the full measure of blessing it was intended to produce.

Revival must be partnered with a *culture* in order for it to be sustained and go where it needs to go. In fact, one of the key reasons past revivals have failed to sustain momentum beyond a few short years is the limitation of revivalists to create healthy revival culture.

A Closer Look at Coffee Culture

Coffee has recently experienced its own "revival." It has always been a point of delight for some, but in the last 20 to 30 years the desire for coffee has become universal, and the coffee industry has grown into a multi-billion dollar business. Along with the growth of the industry, we have also grown in our understanding of the power of caffeine and the way it works. A good dose of caffeine can spark us, move us forward, and get us going where we need to go. Caffeine has value.

At the apex of the coffee revival is a company called Starbucks, which was founded in Seattle in 1971. Starbucks was able to get ahead of the game, and today it is a significant force in fostering the coffee revival that has spread around the world. The interesting thing about Starbucks is that the company doesn't just sell coffee but also a cultural experience. Each Starbucks has a common culture, regardless of where it is located in the world. I have visited Starbucks in Thailand, Hong Kong, Europe and Latin America, and almost every shop is the same. Each locale has similar graphics on the walls, similar pastries behind the glass counter and, for the most part, the same type of coffee, the same environment, and the same music playing on the sound system. Starbucks has created a *culture*.

In fact, the company even has its own language. It uses unusual terms such as "venti" and "tall," and it sells strange-sounding products such as "soy caramel macchiato frappuccino." Having a number of college-aged children in my family, many of whom have worked at Starbucks at one time or another, I have come to realize that even their business culture is tremendously honed and cultivated. This is why they are consistently able to be the most prolific coffee shop in the world.

Like Starbucks, the Church needs to create a culture in which it can develop and sustain the coming revival. God is about to move on the earth in a powerful way, and it is time for the Church to get ready. If we, as a people, can prepare for what God is doing, we can maximize His impact in our lives and the lives around us.

Understanding the Power of Culture

Culture, as we have stated, is a common set of values, priorities and practices that guide the beliefs and behaviors of a group, organization or community to fulfill a common vision. It is present in every group or community of people, whether we like it or not. It exists in families, businesses, clubs, cities, regions and nations. It can be intentional or accidental, positive or negative, helpful or harmful. It can be cultivated and transformed or it can be ignored and neglected, but in either case it will continue to function and affect the effectiveness of everything we think and do.

Culture is rooted in *values*, those often-intangible assumptions and ideals by which we determine the relative worth of all we do. Values are much like the DNA in our bodies—they are unseen but

absolutely influential. They are essential in defining our priorities, which ultimately dictates our allocation of time, energy and
resources. Values and priorities express themselves in *practices*,
which are the things we naturally desire to do, not just because we
"should." Our practices are the truest indicator of our *actual* values and priorities, as opposed to our *aspired* values, which rarely
seem to find their way into our calendars or our checkbooks.

Culture is to community what discipline and habits are to
individuals. For instance, in my own life, I don't always feel like
doing what I "should" do. I don't always feel like rising early, praying, reading the Word, exercising, limiting my food intake, doing
chores or going to work. However, I have built discipline and
habit into my life, which supports me in my desire to become the
person I intend to be. As I use the power of habit, I can find my
discipline turning into delight because of the goals I accomplish
and the people I impact.

In the same way, once a culture has been firmly established in
a community and has been reinforced over a period of time, the
community begins to move in greater unity toward the common
goals that have been established. If a culture is chaotic and scattered, the members in the community will have a difficult time
accomplishing anything important. However, if the people work
together with others to establish a revival culture, they can save
themselves a lot of work and a lot of grief.

Culture is like the banks of a river that keep the random and
individualized streams of community flowing in the same general direction for the benefit of all. Without banks, a river becomes a stagnant and directionless marsh. As Proverbs 29:18 tells
us, "Where there is no vision, the people perish" (*KJV*). When vision and values are not clearly upheld in communities, churches
and ministries, the people suffer from a "marshy malaise."

In my estimation, the biggest mistakes we can make are to
underestimate the power of culture and fail to cultivate the kind
of culture that will effectively empower our community to fulfill
its mission. In the absence of culture, we must expend more energy and battle more anxiety. But as we embrace the value of cul-

ture and use its power to transform families and communities, we will see the power of God released in a much more effective and efficient way.

Bethel Church and Revival Culture

One of the best examples I have seen of a church that is actively building this type of revival culture is Bethel Church in Redding, California. I first began to hear about Bethel in 2000 when several leaders from our church attended conferences held there. It wasn't until a few years later that I first visited Bethel to attend a Jesus Culture conference with a couple of my teenage children. The Lord touched my kids in a powerful way at this event, and, to be honest, He touched me powerfully as well.

During the next two years, my kids and I traveled to Redding a few times each year to be a part of Jesus Culture and receive a fresh touch from the Lord. Diane and I also began to attend adult conferences in 2006. The more I visited Redding and hosted Bethel leaders in our church in San Francisco, the more I began to realize I was seeing a new and fresh expression of revival culture unlike anything I had seen in the past. It wasn't long before we decided to fully align our hearts and our ministry with Bill Johnson and Bethel Church.

In 2009, after 30 years of uninterrupted ministry in the city of San Francisco, Diane and I decided to take a three-month summer sabbatical. God opened up a beautiful house for us in Redding, and we decided to spend our sabbatical building a deeper relationship with our Bethel friends. Near the end of this amazing summer, I had a vivid dream in which the Lord seemed to be guiding our family to extend our sabbatical to a full year in Redding. I submitted this direction to my staff in San Francisco, and they agreed it was the word of the Lord. So Diane and I enrolled our children in school and settled into the Bethel Culture. Over the course of the next year, I commuted to San Francisco two to three times each month to meet with leaders and speak to our church.

Once our family was settled in Redding, Paul Manwaring, the director of Global Legacy, invited me to sit in on his team meetings and be part of his ministry. Paul and a few other leaders began to speak into our lives about our past, present and future. During the course of a year it became clear that our grace to continue ministry in San Francisco had lifted, and in May 2010—the end of our first year at Bethel—the Lord spoke to us to pull out of the city for the time being. In response, Diane and I met with our church leaders and began outlining a succession plan. Within a year, I was invited to serve with Paul Manwaring in Global Legacy and with Banning Liebscher as director of development for Jesus Culture.

The Components of Revival Culture

As I have had the privilege of working with many outstanding leaders at Bethel, I have come to have a unique respect and appreciation for what God is doing in and through the church. I believe the key to Bethel's fruitfulness and impact comes from the revival culture they have built. In the next few pages, I will outline some of the components the church has put in place that may account for the blessings people are finding there.

The Favor of God

In every move of God, there is a human element and a divine element. Unless the Lord builds the house, human efforts will matter little (see Ps. 127:1). In Bethel's case, I believe the primary key as to why the church has attracted God's favor is that it has consistently placed value on the presence of God above all else. This church has cultivated an experience and expression of worship that is honored around the globe. Bethel's emphasis on hosting God's presence is the foundation of its revival culture.

The Leaders

Another key to the powerful culture at Bethel can be found in its senior leaders, Bill and Beni Johnson, who walk in a level of authenticity and integrity that is rare in the Body of Christ. Bill is an unusual leader who is consumed with extending God's kingdom, and he has no time or interest in extending his own. As a result, God has entrusted him with great favor and influence throughout the Church. Bill has cultivated an environment of permission that empowers people to reach their highest potential in Christ.

When the Johnsons first moved from the small town of Weaverville to assume the leadership of Bethel Church, Bill declared four principles that would guide the development of this congregation:

1. God is in a good mood.
2. Every believer is significant.
3. Nothing is impossible with God.
4. The cross of Jesus did it all.

These four foundational points have created the bedrock of the revival culture of Bethel and have fueled every aspect of this ministry, both locally and globally.

The Team

The next key to the quality of Bethel's culture is the leadership team that works with the Johnsons. There are a number of powerful couples that are part of the senior team, including Kris and Kathy Vallotton, Danny and Sheri Silk, Eric and Candace Johnson, and Paul and Sue Manwaring. These and other leaders at Bethel have done an amazing job of taking Bill's core message and building a culture and community to sustain it. Because of the environment of permission and empowerment that the Johnsons have created, these leaders have also been released to pursue their own dreams and develop their own messages, which are also blessing the Body of Christ around the world.

The School

Perhaps the most powerful generator of revival culture in Redding is the Bethel School of Supernatural Ministry (BSSM). This ministry started in 1998 with only 36 students and now numbers more than 1,500, with more than 600 attending from foreign countries. BSSM is more than a Bible School—it is a place of transformation where students learn who they are in Christ and who Christ is in them, and they are empowered to demonstrate the words and works of Jesus in the real world. One of my greatest delights is to teach the Bible at this school.

The Healings
Bethel Church is perhaps best known for the amazing miracles and healings that occur on a consistent basis. Two of the ministries that foster this environment of healing are the Healing Rooms and the Transformation Center. Every Saturday hundreds of people, many from around the world, come to the Healing Rooms to receive a blessing from the Lord. Many are healed each week, while those who are not leave knowing they are loved. The Transformation Center houses several ministries, but the best known is Sozo, led by Dawna DeSilva and Theresa Liebscher. Every day, the Spirit of God sets free people who have been bound by the pain and disappointments of the past.

An Atmosphere of Permission
A number of other components have also helped create the culture of revival that exists in Redding, including Dann Farreley's teaching on Brave Communication, Kevin and Theresa Dedmon's ministry of Firestarters and Treasure Hunts, Chris Overstreet's work in evangelism and outreach, and Steve Backlund's teaching on Joy and the Victorious Mindset. Steve has also worked closely with Paul Manwaring to create the Leader Development Program that has distilled many elements of Bethel's revival culture into a dynamic curriculum for ministry leaders around the world. Who would have expected that a church would emerge in a small town in Northern California and bring so much blessing and impact around the globe.

In addition to Bethel's growing influence, this atmosphere of permission creates an environment in which people take risks and occasionally make messes. While this has drawn scrutiny from some self-appointed watchdogs who wait in the wings to pounce on mistakes when they are made, we have to remember there will never be innovation without experimentation and there will never be experimentation without some messes. Thomas Edison made 400 "mistakes" in creating a light bulb before he ultimately succeeded, but most of us would agree that the final result was worth the process.

As we stand on the cusp of another great awakening, it is time for the people God to recognize that with all of our sound doctrine and polished programs, we are barely keeping pace with the world around us. We have a long way to go before we are reaching the lost, healing the sick, freeing the captives and transforming the world at the level God desires. In pursuit of this goal, the leaders at Bethel have determined not to limit the experience and expression of the power of God. They would rather allow a bit of excess than throw the baby out with the bathwater. They maintain an atmosphere of permission in public and bring correction to excess and error in private.

In order for us to understand the perspective of God, host the presence of God and walk in the power of God at a new level, it's likely we will make mistakes along the way. I pray we have the courage to take risks and the care to clean up the messes so we can bring the full power of heaven to earth.

Church: Inside Out!

John Wimber is widely regarded as one of the forerunners of the Bethel Movement. He was also one of the premier experts on "doing Church" in our generation. As I noted earlier, Wimber was an expert in both the *art* of church and in the *science* of church. He equipped the Body of Christ in the gifts of the Holy Spirit, signs and wonders, and the power and presence of God. At the same time, he was one of the most knowledgeable leaders concerning the sociological and structural dynamics of the Church. In one of Wimber's teachings on building healthy churches, he presented the following pyramid:

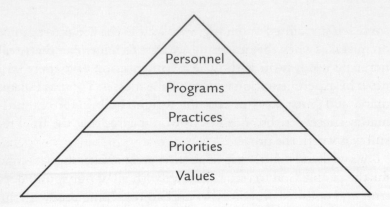

Wimber believed the foundation of every ministry should be the *values* its members hold in common. From there, priorities, practices, programs and personnel should be added on to build the ministry "from the inside-out," or from the ground up. With all due respect to Wimber's model, I would add one more layer that I believe is even more fundamental than values: *vision.* In my experience, without a shared vision of what you are building as a team, the shared values won't help you very much.

Wimber felt the mistake most leaders make is to focus on external things such as programs and personnel. He held that the effectiveness of a ministry or organization is most affected by values, priorities and practices, which are the three primary elements of culture. It was his conviction that the powerlessness of a church or ministry is directly related to the lack of consistency between its culture and its programs. He saw that leaders of churches and organizations were often overwhelmed by the tyranny of the urgent and the demands of people, which caused them to address the symptoms of organizational problems rather than the causes that were rooted in cultural weaknesses.

Here's an example to which most of us can relate. Let's say we hear from various people in our church that they are feeling lonely and relationally disconnected. So, we hold a leaders meeting and decide to institute a small-group program. Next, we appoint a leader to run it, find a program we feel good about, hold a series of information meetings, and preach every Sunday for eight weeks on the need for relationship in the Body. Finally, we launch our new small-group ministry with great pomp and circumstance. Unfortunately, in spite of our best efforts, only a small percentage of our membership joins the new groups, including almost none of the people who were complaining about disconnection in the first place.

This same scenario can be played out in other ministries the church attempts to establish, such as evangelism, healing rooms, children's church and family ministries. In each case, the reason the programmatic approach to leadership failed is that the community lacked the core values of relationship and accountability. Programmatic solutions only succeed to the degree they correspond to the actual cultural values, priorities and practices of the community.

How to Cultivate Kingdom Culture

True and lasting change, in any family, group or organization, comes about not by changing external things such as personnel or programs but by carefully implementing internal changes. However, changing internal things—such as core values, priorities and practices—requires a level of dedication and commitment that many people are unable to manifest, primarily because internal change must begin in the heart. Cultural transformation is *concentric*, which means it begins in the heart of the individual, then radiates to the next ring of friends and family, and then ultimately impacts the wider community. It all begins in the heart.

Personal Transformation
Given this, the first step in cultivating revival culture is to examine ourselves in the light of Scripture. As we look at the life of Jesus and the Early Church, we become aware of the gap between our values, priorities and practices and the ones we see in the Bible, and from there we are able to begin to make adjustments. The next step is personal prayer and alignment with God. Prayer is the crucible in which our desire is refined, and as we pray God begins to change our hearts. Next, we begin to change the way we speak about ourselves and our community in relationship to the cultural changes

we are pursuing. Finally, we become willing to implement personal disciplines that assist us in turning the value into a priority and then into a practice. Full transformation begins in the "root" but ultimately must manifest in the "fruit" of our lives. Once we are able to express the new value through a tangible lifestyle change, we are ready to impart this value to others in the community.

Team Transformation

Team transformation is similar to personal transformation in that it must be an inside-out process. The first step is to join or create a team of friends who recognize the need for change and are willing to pursue the process with us. The second step is to pray and begin to foster the particular aspect of Kingdom culture we are seeking to make a deeper personal value in our friends and our team as a whole. The next step is to change the way we speak about ourselves and begin to boldly confess what the Word of God says about us in this matter, for our declarations matter to God and to the process of transformation. Finally, we move from "root to fruit" by implementing a group behavioral change that can be supported in the larger community.

As a practical example of how this works, consider a team that wants to implement a culture of honor. First, the team must evaluate and expose the fears and pride in its members that lead to control. Second, they must pray for one another in ways that reveal the honor that God has for each individual. Third, they must begin to speak identity and destiny over one another and celebrate each other's victories. Finally, they must create an environment in which honor can be fostered and sustained on a consistent basis.

Church and Community Transformation

Once we have cultivated values, priorities and practices into a team, we are ready to begin to influence the whole congregation or organization. Here is where teaching and testimony about the issue make a huge difference. We begin by calling the congregation to pray and to consider the problem, and then we help them evaluate their shortcomings on a personal basis. We encourage them, enforce a new way of speaking about the subject, and *then* institute programming that will reinforce the topic.

As an example, the church I previously pastored in San Francisco recently hosted Steve Backlund for a weekend conference on the subject of joy, hope and the victorious mindset. The impact on our congregation was amazing, and many repented of "victim thinking" that had brought hopelessness to their lives. In order to deepen the impact of this weekend, we implemented a 40-day negativity fast (or "positivity feast") to help everyone think and speak differently. By the end of this season we had a distinctly different culture than before, and we had implanted one more element of revival culture in our church.

Developing a Kingdom Culture

We are called to partner with God to bring His kingdom to earth, and one of the most effective ways we can do this is by developing Kingdom culture. As we cultivate the vision, values, priorities and practices of heaven, we will create the relational soil in which every fruit of the Kingdom can grow. As we look forward to the coming harvest, the most important way we can prepare is by building revival culture from the inside out. In the next chapter, written by Banning Liebscher, we will focus on the challenge of discipling the emerging generation to bring about a true Kingdom culture and lifestyle.

Discipleship and the Coming Harvest

Banning Liebscher

As I am approaching my late thirties, I am realizing that what brings joy or grief to my heart now is very different from what brought joy or grief to me back in my early twenties. In years past, I would celebrate when attendance was up at our youth meetings or when our programs were running smoothly. Alternatively, I would be grieved when numbers weren't so high or our structures and programs were not working well.

In contrast, after many years of ministry, what brings the most joy to my heart now is seeing those young people still following the Lord. I rejoice over those who have remained in love with Jesus—those who are dedicated husbands and wives, incredible parents, and who are plugged into their church communities. And what saddens me the most (even though their stories are still being written) are those who have fallen away from the Lord. The truth is that numbers and performance has become increasingly less relevant, because what brings the deepest delight to my heart is the lasting fruit I see in the lives of the people I have walked with.

Chris Quilala is one of those people in my life. He was just a junior high kid (12 years old) when I started youth pastoring. Over the years, it has been one of my greatest joys to be able to pour into him and to walk with him. Even though he is honored to lead worship all around the globe, what fulfills me the most is that he is a phenomenal husband and a devoted dad who serves the Lord faithfully in his local church.

When I am in my seventies and look back on my life, I want the
fruit I see to be people! Sure, I want to look back and say we filled
stadiums and sold hundreds of thousands of CDs, and I am grateful for those aspects of leadership. I genuinely believe the Lord has
given us a mandate to inspire nations through mass gatherings,
and I am passionate about that aspect of ministry. But if my experience so far serves me correctly, when I am in my seventies, what
will most bring joy to my heart will be the lasting fruit—the *people*—
with whom I shared my life.

For this reason, I believe a major key to establishing and sustaining a culture of revival is by making disciples of this emerging
generation. As Michael has presented throughout this book, because of the unique challenges of the coming harvest, the key to our
success depends our ability to bring authentic, transformational
discipleship to every person we reach. I have spent half my life ministering to youth and young adults, so I understand firsthand the
absolute importance of this process. If we are to build an enduring
revival culture, we need to rethink the way we reach people with the
gospel and renew our ideas about how we make disciples.

Program or Process

Personally, I am a linear thinker. My wife, SeaJay, on the other
hand, is not! One of the more apparent demonstrations of this
difference is our approach to radio stations. I was in the car with
her one time and noticed her radio stations weren't in order. So,
being the awesome husband I am, I offered to help her out by lin-
ing them up. Unbelievably, she said, "No thanks." I couldn't understand this, because here I was trying to do her a favor and serve
her. Aren't radio stations created to be left to right in ascending order? It seemed to me that this was common knowledge and that
everyone was aware of the proper order for radio stations.

I want to go from point *A* to *B*, from *B* to *C*, and from *C* to *D*.
I want to go from start to finish. But one thing I have learned
about discipleship is that it is *not* linear. It is point *A* to *G*, and then
possibly *C* to *P*, and then back to *G*. It is impossible to confine dis-

cipleship to a program or predictable process because it is sponta-neous and flows like a river. It is alive and breathing and, most im-portantly, it doesn't take place in a classroom.

I don't mean to sound as if I am downplaying current models of discipleship. I absolutely agree that discipleship is a God-or-dained and effective tool in connecting, training and releasing oth-ers. I simply believe that discipleship should be based on real relationships with real people—what I call *life on life*.[1] I do not be-lieve we can successfully disciple people by teaching a biblical les-son. While that is a part of imparting revelation, it is not enough to just fill heads with information.

In the New Testament, we find that Jesus made disciples by sharing life together. The best example of this is found in Mark 3:14-15, which states, "Then [Jesus] appointed twelve, *that they might be with Him* and that He might send them out to preach, and to have power to heal sicknesses and to cast out demons" (empha-sis added). Jesus gave us a model for life-on-life discipleship that is *caught* as well as *taught*. Discipleship is not a series of steps and then—*BAM!*—you're done. Discipleship means sharing life.

Awakening Life

In 2 Kings 4, we read a story that illustrates the life-on-life princi-ple. One day, the prophet Elisha was travelling through a remote region when he met a Shunammite woman and her husband, who gave him some food. The couple began to host him every time he came to their town, and they even built him a room. Because of all the kindness and care this woman showed, Elisha said to Gehazi, his servant, "Find out what I can do for her."

Gehazi answered, "Well, she doesn't have a son."

So Elisha prophesied, "Next year, you are going to have a son."

"Look," the woman replied. "I need you to be straight up with me. This isn't funny if you're joking right now."

Elisha replied, "No, really, you're going to have a child."

Sure enough, the following year the woman gave birth to a baby boy. But unfortunately, while that child was still young, he came home with a headache and died in his mother's lap. She rode off to find Elisha, fell at his feet, and said, "Why did you lie to me? My son is dead."

This is such a powerful picture. Just like so many people today, the boy was dead when he should be alive. The mother came to Elisha in her desperation and faith. The prophet's first response was to tell Gehazi, "Get ready to depart. Take my staff to where the boy is, and put it on his face."

As instructed, Gehazi travelled back to the woman's home, where he put Elisha's staff on the boy. But he didn't awaken. Elisha had tried to send his "gift" ahead of him, but to no avail. Nothing happened to change the lad's condition until Elisha himself arrived and lay over him—mouth to mouth, eye to eye, cheek to cheek. Then the boy was restored. Life-on-life had begun the awakening.

I am learning more and more about how discipleship *awakens* life. God doesn't need our gifts . . . He wants our lives! The Lord isn't looking for our *gifts* to ignite a generation; He is looking for our *lives* to revive and animate those with whom we have been entrusted. If we are going to fulfill our calling and transform a generation, it will require life-on-life.

The Holy Spirit Flows Through People

One of my favorite authors is E. M. Bounds. He wrote the book *The Power of Prayer* for preachers about prayer, but it also goes hand in hand with this subject of discipleship. In one passage, Bounds writes:

> What the Church needs today is not more machinery or better, not new organizations or more and novel methods, but men whom the Holy Ghost can use—men of prayer, men mighty in prayer. The Holy Ghost does not flow through methods, but through men. He does not come on machinery, but on men. He does not anoint plans, but men—men of prayer.[2]

The Holy Spirit anoints *people*, not methods. He doesn't move upon machinery; He blesses and partners with men and women. It is *our lives* that make an impact. This is so important for us to understand because as we do, we will naturally begin to change our perception and methods about discipleship. And as we begin walking out this revelation, we will see revival flourish.

This truth about discipleship becomes even clearer as we approach the prophesied great harvest. Because of the pain that has ravaged the earth, those who will be meeting Jesus and joining our Christian communities will often be fractured and alienated at a level we cannot comprehend. We need to prepare our hearts to share our lives with these new believers. We must be authentic, open and willing to embrace their lives compassionately and allow them in to our world. This is what will help heal and transform them.

When I picture life-on-life discipleship, I often think of coaching. My wife and I coach basketball, and we have a passion for it. I think one reason I enjoy it is that when I was a young man, my high school basketball coach shared his life with me and helped shape me. Twenty years have passed since that time, but I still remember him pulling me into his little office off the gym and challenging me to be a leader. I remember sitting in that room as a 17-year-old kid, crying because I knew I wasn't living up to the leadership mandate on my life, and he was calling it out of me.

Again, I don't want to downplay gifts, talents or programs, but I do want to emphasize how much our *lives* are the impacting force. It is our *lives* through which God flows. To truly make a difference in our communities, the Lord requires our *lives*.

Classroom Verses Reality

Our western mindset is very classroom-driven. Teachers pass on knowledge to their students, which they expect will train and transform them. After presenting the information, the instructors then step *out* of the equation, because they assume they are no longer needed in their students' lives.

If we are going to produce sustainable, long-term fruit in the Kingdom, we have to shake this premise. Teaching is good, but for truth to be fully lived out in people's hearts and lives, it needs to be imparted and processed in the context of real life. As Paul writes in 1 Corinthians 4:14-17:

> I do not write these things to shame you, but as my beloved children I warn you. For though you might have ten thousand instructors in Christ, yet you do not have many fathers; for in Christ Jesus I have begotten you through the gospel. Therefore I urge you, imitate me. For this reason I have sent Timothy to you, who is my beloved and faithful son in the Lord, who will remind you of my ways in Christ, as I teach everywhere in every church.

Note that Paul does not say, "Timothy is going to come and remind you of what I teach," but instead, "Timothy is going to come and remind you of *my ways in Christ*." Because Timothy had been with him and they had experienced life together, Timothy could actually come to the believers in Corinth and show them Paul's life in Christ."

For the most part I can't recollect sermons from my younger years, but I can remember when the fathers in my world broke off pieces of their lives and shared them with me. Those were the times, the situations and the friendships that impacted me the most. For instance, I clearly remember my youth pastor, Scott Anderson, coming to one of my basketball games. I was already on the court, but saw him walk in the door. It was a simple and seemingly insignificant moment, but I remember it to this day. I could still take you to the school gym and show you exactly where he sat. His focus and support made a huge impression on me.

Dann Farrelly has been another father in my life. I watch as he interacts with people, and I have had the opportunity to observe his extreme grace in the way he communicates and interacts with them. What God has shown me through him about communication has *radically* changed my marriage and my leadership.

Bill Johnson is yet another father figure. About eight years ago, I went on a trip with him and his wife, Beni. It was just the three of us. We were on our way to a meeting, but we didn't know how to get there and were running late. From the back seat, I watched how

Bill—unstressed, full of grace and totally relaxed—interacted with his wife. I remember thinking, *Wow, that is not how I interact at all! This is super foreign to me!* Without meaning to do so, Bill showed me how to live. He was discipling me in that moment, life-on-life.

I don't think we realize how much our lives impact others when we just *share* them with people. But the truth is that we literally shift and regenerate the world around us as we allow others to see us and access our lives. The accomplishments of my life have occurred because certain men and women of God were willing to allow me to *see* them and connect with their world.

In Scripture, the constant example we see is not just teaching alone, but of counsel and learning in the context of day-in-day-out real life. Advice and explanation has its greatest impact within the surroundings of community. In that environment, it *sustains* long-term fruit.

Jesus and His Disciples

E. M. Bounds once said, "The training of the twelve was the great, difficult, enduring work of Christ." While on Jesus was on earth, He gave the world phenomenal teachings and incredible hope, but the training of the 12 disciples was His greatest and most permanent handiwork. They lived together, ate together, ministered together and experienced life together. They shared life in an everyday environment, and they were apprenticed in the gospel of the Kingdom.

One of the key things the disciples developed was how to pray. When they woke up in the morning, Jesus wouldn't be with them. Scripture says He would often rise early, separate Himself, and go spend time with the Father (see Mark 1:35). He would pray all night long, or He would get up early in the morning to be with His Father. When the disciples finally found Him, they would discover Him praying, so it is no surprise that they eventually asked, "Lord, teach us to pray, as John also taught his disciples" (Luke 11:1). The disciples encountered Jesus' life, and it stirred in their hearts a passion to pray as He prayed. His example compelled them to learn more.

Again, discipleship doesn't only take place from the pulpit. It is not solely the pastor's mandate. It is the *community*'s responsibility. Jesus invited a handful of men to participate in life with Him. As Michael has said, the Lord revolutionized the world by changing the lives of 12 men.

I want to deposit within you the desire to get life-on-life with people . . . to pour yourself into others. You are called to disciple, and you need to allow others into your life so they can see you demonstrate what God has taught and invested in you.

The Gospel Plus You

In 1 Thessalonians 2:8, Paul writes, "We loved you so much that we were delighted to share with you not only the gospel of God but our lives as well, because you had become so dear to us" (*NIV*). The glimpse of discipleship Paul gives us in that verse blows my mind. Paul is saying, "We loved you so much that we didn't want to just share the gospel with you . . . we wanted to share our *lives*. We purposed to take from our life and give it to you." We can break open the gospel without opening our lives, but we are called to release our hearts as we dispense heaven's good news. If we truly hope to transfer revelation, we need to reveal our lives!

Along those similar lines, the writer of Hebrews says, "Remember your leaders, who spoke the word of God to you. Consider the outcome of their way of life and imitate their faith" (Heb. 13:7, *NIV*). In other words, even though we are to pay attention to the words of our leaders and teachers, we are actually instructed to consider their *way of life* and imitate their faith. We are prompted to notice *how* they live.

As we allow people into our lives to *see* how we live, they are more able to emulate our faith and way of life, not merely our words or ideas. Just as in the story of Elisha, where *life-on-life* awakened what had been dead, life-on-life discipleship will transform others, bear fruit in their lives, and build momentum to affect the course of history.

In the Bible, Joshua went with Moses to places nobody else would go. As a result, Moses opened his life to him, inviting Joshua to get life-on-life and spend time with him. Deuteronomy 34:9 actually says that Joshua was full of wisdom *because* Moses laid his hands on him. There was an exchange of life between the two, because Moses engaged Joshua and poured his life into him.

Paul told the Galatian church, "I labor in birth again until Christ is formed in you" (Gal. 4:19). In true discipleship, we allow our lives to be instruments through which God develops Christ in others. We labor alongside them until Christ is seen. "As iron sharpens iron, so a man sharpens the countenance of his friend" (Prov. 27:17).

This is an incredibly important principle. Be *deliberate* about having a Barnabas in your life who can help define and enhance you as well as a Timothy into whom you are pouring your life. We need to access people who are sharing their lives with us and permit people to engage in our lives. As we coincide, true discipleship happens.

Enlarging Vision

An important foundation in discipleship is not to allow fear to dictate our motivation or leadership style. Instead of trying to control and manipulate others into moving away from temptation and doing good, we need to encourage them to have their own intimate relationship with Jesus and be in the Word every day. Sin is pushing at our door, and if we do not have the Word fresh *in* us, we will be overtaken or overwhelmed by it. However, when we are passionately focused on the Lord, choices become simpler—to love and pursue Him and His ways.

So much of discipleship and ministry has become survivalist—like a sin management system. In general, the idea has become, *If I can just keep others saved until they get to heaven, I will have done my job.* But true discipleship is so much more!

Mario Murillo, a good friend of mine, has said that people don't have a sin problem; rather, they have a *vision* problem. So, as we pour into the youth around us, we must be committed to encouraging them in their dreams. We must challenge them as to how they are going to change the world and how God wants to use them, and then show them how to invite the Lord to go deep in them. Why? Because they are worthy and have a high calling! We need to shift their thought processes from constantly steering away from sin to focusing on the Lord and allowing Him to deal with heart issues because of the world-changing call on their lives.

Young people tend to quickly lose focus and become vague in their sense of purpose. Where there is eroded vision, people can become scattered, vulnerable and perish. So discipleship must include coming alongside them and helping them remember the mandate and *size* of the vision the Lord has placed on them. Discipleship can be stoking that fire whenever they begin to lose their heavenly Father's perspective of who they are and for what purpose they were created.

To achieve success with discipleship means to believe in people and persist with validating and affirming them over the long haul. With our lives, as well as our words, we tell people, "I believe in you. You have greatness on your life. The Lord is going to use you to imprint heaven upon the earth. I said that to you 15 years ago, and I'm still repeating it today. You are valuable and beloved."

As we prepare for the coming revival, we need to be praying for the millions of newcomers who will be established in the Church—for the thousands in our cities. When they come into the Church, they need to encounter life-on-life. They are not called to come in, sit down and just listen to good teaching. They are called to encounter life.

Regular People Doing the Extraordinary

What does this mean for the average believer? At wherever stage of life we find ourselves, there are people around us who are either younger or not so far along in the Christian faith. We need to go and get life-on-life with those people. We need to encourage them, pour the Lord's acceptance and hope into their hearts, and remind them of the greatness of God's call on their lives. *That* is what is going to change them forever. *That* is what is going to transform them.

Keep in mind that discipleship involves a platform. The kid who is called to be a drummer needs a drum set, so *show* him you believe in him and go buy him one! We have the opportunity today to open doors for the youth around us that would never have been accessible in the past. We need to pour resources, time and life into them and make sure they feel our support. We need to be saying to them, "Because I genuinely believe in you, I am going to give you opportunities. I've poured into you for a lot of years. I'm telling you that you have greatness on your life, and now I am going to use whatever favor and influence I have to help you step into that call."

The Greatest Joy of Growth

Because true discipleship is life-on-life, it is crucial we allow God to develop us. Why? Because fundamentally, our lives are all we have to offer to someone else. As the author of Hebrews says:

> We desire that each one of you show the same diligence to the full assurance of hope until the end, that you do not become sluggish, but imitate those who through faith and patience inherit the promises (Heb. 6:11-12).

The writer is saying, "Hey, look! Do you see those guys over there? They've persevered. They've had faith and patience. They're inheriting what has been promised. Imitate those guys. Mirror their lives."

It is so important for us to nurture a fresh desire for allowing the Lord to go deep inside to mature and advance us. Being *constantly* stretched and grown can feel incredibly frustrating, but at the end of the day, the growth in our lives is all we have to give people. In my own life, I have learned that the battles I encounter and the broadening I endure has tremendous impact not only in my life but also for the people around me. And as I become older, I find there is so much joy in being able to give others for free what I had to fight for. This understanding enables me to keep

the long-term objective in my heart when I'm feeling as if I'm being stretched beyond my capacities. Even when I'm feeling stretched,
I know that eventually I will be able to break a piece of my life off
for somebody and share it with them. I will be able to give them access to this experience, and it could change their life forever. This
places a priceless value on my challenges and enlargement, which
makes the discomfort of my growing pains worth it.

Danny Silk, one of the fathers in my life, went through a rough
patch with his daughter when she was a teenager in high school. I
watched him interact with her during that process and listened to
the phrases he used. He would sit on the couch next to her and
just pull her in close. While he could have chosen to react with fear
and control, I watched as he moved toward her in this very messy,
sticky, vulnerable, raw and scary situation.

My own little girl just turned 13, and Danny's example has
given me so much confidence as my wife and I walk into the
teenage years with her. He broke off a piece of his life and shared
it with me, igniting my heart and radically affecting me as a parent. *My* daughter gets for free what Danny had to contend for with
his daughter. That is discipleship. He didn't just sit down and
teach me everything he had learned about parenting but actually
shared his life with me.

I have experienced this in my marriage as well. My wife and I
have been married for 14 years, and admittedly, the first few were
an emotional struggle. We had no idea how to communicate. But
the breakthrough we eventually experienced now allows us to
come alongside young couples and give them contact with what
we have secured. We can break it off and share it with them. Now,
as my wife and I press in for certain things, I find so much pleasure in it because I know that as I reach victory and progress, my
kids are going to get it for free.

Every rough spot and challenge I wrestle through is worth it if
I can share my discovery and gain with another life. That is fruitfulness, gain, multiplication and momentum. That is life. That is
Kingdom! There is nothing better than being able to share our
lives with someone else.

Where Structure Holds Life

So, how do we do this? How do we come alongside and disciple someone in an organic, real-life setting?

I know a whole lot of fathers and mothers who have no connection with the younger generation. Relationship may have happened quite naturally in the past, but today, in our Western culture, it has become incredibly difficult. Kids want to make it on their own. They desire more independence, while parents are often just trying to survive. There is heartache and brokenness on both sides, and even in the Church there is a significant amount of distrust. So, how do we create a *structure* to link spiritual parents and spiritual children amicably so life-on-life discipleship can take place?

While I don't believe discipleship is based on a structure, at the same time, structures are a bridge or framework that connect people. My job, therefore, as a spiritual parent is to create a structure that connects people in a way that is functional and productive. For example, when I was a youth group leader, we would organize social activities that had zero spiritual foundation or intent—like going bowling. The *only* reason we would hold these social events was to be with the teenagers for two hours. In those hours, we would make connections that we otherwise would likely not have been able to make. Obviously, true discipleship isn't going to happen in a short time frame, but those particular moments helped us to get connected.

Structure is important for discipleship in college settings as well, though it will tend to look a bit different. There is a spirit of independence on college campuses, and often the older generation is not represented and connected with the younger generation. I believe the *full* Body of Christ includes both the younger generations *and* the older generations together, so in order to disciple people in a college setting, we need to have leaders on the campuses who can demonstrate the value of younger people connecting with the older generation. When this is done well, the students will begin to realize they need something more if they really want to succeed. They need spiritual mothers and fathers in their lives. They need to find that *connection*.

The Next Thing

Who has God put on your heart? Who are the people you are to labor for until Christ is formed in them? I believe that the Lord gives
every one of His sons and daughters a mandate to disciple. It
doesn't have to be 50 people, or even 10. We simply need to make
sure we are sharing our lives with others.

Trust me when I say that you are more experienced than
someone. Wherever you are in your journey, you are further along
than somebody else. You can come alongside that person, break
off a piece of your life, share it with him or her, and change that
person's world forever. We want to see a generation awaken, and
I believe the only way this dream will be realized is through life-
on-life discipleship.

13

Spiritual Sonship in Sustained Revival

Banning Liebscher

In the summer of 2011, Jesus Culture stepped out in response to a word from the Lord. For several years, God had been talking to us about arenas and stadiums filled with passionate revivalists going after Him with all their hearts. In response to these different words, we put out a call to believers all across the nation to join us to seek the Lord at the Allstate Arena in Chicago for three days. More than 14,000 people joined us, and the Lord moved in mighty ways.

As we conducted the lead-up preparations for the event, and during the platform ministry throughout the event, we welcomed input from several spiritual fathers—giants in the faith—to guide us and speak into the lives of a generation. The reason we drew so strongly on seasoned leaders was out of our belief that the coming revival will be established and sustained as a result of *intergenerational partnership*.

At the end of the Old Testament, the Lord gives us a stunning promise. In Malachi 4:6, He declares that He will "turn the hearts of the fathers to the children, and the hearts of the children to their fathers." This intergenerational partnership will unite the wisdom of the old with the zeal of the young, removing the disconnection of independence and releasing the promised revival.

Submitting My Own Life

Let me share a portion of my story to help you understand why this is so important to me. I started as an intern at Bethel Church

in Redding when I was 19 years old—the year Bill Johnson became the senior pastor. I was new to church leadership, but
through my relationship with Bill, I began to understand the
value of having a spiritual father. A little later, when I was 23, I began connecting with Kris Vallotton, and my appreciation for his
wisdom, gifting and invaluable input has grown over the years.

Danny Silk started speaking into my life and ministry when
I was 26. His approach to relationships literally revolutionized
my own. Dann Farrelly came along soon after that. He taught me
about walking in truth and grace in a way I had never experienced
before. If I understand intergenerational ministry at all, it is because of these four spiritual fathers in my life: Bill, Kris, Danny
and Dann. Their lives have deeply impacted mine.

God has blessed our ministry in many ways, but I know we
didn't achieve any level of influence through our own strength.
I am aware and thankful of how integral the covering and partnership of spiritual fathers and mothers has been to us. Any success we have had is largely due to our connection with them.

Sons and Daughters

So, what does intergenerational partnership involve? First and
foremost, it means sons and daughters coming alongside fathers
and mothers to support, strengthen and serve the vision of the
older generation. They do not do this so they can get something
out of the older generation, but because they sincerely want to
see the desire of that generation's hearts come to pass. To receive
the full blessing of spiritual mothers and fathers, the younger
generation must learn how to position their hearts as spiritual
daughters and sons.

In my life, this journey into sonship began when I postured
myself as a learner.[1] Even though I had many dreams and aspira-
tions of my own, I recognized early on that I would never fulfill
God's call on my life until I began to glean from the experiences
of my elders. This learning primarily took place in church, small
groups and one-on-one times with my leaders, but it also devel-

oped as I read the writings of amazing men and women of God who went before me. I believe that intergenerational partnership can never take place until we embrace the heart of a student—one who assimilates and outworks the lessons he or she is shown.

The second step in embracing sonship was for me to intentionally make myself available to serve my leaders in both spiritual and practical ways. This service began by accepting their vision as my own and aligning my personal goals with theirs. It included maintaining a good attitude even when service was hard—being faithful in the little things—and receiving correction with humility. I have found that when I am faithful with the smaller areas, God entrusts me with larger territory. I began my ministry with this attitude, and even years later the principles of sonship remain some of the highest priorities in my life.

In the third stage of sonship, I sought to move into partnership without becoming disrespectful and rebellious. In our Western society, we have a myth we refer to as "teenage rebellion." We accept this problem as an unavoidable stage of emerging from childhood into adulthood, but personally I don't believe it is a necessary season of life. My opinion is that sons and daughters can mature into adults without rejecting the parents who raised them. This same fabrication of a generation gap also exists in the Church, but it is not God's plan. The Lord desires to infuse our leadership teams with a culture of honor that allows older leaders to welcome the younger ones into a peer relationship. This empowers younger leaders to step into their destinies while preserving their respect for those who have gone before them. This breakthrough is the key to building a culture of revival in our churches and ministries.

Throughout the years, my spiritual fathers have consistently turned their hearts and extended their favor toward me. They believed in me and affirmed the calling I have in Christ. As I matured, they gradually released me into greater responsibility and authority, and they have continued to enable and support me as my leadership abilities grew. Because of their wise and generous input, I never felt wedged into a position where I wanted to resist or rebel in fulfilling my calling.

To be honest, this didn't always come easily or naturally to me. It was the result of a long 17-year process, with both sides being committed and persisting in working through difficulties with love and honor. I am confident that I could not have become who I am apart from my mentors. The role of these spiritual fathers in my life gave me an identity that cultivated stability, confidence and authority.

These are just a few reasons intergenerational ministry is so important to releasing healthy leaders and establishing a revival culture in the Church.

Grace on Your Journey

I want to pause for a moment to recognize that each individual has different circumstances and comes from a unique background and variety of experiences. I am sensitive to the fact that some individuals who are reading this may not have access to the healthy form of relationship I am describing. But first, I want you to remember that nobody is perfect—including you and me. We are all at different stages of surrendering and moving beyond our personal shortcomings and weaknesses, fears and insecurities, baggage and pain.

When it comes to relationships, there are many dynamics involved, and trust and honor is necessary. The enemy's plan includes disillusionment and division, and there are people who simply lack the personal tools and insight to demonstrate the kind of wholehearted connection for which we are designed. In many ways, the Church as a whole is still in the embryonic stages of developing a healthy demonstration of intergenerational partnership. In some circles, we are still pioneering it as a priority.

So, if you lack the opportunity to connect with a father or mother whose heart is to love and empower you, I want to encourage you to focus on *your heart*. You can overcome the frailties of others when your focus is turned toward things above. Ultimately, God the Father is the perfect parent, and He will protect and lead you. He is the One who fashions and anoints you. He will also guide, correct and comfort you as you remain aligned with His heart. In this relationship, the principals involving your response remain the same as those I outline for spiritual fathers and mothers.

As you open your heart and refresh your perspective, perhaps the Lord will bring people into your world that will allow you to break the cycle of independence and fatherlessness within your own Christian community. Negative patterns can be overtaken with persistent love. Our initiation and growth in this area requires courage and grace, but it is well rewarded with strength, blessing and multiplication.

Turning the Hearts of the Fathers to the Sons

If you read through Malachi 4:6 again, you will see that the prophet puts most of the weight of responsibility on fathers. In the outlined progression, the father's hearts turning toward their sons comes *first*. After all, they are the more mature and should set the lead in pursuing connection. Elders must turn *first* in order for the hearts of the children to respond.

Some people who predict the coming revival have mistakenly said that it will be a revival led by youth. Their advice is to release young people and set them free to do their own thing. But clearly, the prophet Malachi believes that God is going to use intergenerational partnership to extend the Kingdom. It is the generations coming together that hold power to remove the curse from the earth. This means that fathers and mothers must choose to run *with* the sons and daughters instead of just releasing them. Spiritual parents need to come alongside emergent leaders to minister *with* them. They need to equip and accredit the next generation to lead and further advance what they constructed together as an alliance.

To do this type of intergenerational partnership effectively requires a deep level of trust. Trust is imperative because we must have credence in one another's motivation and commitment to the task at hand and, even more importantly, to each other. When the foundations of a relationship are not compacted with trust, the walls can erode and crumble at any given pressure along the way.

Parental Responsibility

In the last chapter, I gave you a condensed version of the story of Elisha and the Shunammite's son told in 2 Kings 4. One part of the story I didn't mention was that one day when the boy was out in the field working with his father, he began to complain, "My head hurts." In response, the father sent the boy home alone while he stayed in the field working. The father neglected to follow through responsibly with his child, as if somehow plowing the field was more important than taking time to care for his son! This is the last we see of the dad, even though his son died shortly after returning home. Thankfully, the story ends well because the mother persisted in pursuing hope and restoration and Elisha responded to her plea for help by raising the boy from the dead. God rewarded her faith, perseverance and courage with life.

I believe this is a story for our times. The transpiring generation is stunted and dying from the wounds of fatherlessness and orphanhood. The majority of young people in the world are growing up with physically or emotionally absent fathers and mothers. This deprivation leads to a host of problems, including depression, aimlessness and hopelessness. However, the issue of orphanhood did not begin in this generation. It has been a recurring problem throughout history.

Many of our parents were limited in their ability to mother and father us because they weren't protected, nurtured and guided themselves. Those who are not fathered well often follow the generational pattern and are ineffective and sometimes even damaging parents themselves. The majority of people who provide spiritual parenting in our generation have never experienced healthy spiritual covering themselves. So, we now have a generation who has never been parented trying to parent, and in many cases they simply don't know what they are doing.

We must be committed to helping the older generation catch the vision and learn how to provide the kind of mentoring and leadership they never received. However, we must also understand that when these leaders finally begin to reach out to sons and daughters, they will sometimes find themselves facing a younger generation that has learned not to trust or rely on them. When this happens, those who are trying to be effective spiritual parents will run headfirst into a major obstacle. They will be confronted with a withdrawn and independent generation that is struggling in its own blood, sweat and tears.

Where There Is Pain

Because of the deficiency in empowering leadership, many young people have learned to survive on their own. Sadly, some have a resistance to fathers and mothers because of the brokenness of family and other fractures in our society. Experience has shown them that the older generation is often so submerged by their own challenges that they don't have time to surface, let alone deal with them. They find that their elders are often inconsistent, break their promises, and overlook commitments they have made. These younger leaders feel neglected by the older generation, whom they love and need.

No one can function consistently at full capacity when they have ongoing unmet needs. So, in order for young people to survive their formative years, many just shut down and ignore their desire for fathers and mothers. They think, *I can do this on my own. I don't require a father and a mother in order to survive. In fact, needing a father and a mother is a sign of weakness. If I lean on them, I will end up hurt, so I just don't need them.*

When people with this mindset accept Christ, we bring them into the Church and tell them, "You need a father and mother!" To which they reply, "Actually, I don't. I appreciate it, but I don't really need them. In fact, I can't need them, because if I do, they will probably just disappoint me or even hurt me and leave." This response isn't necessarily birthed out of rebellion; it is just a defense mechanism they have set up to shield their hearts and protect their lives. They reject the idea of having a spiritual father or a mother because they do not want to be rejected and wounded.

Unfortunately, the older generation doesn't always understand this attitude. To them, the young person can appear defiant. When I was a youth pastor, teenagers were some of the most intimidating people in the world! They were often upfront with their opinions and resistance—"I don't want to go on that retreat!" or, "I don't want to listen to that teaching!" I tried not to take it personally, but it still grated on my desire to connect with them, see them restored, and serve their future. I had a lot of work on my hands to provide effective fathering to young people with this level of distrust toward leadership. I had to be willing to spend time hearing their hearts as I gently and consistently demonstrated a different form of leadership. I had to prove I was not going anywhere. I had to jump over some walls and tear others down.

Those of us who are called to father and mother this generation need to press through the barriers and make genuine connections with young people. This is the reason why most of us can't handle more than a handful of kids. While we can *teach* young people, we can only *parent* a handful. It takes a lot of time to convince a young person we mean it when we say, "I really am with you. You can trust me in this. This isn't just about me sharing all my life lessons with you. This is me choosing to stick by you to help you, honor you and support you."

Accelerated Growth

If the younger generation can figure out the importance of submission and honor, and how to walk in these two things with the older generation, they will experience *acceleration* in their lives. I am convinced that I am where I am right now because I am connected with the older generation—because I have persisted for the past 17 years in really listening to and applying wisdom. In the same way, my family is healthy right now only because I adhered to the advice and example of the older generation. Potentially, it would have taken me many more years to reach where I am if I hadn't had such a value and honor for submitting to those who paved the way before me.

As a son, the joy set before me is to say at the end of my life, "I honored well. I served well. I took care of the legacy of my fathers. Like Elisha, even when I had the chance to build my own ministry and my own school of prophets, I was with Elijah to the end, serving him well. I wasn't just building my own kingdom. I loved and honored the older generation. I was with them to the end." As a father, the joy set before me is that my legacy will remain—that what I gave my life for is not ending with me, because my children and grandchildren are alive and thriving in Jesus.

Securing Longevity

I think what the Lord is doing right now is so massive and unprecedented that it has to go beyond a single generation. He desires to sustain what He is doing and what He is about to do, but achieving this level of *longevity* will require a partnership between multiple generations. If the younger generation is not connected with the older generation, they will lack the authority and grace necessary to perpetuate anything long-term. The reverse is also true. Without the younger generation, the older will not have anything that continues. The older generation can teach, train, equip and deposit all they want, but it will have a short life without intergenerational partnership.

Children Becoming Parents

One of the people who impacted me greatly during my teen years was an intern named Kurt Fry. He was probably 20 years old when I was a senior in high school. What I remember most about him is not a sermon he preached but the video games I played at his house. And playing baseball . . . I could take you to the field at a local high school and show you where we did batting practice together. He helped to shape and mark me just by investing in me. Kurt was not yet a spiritual father, but he was growing into that role. Along the way, he served as an older brother to me, and God used him to guide me forward by example. The apostle Paul told the Corinthians believers, "Though you might have ten thousand instructors in Christ, yet you do not have many fathers" (1 Cor. 4:15). He went on to tell them that he was their spiritual father, but throughout the letter he affirmed the role of other leaders who helped guide the church as well.

Transitioning
It can sometimes be difficult in intergenerational ministry for young people to schedule face time with spiritual fathers and mothers. Many make up for this by spending time with older brothers and sisters—people like Kurt who are on their way to becoming fathers and mothers. During the first few years of my ministry, I served as a spiritual big brother, and then, in my twenties, I started transitioning to a spiritual father. As my leaders at Bethel gave me more freedom and authority and encouraged me to take greater risks, I slowly progressed from being a son to a father. These leaders empowered and released me with a sense of ownership in what I was establishing.

Risks Required
Now that I am a father in my own right, I realize how this transition from son to father and daughter to mother can be a scary and challenging process. I have more options now, which can be a little unnerving because I have been trusted with spiritual sons of my own. As a spiritual father, I am learning to trust that my spiritual sons desire to protect what I have put into their hands. As I give them freedom, I have to believe they will honor that liberty, not because I have the power of their paycheck but because they respect me and want to protect the responsibility and honor I have given them.

A lot of spiritual fathers and mothers have difficulty making this transition as their children grow and become fathers and mothers themselves. Often, they continue to see them just as children. As a result, when these emerging leaders come into parenthood, many feel they have to disconnect and start ministries of their own, because their senior leaders were not willing to make the transition with them. I do not believe all young leaders who start ministries on their own are doing it too early, but I think we would see a lot more fathers and mothers investing in a younger generation if the senior leaders knew how to navigate the transition from son to father and daughter to mother. This seems to be a substantial issue for many leaders in the Church.

I believe that if we truly want to release our spiritual sons and daughters into their destinies, we must be willing to take *risks*. Releasing young leaders requires risk because there is a high possibility they are going to make some messes. After all, who doesn't make mistakes while they are learning?! However, if we understand that our spiritual children are our *legacy*, we will be willing to work through the awkwardness and messiness of the process to see them become spiritual mothers and fathers.

Remaining Fruit

In John 15:16, when Jesus called the disciples to bear fruit that would remain, He wasn't talking about organizations or buildings. He was talking about *people*. My spiritual sons and daughters are the "fruit that remain" in my life and ministry. Yes, it may be messy at times when young leaders step into maturity, and we may not always know how to guide them or protect them from making errors, but we must learn to make the transition. There is a development and enlarging required for both the son and daughter and the spiritual parent.

Much of the mess the Church has experienced with intergenerational ministry is because the older generation doesn't understand this truth about their legacy. Sometimes leaders mistakenly think, *I'm protecting what I've built, and I don't want them to mess up what I've created. I don't want them to change the structure I have labored to build.* However, if we adopt a Kingdom perspective of fruit bearing, we will realize that what we've contributed is not a building or organization we are leaving behind . . . the younger generation is what is left of our work and ministry here in the earth. So, if they choose to tinker, change, blow up or even misrepresent what we've built, we won't be protective because *they* are what matters most. They are our legacy.

Biblical Examples of Intergenerational Ministry

The Bible is filled with examples of intergenerational partnerships, and each relationship has something to teach us. However, out of the dozens of partnerships we see in Scripture, I think the most profound is that of Mordecai and Esther. God used Mordecai and Esther to save a nation. They were able to work *together* to accomplish God's purposes, and it was the two *united* who ultimately saw a nation saved.

It is obvious from the story in the Bible that Esther honors Mordecai. In fact, she was brought up in his house as a daughter and learned to obey him. She follows his counsel when she is taken from his household to join the king's harem. Even after she is made queen and has access to great wealth and power, she continues to honor Mordecai as he coaches her how to convince the king to spare the people of Israel. The story ends with the Jews being delivered and Mordecai being exalted, and none of it would have happened without intergenerational partnership.

Moses and Joshua provide another important example of intergenerational ministry. For 40 years, Joshua served Moses as a servant, a warrior and a son. Joshua would accompany Moses on the mountain and into the tabernacle, and sometimes Joshua would remain there, ministering to the Lord long after Moses had gone home. As Joshua matured, he was given increasing amounts of authority and responsibility, and ultimately he was commissioned to lead the people into the Promised Land.

Other examples of intergenerational ministry in Scripture include Elijah and Elisha, Naomi and Ruth, Barnabas and Paul, and Paul and Timothy. In each of these relationships, the younger generation allowed the fathers to come and do life with them. They resisted the urge to leave when things got tough and wrestled through the process. And the fathers, for their part, were not so busy *building* that they neglected the younger generation who needed their guidance. They established credibility with the younger generation. They didn't just interact to correct them, but championed them as their biggest fans.

In the end, I think the battle comes down to this. Can the older generation really invest in, encourage and support the younger generation and challenge them where they need to be challenged? And can the younger generation not withdraw or run away when that happens? Can they open their hearts to receive input? Can they welcome correction? Can they receive rebuke? Can they apply instruction?

A Long-Lasting Effort

Building a revival culture that brings genuine societal transformation is a long-lasting effort—a work of the Holy Spirit that must be strategized and stewarded from generation to generation. Any time the older generation begins to think they don't need the young, they are assuming revival is some type of short-term entity—when it isn't. Revival isn't a two-year event but a long-term covenant.

Sons and daughters desperately need fathers and mothers whom they can follow and run with and from whom they can learn and receive wisdom. At the same time, fathers and mothers desperately need sons and daughters. Ultimately, what we are praying for and pressing toward may not be fully manifested in our lifetime—but it could happen in our children's. Elijah, for instance, never saw the complete fulfillment of his call. The kingdom did not shift in his lifetime. In the end, it was his sons, Elisha and Jehu, who saw Jezebel dethroned.

Intergenerational ministry only makes sense if we have a long-term concept of revival. Again, the true fulfillment of what we are looking for may not be satisfied within the next two years, but it might be established in 20. We *have* to have an intergenerational mindset and ministry.

I think God is highlighting intergenerational ministry right now because power is released when the generations work together. There is an untapped strength in genuinely pursuing revival together.

The Rod and the Sword

In Exodus 17:8-16, as Moses held the rod of God in his hand and commanded the battle against the Amalekites from the top of the hill, he relied upon Joshua to be fighting against the enemy in the valley with the sword in his hand. Joshua, in the midst of warfare, desperately relied on Moses with the rod in order to win. The two had to be connected. The rod apart from the sword wouldn't lead to long-term victory, and the sword without the rod couldn't sustain victory. One required the other. In the same way, for true victory to occur today, we need the younger generation to wield the sword and the older generation to wield the rod.

In Scripture, a rod usually represents *authority*, yet there are different types of authority. The authority to heal the sick is different from the authority to take cities—one assignment requires more time, experience and perseverance than the other. The younger generation has a realm of *personal* authority, but for true, lasting transformation to occur, they need a level of *seasoned* authority they can only obtain by being connected with the older generation!

Let me give you an example. As a 36-year-old, I could be preaching some of the same sermons I preached as a 22-year-old, but those sermons would now have a completely different authority. While they contain the same concepts and biblical truths, the transformative power they carry has radically changed. The difference is simply due to the fact that I am stepping into greater authority as I get older. The sermon is no longer simply a concept I preach but something I have experienced.

E. M. Bounds once said, "Preaching is not the performance of an hour. It is the outflow of a life. It takes twenty years to make a sermon, because it takes twenty years to make the man. The true sermon is a thing of life."[2] So, at some level, that 22-year-old preacher cannot access certain realms of authority on his own, whereas he can access them through intergenerational partnership.

While the older generation walks in mature authority with the rod in their hand, the younger generation walks with the sword. They take pleasure in the battle. There is a natural risk-taking in the younger generation . . . a characteristic *zeal and passion*. They just believe God and step out in faith. We all need that alongside us—no matter our age. I love passion around me, and I never want to lose that.

Honestly, the older generation can do many things without the younger generation, but those things *will* eventually die out.

The prophetic words over this coming revival declare that this move of God will *not end*. Therefore, we need to break out of the mindset that revival pops up for a few years and then reappears 40 years later—and the only way we can do that is if we run hard *together*. This is what will propel the Kingdom forward.

14

Spiritual Fatherhood in Sustained Revival

Bill Johnson

A few years ago, I had an experience that dramatically impacted my understanding of revival. I went to a city that is home to the headquarters of a well-known cult. This cult had affected the entire city, including those who weren't part of their particular group. It even affected those people whose lifestyles were completely opposed this cult's belief system. Somehow, this group was able to produce a blanket effect on the entire culture of that region.

This particular cult believed things that were laughable to me. But somehow, even with their theological errors, this group succeeded in creating a culture that has sustained their movement. In a case like this, it is helpful for us to do some "reverse engineering" to try to understand the reason for their success. These people, in spite of their strange beliefs and behaviors, tapped into a true Kingdom principle and were able to develop a culture that sustained their movement, making them a force to be reckoned with around the world. If the principle of sustainable culture works with a lie, how much more could it work with the truth.

God's Nature: From Glory to Glory

Two things originally inspired me to start thinking about the *sustainability* of revival. First, I was frustrated with the conclusions that the students of revival were making. Many of them seemed to believe that it was God's will for revival to end after just a few years. The common idea was, "If we're lucky, maybe we'll make it 10 years or longer."

That idea didn't feel right to me, as it is based on *what has happened* and not on *what is possible*. In other words, when we limit God's plan for the future to what He has done in the past, we are automatically saying we are not prepared for the new thing. This way of thinking frustrates me.

The second thing that started me thinking about the sustainability of revival was God's nature. What is His nature? He leads us from glory to glory (see 2 Cor. 3:18). The Bible clearly says, "Of the increase of His government and peace there will be no end" (Isa. 9:7). It doesn't say simply that His government will never end, but that the *increase,* or the forward motion, of His government will never end. Revival was never meant to last only a few years. It was meant to mimic God's nature—everything is in forward motion, moving from glory to glory.

I realize there will be setbacks in this revival process, or experiences that *appear* to be setbacks, but sometimes the biggest setbacks are the shortcuts to our biggest promotion—if we use them well. Where does the Bible *ever* say that a move of God is only for a season—to give the Church a "shot in the arm" so that we can face the next season? Just to be clear, I do believe there are seasons in revival, but I don't believe they are seasons of "on" and seasons of "off." Instead, I believe we go through seasons in which God seems to shift our focus—that is, there is a shift in what the Holy Spirit is doing at that time. Some expressions of revival may focus on physical healing or deliverance, while others may focus on the salvation of the lost or building up the community of believers.

When God is doing something new, the Church tends forget what we just learned and put all of our focus on the new thing. But whenever the Lord reveals something new, He doesn't abolish what He revealed in the last season. Once I have learned something and it becomes a part of me, He is able to change the subject and lead me into the next season. That is why Hebrews 6 tells us to not go back to the former things that have been established, but to move on. The writer is not recommending we abandon the foundation but rather we build upon it.

I believe God is moving all of us into an experience of sustained revival in which we will no longer see shifts in seasons. The more we advance, the more we will bring the age to come into this age. In the age to come, Scripture tells us the trees will bear fruit 12 months of the year (see Rev. 22:2). That is a prophetic picture of sustained revival.

It is important for us to realize there is no spiritual "winter" in heaven. In my personal life, I have not had a shift in season for 16 years. I see where the Lord has added line upon line and precept on precept. I can see where He has shifted my *focus* at times. But I can't see a shift in seasons where something stopped and something else began. I believe God is moving all of us into a similar experience of sustained revival.

What Is Revival?

To me, *renewal, reformation, awakening* and *revival* are all essentially the same thing, but they reflect different levels of maturity within the same experience. I consider the outpouring of the Holy Spirit in *renewal* to be an *infant* form of revival. Revival allowed to grow from adolescence into maturity will eventually become a *reformation*.

Our definitions of revival, or any other move of God, need to be adjusted because we have accidentally begun to define revival by its manifestations instead of by its core values. In some circles, the manifestation of revival may be physical—falling under the Spirit and things of that nature. In other circles, its manifestation may be public repentance. All these things are brilliant evidences of a move of God. But when the *manifestation* becomes the *definition* of a move of God, we get into problems.

For instance, if we define revival as the public confession of sin, we actually need *more* sin in order for revival to continue because it is now based on exposing a negative. In other words, we have created a definition that feeds off the negative. Much of the

Church feeds off negative circumstances that are happening around the world, in order to believe we are in the Last Days, but that is a perversion of God's intent. The result of this perspective causes some believers to celebrate wars, natural disasters and negative events because of the end-times implications. But the intent always was, "Arise, shine; for your *light* has come" (Isa. 60:1, emphasis added). Yes, darkness will cover the earth, but the light is what we feed on because it is what God is doing. This light—God's government—*increases* until the darkness is no more.

This posture of faith and anticipation fuels prayer and vision. It makes me want to stay in a city for the rest of my life to make sure something can be accomplished that has long-lasting impact and subsequently causes a domino effect that touches other cities around the world. There is a long-term thinking that comes with the commitment to sustained revival.

Revival, then, *can't* be just what happens to the negative. Certainly, it has to include deep repentance, dealing with sin, and the public confession of sin—revival depends on making things right with people who are at odds with one another. All of these things are excellent manifestations of revival. But if we define revival only as a move of God that fixes bad things, we don't yet know what revival is.

Revival is the fiery presence of God having a deep influence on those who are touched by it. Often that influence deals with sin, but after people have fully repented, it means more than just attending services six to eight times a week. Personally, I like ongoing revival meetings because of the discipling effect it has on people, but revival has to be more than this. It has to be something that is transferrable to the city itself. It has to impact *how* we work—not just the fact that we now witness while we work.

Proverbs 22:29 says, "A man who excels in his work . . . will stand before kings." But two verses later we read, "Put a knife to your throat if you are a man given to appetite." In other words, when revival affects our lives, we become excellent in all we do. Our excellence inevitably leads to favor and promotion with leaders. However, it is important to make sure that when promotion comes, we live with self-imposed restrictions so we can operate in this new world without being seduced by it. It is important to place restrictions on ourselves so we remain an influence—the salt, light and leaven in an environment that needs salt, light and leaven. Once we conform our values to the values of that system, we have lost our ability to be an influence.

Sustainable Revival: Building a Revival Culture

There are many kinds of hindrances to sustained revival, but most of them are just between our ears—it is a matter of how we think. A renewed mind makes anything God is doing sustainable. For this reason, my approach to sustainable revival is to focus primarily on building a revival culture. Culture is important to God, and it is important to the way He works in different groups of people around the world.

For example, when the power of God falls on an Anglican church in one city, it seems to spread much more easily to Anglican churches in other cities because there is already a network of communication and culture between them. God created our ability to generate culture for this purpose. Originally, there was only one language and one culture, but when God separated the languages in Genesis 11, He also separated the cultures, for language does have an impact on defining the culture. The result was a wide variety of human cultures that can express His heart in a myriad of different ways. When God sends revival, it often affects whole cultures, and it most easily travels through cultural connections. It should not surprise us that the best way to sustain a revival is to build a culture that supports it.

At the same time, there is also a geographical effect of revival—or at least there is supposed to be. When God's presence is poured out on one church or people group in a region, it should have an impact on the other churches and various other groups that surround it. I think you can see this happening in revivals of the past. In the Toronto Outpouring, for instance, the power of God fell on one church and affected completely different churches and groups that were close to them geographically. They became a part of the move of God because they were geographically close, and they were impacted by the environmental shift. Revival clearly spreads through geographic proximity, but it moves most easily through the channels of culture.

We don't invent culture; we *discover* culture. We don't invent what looks good to us or what will become a wineskin to sustain an outreach, a healing ministry, multiple services, or whatever else. True culture is not that short-sighted. It is developed after heaven's model; therefore, we *discover* it. As we seek to bring heaven to earth in a sustainable way, we need to ask ourselves, *What are the values of heaven? How can we bring those values into this world?*

Jesus demonstrated heaven on earth. That is why He put a towel over His shoulder and washed the disciples' feet (see John 13). He modeled what it was like in heaven. He modeled the value of the presence. He did only what He saw His Father do. As Jesus explains in John 16, it was the Holy Spirit who revealed things to Him, just as He reveals things to us.

So, building a culture of revival begins with discovering the values God carries for His people and community life. In a culture, we develop ways of living in relationship to one another that also affects our personal lifestyles.

A Culture of Honor

One of the most important elements in true revival culture is what we call the "culture of honor." In this type of culture, every single person is celebrated and valued, even before they deserve it. This is a huge step in building a culture that sustains revival, because when we honor and value others before they deserve it, it draws them into their God-given potential and helps them achieve significance and greatness in the Lord.

As I began to study this topic in Scripture, it was almost shocking to find the kind of value that God places on the concept of honor. At least, it was shocking for me. Although I had always been intrigued by the idea of honor, and as a church we have always sought to practice it, I was still astounded every time I would see it in the Bible. The God of heaven actually celebrates His people. He gives rewards and says, "Well done, good and faithful servant" (Matt. 25:23). Even while on earth the Lord honored people, such as the Syro-Phoenician woman who had great faith (see Mark 7:24-30), and the centurion who believed that if Jesus only spoke the word, the servant would be healed (see Matt. 8:5-13). There is an honor in heaven *and* an honor on earth.

We have been called to steward the realm of honor, and we do so mainly with our words. As Paul writes in Ephesians 4:29, "Let no unwholesome word proceed from your mouth, but only such word as is good for edification according to the need of the moment, so that it will give grace to those who hear" (*NASB*). Our words give grace. Grace is God's gift, so *He* allows *us* to steward His gift through our choice of words. This is an amazing truth. As we learn to honor God and honor one another through our words, we become dispensers of God's grace on the earth.

The Heart of Honor

People often invite me and other Bethel leaders to come to their churches and teach on the subject of honor, but it is not always with the best motives. Every so often, pastors will invite us to teach on the subject so their board will treat them better or so their members will be less resistant to their leadership. Their thinking is, *We don't have that kind of culture here. I don't have the respect I should have.* And they are right; it is just the wrong way to go about getting the honor they think they deserve. The purpose of the culture of honor is *not* to have more control but to cultivate an *environment* in which God's people become their best.

Revival is the life of God being experienced and expressed in His people, and honor releases life. It is the pattern of sustainable life, and it is a huge part of sustainable revival. In order for a culture of honor to work, it has to stay servant-based. It has to stay focused on serving and blessing other people.

In a home, the wife influences and sets the atmosphere, and the husband establishes the standard of love and sacrifice. Good leaders will always fill these two roles. We do not bestow honor in response to how well people are doing—we honor them *in spite of* how they are doing. As a leader, I have been appointed to be a blessing to others. All authority and favor are given to me for that purpose.

In revival, the Lord increases our awareness of the abundant resources He has made available to us. However, we do not use that increased awareness to make ourselves the focus of people's admiration or to build a loyal following. Rather, we use the resources of God to bless others in greater ways. This is the culture of honor, and it is what sustains revival.

King David was a man who tapped into the Lord's heart (see Acts 13:22), but the Lord wouldn't let him count his troops (see 1 Chron. 21). Your identity should never be in the number of people who follow you but in the fact that you have done what God has told you to do. Obviously, a culture of honor does create an environment in which leaders will receive greater respect, but that is not the main goal. The main goal is to foster the pattern of sustainable life.

Denominational Boundaries

I think the Lord uses movements like Bethel's as resource centers for people from other movements. Even in our own network of churches, we don't ask people to leave their denominations to be a part of what we are doing. Instead, it is our desire that these leaders stay true to their denominations. In some cases, leaders and churches may decide to make a change, but getting them to leave their group and join our network is not the goal. It is not even a hidden, secret goal. My goal actually is the opposite.

Movements such as ours tend to attract people in other movements who realize there is a vitamin deficiency in their "meal." Their meal is a good meal, and it is taking care of certain areas in their overall health, but it is deficient in certain things. We are the orange juice for those who have that issue in their spiritual health.

As a result, we end up attracting people from other movements. Sometimes we attract them for the long term, and sometimes after they get what they need they return home. In my opinion, this is the way it should be, because God desires to preserve the uniqueness of Calvary Chapel churches, the uniqueness of Foursquare churches, the uniqueness of Episcopal churches, and the uniqueness of every other stream. Yet at the same time, our ability to cross-pollinate provides a way to share elements that every stream needs. I don't want other groups to become like us, but I sure would like them to experience what we are experiencing.

Revival and Resistance

Throughout history, when the devil has opposed a revival, it has increased. However, when the Church has opposed a revival, that revival has been compromised. The recent move of God in Mozambique caused 10,000 churches to be planted. Why? Because the only opposition to the movement was militant Muslims and witch doctors. There was no Church to oppose it, so all it did was thrive. When one person is martyred, a thousand more take his or her place. We see the same thing happening in China, where the only opposition is the government.

But when we take that exact same move of the Spirit—that exact same manifestation—and put it in North America, Europe or the United Kingdom, that move of God is compromised when the Church rises up against it. That does not mean the Church can kill the revival, but it does hinder it.

It is important for us to remember that Jesus commissioned the Church to steward His authority on the earth (see Matt. 28:18). Life and death are in the power of the inheritance we have been given. When leaders in the Church who occupy *genuine* places of authority in God stand against a move of God, they can actually bring about a hindering effect. They can also bring confusion to the hearts of average believers, who end up waffling between their decision to pursue revival and their fear of error or excess. This doesn't mean those who oppose these leaders can control what they are experiencing in God, but it is vital for us recognize that in the Body of Christ, we all affect one another.

The Violent Take It by Force

If we are going to influence and impact the world around us, spiritual warfare will always be involved. Spiritual warfare is a key element in every revival; however, I resist emphasizing this subject because I hesitate to give any attention to the devil. On the one hand, I don't want to be ignorant of his devices, but at the same time I don't want him to become my focus.

I once heard of an artist who refused to look at a bad painting twice because he didn't want what he saw to affect what he could paint. This is a principle I really believe in. Although we are in constant warfare, sometimes it takes a deliberate decision for us not to be preoccupied by that warfare. We need to have the same attitude as Smith Wigglesworth, who was awakened one night by the devil and responded by saying, "Oh, it's only you," and then turned over and went back to sleep. We need to cultivate an attitude that tells the enemy we are not impressed with his plans.

But again, at the same time, we do not want to be unaware of the devil's schemes (see 2 Cor. 2:11). The enemy hates revival, and he will do everything in his power to distract and diminish our experience of God's presence and power. We need to stay mindful of the tools he uses. When we are unaware of him, we can be lulled to sleep or become isolated and ignorant of what is happening around us. All of this, obviously, will make us ineffective.

There are some teachers in the Body of Christ who are proclaiming some wrong concepts about grace—and the result is that they don't have any fight left in them. While it is true that all we need was provided for us at the cross, this truth does not mean we are exempt from the possibility of spiritual battle. There is a tension that exists between the doctrine of the finished work of Christ and the work He calls us to do. Jesus did it all, and yet He commissions us to fulfill His purposes on the earth.

The way I reconcile this tension is by remembering there is a difference between what is in our possession and what is in our account. Sometimes, moving something from our account to our possession requires that we change—and that we activate that change through passion with faith. When Jesus declared, "It is finished" (John 19:3), He was stating an absolute truth about God's grace. Because of what He accomplished on the cross, we no longer have to fight to get favor. Now we fight because we *are* favored. Our new position in Christ changes everything. It makes everything available to us according to the maturity we have to apprehend and use it.

The Power of Prayer

We need to *fight* for revival. We need to be desperate. But when I use the word "desperate," I am referring to a true spiritual desperation, not a fleshly emotion. In other words, we are not desperate because we don't know who we are, for that will only work against us. Natural hunger can produce emotional frustration, which inevitably leads to unbelief. True desperation comes from knowing who we are and who is in us, and it produces a deep desire to align ourselves and our communities more fully with Him.

Sadly, as I have observed this current renewal around the globe, I have witnessed many cries of desperation that were nothing more than expressions of unbelief, and they never produced any positive results. Our hunger has to be filled with anticipation. There has to be some sense that *God is about to do something*. There has to be a *positioning* and a *readying* of our hearts for the fulfillment of what we are praying for.

Whether we call this *desperate hunger prayer* or *enduring persistent prayer*, it develops a muscle that can contain the answer when it is released. It is like the chick in the egg. The time may be right for the chick to emerge, but if we open the egg for him, he will die. It is the fight out of the shell that strengthens the chick and increases the circulation to his limbs, enabling him to live. In the contending, there is something strengthened within us that actually positions us to live in the promise once we get it.

As Michael noted in chapter 10, Jesus said the Kingdom allows for violence, and the violent take it by force (see Matt. 11:12). I believe strongly in the power of prayer, but I have seen many instances in which fasting, prayer and crying out to God did *not* work because they were not followed by equal risk. If we desire the walls of Jericho to fall through prayer and prophetic obedience, then we also need to position our soldiers to go in and take possession of the city. If we do not go in and take possession, the victory we achieved through prayer will be useless.

The risk factor has to follow the prayer factor. I constantly tell people, "In private, you cry out to God. In public, you take risk. When you don't get the breakthrough in public, you go back to the private place and cry out to God again." Those are the only two worlds I know. It is the combination of private prayer and public risk that releases Kingdom power on earth.

Sustainable Revival: Intergenerational Partnership

As Banning said in chapter 13, another essential element in building sustainable revival is fostering a true partnership between the generations. Those who are in charge (which is almost always an older generation) have to cultivate a value for the younger generation—not only because of that generation's youthfulness or zeal, but also because they bring something to the table that the older leaders cannot provide on their own.

I like to put it this way. If I were a king, I would raise my children to live responsibly with royalty. I would expose them to public pressure. I would teach them to steward unusual favor. I would help them answer the key questions of royalty: *What traps have been set for those with unusual favor? How can you keep from using that power for yourself? What do you do when somebody wants to buy your attention and your favor? How do you maintain respect but not compromise on your standards and position? How do you manage wealth in such a way that it becomes a blessing not only for you but also for others?* Knowing these things makes us effective in serving.

When my children were young, I would increase their exposure to responsibility so that I could increase their authority. I did this because I did not want to pass away and have a successor who did not have any idea what it meant to rule. History and Scripture are filled with tragic stories of failed succession because the children were not raised in a way that prepared them for what they were destined to become.

This idea of intergenerational partnership is like repotting a plant. When you are transplanting, it is necessary to put the plant into a pot that is bigger than what it needs, as this creates the capacity for growth. The bigger pot brings growth because it provides a more expansive environment than what the plant is used to. In the same way, we need to expand the environment of younger leaders so they have room to grow into the people God has called them to be.

Emerging leaders need to be protected, but at the same time they need to be exposed to challenges and opportunities. This is the key to growing the next generation of leaders. We put them in a larger, bigger environment so they can grow.

Revival and the Emerging Generation

My greatest source of confidence in the emerging generation is their spiritual hunger, and I believe they hunger for the right things. My greatest source of concern, however, is that many younger leaders don't have an awareness of the price the previous generation paid in order to give them their inheritance. An inheritance is something another person paid a price for that we get for free. If we don't understand or appreciate the price that was paid, we will probably not appreciate the value and worth of what we have received.

For example, let's say your dad worked three jobs, lived frugally, never moved into the home he wanted, and never drove the car he wanted, all so he could put money aside for you. He did this so that when you got married, you wouldn't have the pressure of a house payment or a car payment. Instead, you could move into a comfortable life that he had established for you as a gift. This would be your inheritance.

But what if, after you lived in that house for a few years, he drove by and saw the lawn hadn't been kept and the paint was peeling? You had not kept up the house because you didn't have an understanding of its value—you got it for free. What message would you be sending to your dad, who paid way more than you could possibly imagine so that you could have something great? How would your lack of concern affect him?

Right now, the Church is in a season of dramatic change. What took me 30 years to build is taking the younger generation only 6 months because God is accelerating events. We need to help the younger generation appreciate the fact that the momentum they freely enjoy was created during the 30-year journey they didn't have to take. It is the responsibility of those in the older generation to let the younger generation know the worth of their inheritance.

Obviously, we don't want to use guilt or manipulation to do this, but we must tell the story of what the Church has gone through so we can give the emerging generation what they now enjoy. The next generation needs to know how many years we didn't see what they see. They need to know about all the cries for breakthrough that God heard in the middle of the night. They need to know the levels of opposition we endured and what it is like to be misunderstood or falsely accused. They don't need to know these things for purposes of pity but so they understand what it cost and, as a result, treasure their inheritance in an appropriate way.

This is a key to intergenerational partnership and sustained revival. As the next generation realizes the true value of their inheritance, they will inevitably begin to ask, "What am I going to give *my* kids? What price can I pay to increase what I received so I can leave something for them of even greater value?" This is the kind of thinking that will not only sustain revival but also increase it from glory to glory throughout the generations.

Good and Faithful Servant

In his first letter to the Corinthians, Paul corrects his friends for falling into an attitude of sectarianism, saying, "One of you says,

'I follow Paul'; another, 'I follow Apollos'; another, 'I follow Cephas'; still another, 'I follow Christ' " (1 Cor. 1:12, *NIV*). A little later when Paul begins to speak of their inheritance, he starts by saying, "Let no one boast in men" (1 Cor. 3:21). In other words, don't divide over nonessential things. Why does he say that? Because "all things are yours" (v. 22).

When we reduce a beautiful Kingdom concept such as loyalty, submission or honor to a natural fleshly expression, we limit our access to the Kingdom resource that empowers us to do God's will. When this happens, we inevitably resort to getting things done through manipulation and control. Trying to fulfill God's principles through human reasoning and strength will eventually cost us our inheritance, which is what enables us to complete our commission. This is why Paul reminds us we have been given all things. "All things" sounds like a lot, until we remember that we have been assigned to disciple nations. We need *everything* we can get to get the job done!

My goal in life is not to feel good about myself. My goal in life is to hear the Father tell me, "Well done, good and faithful servant." My goal is to have God's assurance that I did everything I was supposed to do. This same goal has to be a part of the consciousness of the next generation. When handled appropriately, the ceiling of the current leaders will become the floor for the next generation, and they, in turn, will be able to deliver a valuable inheritance to the generation that comes after them.

Fathering Spiritual Sons and Daughters

As we pursue the things of the Lord, it is essential for us to include our children. At Bethel, we don't consider our children to be the church of tomorrow—we consider them to be the church of *today*. We believe there is no Junior Holy Spirit, and we include our children in all aspects of ministry. We even include them in our prophetic teams that minister to adult leaders from around the world. (In fact, one of our prophetic teams is comprised of eight-year-olds.) We entrust our children to pray for the sick, and we have

seen many healings and miracles. We give them present-tense responsibilities, yet we also allow them to remain children and play
on the playground and do the stuff that they do. We value what
they carry now *and* value what they are becoming—a strategy that
can be used in raising up spiritual children as well.

This is how Jesus worked with His disciples. He gave them responsibility ahead of time, before they deserved it. At times, He
even changed their names to what they *were going to be*, not what
they were. He often spoke to His disciples as though they were
something they were not.

That being said, many of us in the older generation do a poor
job of handing off responsibility to those we are leading because
we are fearful and want to control them. In the early stages of
training, it is usually necessary to provide more instruction and
control, but as we hand off responsibility to emerging leaders, we
need to learn to release that control and increase their influence.
They need to begin to live out their gifts and callings and pursue
what God has put in their hearts.

At the same time, many younger leaders have difficulty receiving input and oversight from older leaders, because they have
never fully dealt with the father-son issues in their hearts. When
these leaders come into a place of authority, they find it hard to be
counseled or challenged by another person. They may be good
leaders who are celebrated and loved, but they will never achieve
their potential until they learn to receive guidance and instruction
from others. In order for leaders to step into spiritual fatherhood,
they must first learn to become spiritual sons. Sometimes, receiving counsel and correction from a spiritual father can be an un-
comfortable and even painful experience, but a true son or
daughter will welcome the input and treasure the growth it brings.

Entrusting Leadership

Throughout the years, I have had the privilege of being a spiritual
father to hundreds of sons and daughters. I consider this to be one
of my most fulfilling roles.

One of my most beloved spiritual sons is Banning Liebscher, the co-author of this book. I have walked with Banning for many years, and I have seen him grow from being a youth pastor at Bethel Church to the Director of Jesus Culture, touching hundreds of thousands of people around the world every year. It is such a joy to be a part of this intergenerational partnership that is having an impact on the world in such a powerful way.

In another branch of our ministry, I recently passed the senior leadership position of Bethel Church to my son Eric. This is an exciting time of transition that has provided new opportunities of growth and ministry for Eric while allowing me to focus on new dimensions of ministry around our movement and around the world. As I pass the baton to Eric, I know that a healthy transition will depend on my ability to shift my focus and my personal responsibilities and give him the opportunity to step fully into his new role. At the same time, it is important for me to remember that I'm not dying. I am still here, and I'm still committed to building our movement, of which the local church is a central part.

During this amazing transition, Eric and I are running together in a true intergenerational partnership. We meet together on a regular basis to talk in depth about the direction of the church. I want to continue giving input, at least for a season, and bring whatever support I can bring. Because of my history and my ongoing role, I can bring the kind of perspective that someone in a different position may not see. I am excited to walk out this process with Eric as he fulfills his destiny and as we continue to work together to bring revival to our region and the rest of the world.

God's will is revival—sustained revival. He is at work in each of us to increase our sense of personal revival, and He is at work in the Church to increase our experience and expression of revival in the earth. The key to sustaining revival is to build a culture that honors and welcomes the presence of God, honors and celebrates every believer, and honors emerging leaders as they grow into their God-given destinies. As we cultivate and carry this *revival culture* forward, we will see God's kingdom come and His will be done on earth as it is in heaven.

15

The New Wineskin: Revival Culture

Throughout this book we have looked at revival culture from many different angles. In section one we focused on the history of revival and the promise of a new great awakening. In section two we looked at some of the hindrances to revival, the challenges of the coming harvest, and the five primary components of culture on earth so we can create a bridge to the culture of the kingdom of God. In section three, with the participation of Bill Johnson and Banning Liebscher, we examined the power of intergenerational ministry and how we can use it to sustain revival in coming generations. In this final chapter, I will present some additional strategies and final thoughts on how we can build a culture of revival that will exist into the future.

The New Reformation

I believe the Church of Jesus Christ has entered into a New Reformation. Dozens of leaders—including Peter Wagner, Alan Hirsch, George Barna and many others—have spoken about this shift. While I do not necessarily agree with everything some leaders in the movement are presenting, I do agree with the idea that we are in a season of massive upheaval in which the Holy Spirit is preparing God's people for a new great awakening. One priority of the New Reformation is the cultivation of a culture of revival that will propel the Church into the coming harvest.

Five hundred years ago, what became known as the Protestant Reformation rocked the religious world. When Martin Luther presented his Ninety-Five Theses, he ushered in a revolution that has never really stopped. Over the course of the next four centuries, three truths in particular became the cornerstone of evangelicalism: (1) the exclusive importance of Scripture, (2) salvation through faith alone, and (3) the priesthood of every believer. The Reformation was powerful and impacting, but ultimately it was imperfect and incomplete. In fact, those who led this reformation were imperfect as well, and as a result many points of disagreement and division followed.

Perhaps the biggest shortfall of this amazing reformation was the fact that the rediscovery of the priesthood of the believer never went far enough. Although Luther and others rediscovered this powerful truth, they never implemented the changes or cultivated the culture to make it possible for believers to step into their true priesthood.

Let me explain what I mean. After the time of the Early Church, the Catholic and Orthodox movements had evolved over the centuries into religious and ritualistic structures with strict hierarchies. There was a pope, archbishops, bishops and priests. The average believer had no access to the Bible and no personal access to God except through the mediation of these priests. This created a clergy-laity divide that became abusive and oppressive, and it also allowed for many man-made doctrines and policies to be put in place that profited the Church at the expense of the believer.

When the Reformation restored the understanding that every believer is a priest of God, it struck at the roots of man-made religion. Unfortunately, the day after this revelation was restored, the pews still faced the stage, the organist still led the hymns, the pastor still preached the sermon, and the church attendees still sat as spectators. In other words, the vast majority of born-again believers who had been saved by faith and filled with the Holy Spirit remained undeveloped and underutilized for God's purposes. Sadly, this essential truth of "priesthood" never fully affected the way we *did* church. Our doctrine changed, but our practices remained the same.

Thankfully, during the last generation, a change has begun that is empowering believers to recognize who they are in Christ, who Christ is in them, and how they can step into the unique gifts and calling God has prepared for them. Yet while this understanding of personal significance in Christ has started to grow, most would acknowledge that we have a long way to go.

From Pastoral to Apostolic

One of the reasons the priesthood of the believer never caught on is because our churches have been led by pastors and not apostolic leaders. The primary impulse of pastoral leaders is to gather, connect and care. On the other hand, the impulse of apostolic leaders is to gather, train and send. Pastors cultivate community, provide resources and bring care and counsel to the flock. Apostles, on the other hand, see the mission, provide the motivation and equipping and empowerment to mobilize every member according to each person's design and destiny.

As the Church has developed over the centuries, it has become increasingly pastoral. The symbiotic desire of the pastors to lead and the flock to be fed has created an ecosystem of mutual maintenance in the Church that has been hard to break. This has forced those who have a greater sense of personal mission to step outside of the local church and join para-church ministries to fulfill their callings. The problem with this response is that when motivated believers leave the Church for more exciting ministry opportunities, the Church becomes weaker still. This becomes a vicious cycle.

During the past 50 years, we have seen a shift in our understanding of apostolic ministry and the need for this important ministry to be restored to the Body of Christ. Although the gift of apostle never ceased, the use of the term began to decrease after the first century. Through a misguided honor for the original 12 disciples and a careless reading of Scripture, many theologians concluded the gift of apostle had passed away. But all it takes is a few minutes of unbiased study of Ephesians 4 to see that these five aspects of the ministry of Jesus are just as real and valuable today as they ever were.

The Five Ministries of Jesus

I believe God is in the process of restoring *every* gift and ministry of the Holy Spirit to us so we can cultivate and foster true revival culture. Unfortunately, in our desire to see these gifts restored, the charismatic community has made some huge mistakes. We have emphasized titles and positions above roles and functions. We have created full-page ads in Charismatic magazines and websites, proclaiming God's mighty apostles and prophets in a way that can seem self-serving and grandiose. Our preoccupation with what many have called the "five-fold" ministry gifts—apostles, prophets, evangelists, pastors and teachers (see Eph. 4:11)—has, at times, seemed more like a new pecking order or a new corporate ladder to climb rather than a sincere expression of the heart of God. Yet in spite of the misrepresentations that have occurred, I believe the restoration of these ministries is essential to the creation of true revival culture.

The Timing of the Gifts

In Ephesians 4, Paul begins by calling us to unity and humility and then encourages us to recognize the measure of grace that God has given to each of us. He goes on to state the unique time at which the five-fold ministry gifts were given: "When He ascended on high, He led captivity captive, and gave gifts to men" (v. 8). The five ministry gifts were not given on Pentecost with the outpouring of the Holy Spirit, but seven days earlier *when Jesus ascended to heaven.*

In addition, note that all of these gifts were given as a package. In other words, God gave apostolic and prophetic gifts at the same time as the gifts of evangelist, pastor and teacher. From this, we see that the particular gift of apostle was given *after* the 12 disciples were appointed, which removes the argument that only the

Twelve were worthy of being called apostles. In fact, with careful study, we find there are more than two-dozen different individuals listed as apostles in the New Testament, one of whom was a woman (see Rom. 16:7).

It is ironic that so many sincere believers deny the current gift of apostle and yet affirm the gift of pastor. The word "apostle" is mentioned more than 120 times in Scripture, while the word "pastor" is only mentioned in noun form *once*, except when it applies to Jesus as the Good Shepherd. The one and only time "pastor" is used in this way is in Ephesians 4:11. From this, we can see that bias and prejudice have influenced some believers' ability to interpret Scripture fairly.

The Purpose of the Gifts

The five ministry gifts, though different from each other, were given for the same purpose: "The equipping of the saints for the work of ministry, for the edifying of the body of Christ" (Eph. 4:12). It's important for us to understand that these ministry gifts actually represent the ministries of Jesus given to the Church. He is the Apostle and High Priest of our confession (see Heb. 3:1), the Great Prophet (see Luke 24:19), the first Evangelist (see Matt. 4:23), the Great Shepherd (see Heb. 13:20), and the Good Teacher (see Luke 18:18). His purpose is to manifest Himself fully in His Body, the Church, by distributing His ministries through gifted individuals whose job it is to do the specific aspect of ministry and impart that ability to others.

The Duration of the Gifts

Finally, note that these gifts were given "till we all come to the unity of the faith and the knowledge of the Son of God, to a perfect man, to the measure of the stature of the fullness of Christ" (Eph. 4:13). I do not believe there is a theologian alive who believes we have achieved all these results. Given this, we can only conclude that the gifts are *still relevant and essential today*. If teachers still exist, then so do prophets. If pastors still exist, then so do evangelists and apostles.

The most simple and objective reading of Ephesians 4:7-16 leaves us with no other choice than to accept each of these gifts as being valid today and recognizing that without them functioning fully and freely within the Body of Christ, we will never come into the fullness of Christ. The mistakes and errors some have made in pursuing gifts in the past do not excuse us from our responsibility to continue to pursue them into the future. We absolutely need apostles and prophets if we are going to meet the challenges of the coming harvest.

A Full-Spectrum Church Reflects a Full-Spectrum God

Here's another way to look at this set of gifts. Jesus is the white light of truth. When He ascended on high, He shined His light into the prism of the Church, and that light refracted into five distinct colors. These five colors blended with the other aspects of gifting and calling in people to create a full-spectrum expression of Jesus on the earth.

One of my favorite passages in Scripture is Hebrews 1:1-3. In these verses, the author articulates God's passion to be understood by His creation:

> God, who at various times and in various ways spoke in time past to the fathers by the prophets, has in these last days spoken to us by His Son, whom He has appointed heir of all things, through whom also He made the worlds; who being the brightness of His glory and the express image of His person, and upholding all things by the word of His power, when He had by Himself purged our sins, sat down at the right hand of the Majesty on high.

God desires to be known, and He longs to be understood. Throughout the ages He communicated through prophets, but ultimately had to appear in person to be fully known. Jesus is the God who made all things and holds all things together. He is also the perfect expression of the Father. But the purpose of God did not stop there. In order for God to be expressed clearly to every tongue, tribe, people and nation, it was necessary that Jesus return to heaven and the Holy Spirit to come and fill His people on earth.

The ultimate purpose of God was to place His presence and power in the Church not only so we would be blessed but also so we would become a blessing to every person in every nation (see Gen. 12:1-3). In God's quest to be known and understood, He has chosen to display Himself in us, but this treasure is "in earthen vessels, that the excellence of the power may be of God and not of us" (2 Cor. 4:7). The purpose of God is the presence of God in the people of God so He might be known in all the earth.

A number of years ago when Diane and I were ministering in Germany, our hosts took us to visit a castle in Bavaria called Neuschwanstein. This breathtaking building, with its turrets, spires and imposing walls, served as the model for the Disneyland Castle. During our tour, we visited the throne room, which was decorated with a mosaic consisting of a million stones. The floor of the mosaic depicted creation, the walls represented humanity, and the ceiling was patterned after heaven. As I looked, I noticed that each stone was chipped and broken, and none of them looked like anything by themselves. However, when they were placed together in all their diversity, they created an image of great beauty.

The same is true of the Church. We each are living stones who reflect Jesus in some small way, but when we are placed together in right relationship, we display Jesus in a glorious way. To do this, we need to be operating in each of the five gifts so we can impart the various aspects of Jesus' ministry to the whole Church. Historically, the Church has been strong in some of the gifts—especially pastoring and teaching—but weaker in the others. The gift of evangelism has been hit and miss. Today we have many great evangelists who serve throughout the Body of Christ, but most are in their own ministries and not based in a local church. In recent years, the gift of the prophetic, which in times past has been all but ignored, has been restored to the Church, and many believers are learning how to hear the voice of God, encounter His presence and minister in His power. It is time now for the restoration of the apostolic ministry in the Church.

Function and Impartation

As we seek to operate in the full spectrum of Jesus, we need to remember that it is not about tiles and position but about *function* and *impartation*. Many leaders today who seek to develop a "five-fold structure" miss this important point. If we are truly *functioning* in one of these ministries of Jesus, we will bear the fruit of that ministry in the lives of the people we touch. For instance, if we are operating in the gift of evangelism, we will draw others to Christ. If we are operating in the gift of teacher, we will help others grow in the Word. If we are operating in the gift of pastor, we will make others feel cared for and connected to the Body.

In addition, if we are truly functioning in one of these ministries, we will bear the fruit of *impartation*. If we are operating in the gift of evangelism, we will not only lead people to Christ but also impart our passion for winning souls. If we are operating in the gift of teaching, we will not only teach but also impart our love for the Word and our desire to teach others. If we are operating in the gift of pastor, we will not only care for the flock but also impart a love for community throughout the congregation.

It is my conviction that every believer is called to be a minister according to the gifts and calling of God. However, while every person is called to *operate* in these gifts, not everyone will be able to *impart* those gifts to others. That is a unique anointing reserved for those who are called to serve in one of the full-spectrum ministries. Consider the gift of prophecy as an example. All three of the lists of spiritual gifts in the Bible includes prophecy (see Rom. 12:6-8; 1 Cor. 12:7-11; Eph. 4:11), but in each case the context in which the gift operates is different. In Romans 12:6-8, the gift resides in the life of the believer and functions as an aspect of his or her personality and motivation. In 1 Corinthians 12:7-11, the gift is available to every believer as the Holy Spirit leads. Only in

Ephesians 4:11 do we find that each gift has been given to *equip others* to function in the same anointing as the person who has the gift.

The Quintessential Church

One could say that Jesus designed the Church to function in five dynamic dimensions at the same time. These five dimensions make up what I like to call "the Quintessential Church." The word "quintessential" comes from the ancient understanding of the five essentials *(quint)* of creation *(essences)*. In the pre-scientific world, there were four primary essences: earth, air, water and fire, while the fifth essence was a mysterious element that bound the other four together. The term has come to mean perfect, ultimate and complete, and I believe God intends for us to operate in this manner in the Church. Before can we do that, however, we need to understand more about each of these five specific dimensions of Jesus' ministry.

Gift of Apostle

An *apostolic* leader motivates, mobilizes and mentors believers for ministry, mission and multiplication. Apostles are builders who see the heavenly blueprint and are able to assemble the right people, processes and resources to accomplish a goal. They not only mobilize others but also impart the anointing and skills need to help other leaders mobilize people. Apostles keep people connected to God's mission.

Gift of Prophet

A prophetic leader experiences and expresses God's presence, power and perspective and imparts the same ability to others. Prophets are discerners who can see into the heart of God, the heart of people, and the heart of circumstances and declare God's purpose in every arena. Prophets impart a love for worship and prayer and encourage others to move in the gifts of the Spirit. Prophets keep people connected to God's presence.

Gift of Evangelism

Evangelistic leaders declare and demonstrate the gospel in word and deed to bring people to conviction, conversion and commitment to Christ. Evangelists are messengers and recruiters who challenge others to think in new ways and commit to new things. They impart their love for the lost, their boldness in the message, and their courage to take risks in demonstrating the gospel. Evangelists connect people to the unreached world.

Gift of Pastor

Pastoral leaders catalyze and cultivate a caring, Christ-centered community. Pastors are connectors who have a heart for people and for bringing them together for mutual support, encouragement and ministry. Pastors comfort the hurting, bind up the broken, and feed the flock. They impart to others a love for mutual ministry and relational and reconciliation skills to the Body of Christ. Pastors connect people to one another.

Gift of Teacher

Teachers communicate and convey truth that brings transformation. Teachers are trainers who are not content to merely present information—their goal is to not only be hearers of the word but doers as well (see Jas. 1:22). They function in discipling new believers, educating growing believers, and equipping future leaders, and they impart a passion for discipleship and transformation in others. Teachers connect people to the Word.

Apostolic Architecture

Although we could argue that each of these ministries is equally important, Scripture seems to favor two above the rest: apostles and prophets. In Ephesians 2:20, Paul speaks of the Church as a building that shelters "the household of God, having been built on the foundation of the apostles and prophets, Jesus Christ Himself being the chief cornerstone." He states that a building built according to this architecture becomes "a holy temple in the Lord . . . a dwelling place of God in the Spirit" (vv. 21-22).

Those who reject the current ministry of apostles and proph-ets will argue that this passage refers to the original 12 apostles and the Old Testament prophets. However, as we look a little further, it is clear that Paul is not referring to these individuals. In Ephesians 3:5, he goes on to talk about the revelation with which he was entrusted that "in other ages was not made known to the sons of men, as it has now been revealed by the Spirit to His holy apostles and prophets." Clearly, Paul is pointing to the apostles and prophets who were alive at the time when this passage was written (see Acts 15:32-33).

This begs the question as to why apostles and prophets are foundational and what their relationship is to one another in building the Church of Jesus Christ. Furthermore, if apostles and prophets are so important to the purposes of God, why are these two gifts the most neglected by the greater Body of Christ? Could it be that the enemy is aware of the power of these ministries and has infiltrated certain theological circles to build a case against them? Could this also be why the enemy has no problem with well-intentioned but misguided leaders who pursue and promote these ministries in an imbalanced way that undermines the proper understanding of these gifts? These are important questions to ponder.

There are many different definitions of apostles and prophets throughout the Body of Christ. I don't claim to have the perfect perspective on the matter, but I do have the unique vantage point of having known and served in a number of diverse apostolic ministries. My definitions thus combine what I have learned throughout the years.

As I see it, apostles are stewards of the vision and mission of God, while prophets are stewards of the presence and power of God. These two spheres overlap in such a way that while their stewardships are distinct, prophets also value vision and mission and apostles also value presence and power. An apostle is a "sent one who sends," and they are commissioned in the full authority of the sender with a heavenly vision of what they are assigned to build on earth.

Apostles are often seen as pioneers or spiritual entrepreneurs who refuse to build on someone else's foundation. However, in Scripture we find there are two different models of apostle. Paul was clearly a pioneer who started new ministries, but Peter was an overseeing apostle, and there is no record of him starting any church other than the one in Jerusalem. Regardless, in each case an apostle is an architect, or "master builder" (1 Cor. 3:10), of the house of God.

A prophet is God's confidant who speaks on His behalf and trains others to do the same. They promote intimacy with God through worship, dialogue with God in prayer, direction from God in prophecy, and demonstration of God through the supernatural. They serve the apostolic architecture by providing communication and power lines to heaven and the apostolic purpose by keeping people connected to the Chief Architect to continually build his house on earth as it is in heaven.

Apostles and prophets function a bit like the traditional model of the husband and wife. The apostle tends to be a "thinker" who is more strategic and goal-oriented, while the prophet tends to be a "feeler" who is more intuitive and discerning. Apostles are typically more intentional and proactive, while prophets are usually more spontaneously responsive. Apostles tend to be focused more on methods, while prophets focus more on motives. Apostles are generally more proficient in words of wisdom, while prophets tend to function most in words of knowledge.

In giving these definitions, I recognize no two prophets or apostles are alike. Today, we have prophetic apostles, evangelistic apostles, pastoral apostles and apostolic prophets (who are distinct from prophetic apostles). For this reason, my humble attempts to define the gifts should only be held loosely. There are too many dimensions of personal gifting, personality and passion to pigeonhole each other into strict definitions, and I believe we make a huge mistake when we create categories that are rigid and unyielding.

The Quintessential Wineskin

As I stated earlier, when Jesus spoke of wine and wineskins, He was talking about the relationship between substance and structure and function and form. The wine that we all desire is the presence of God that manifests as revival in the Church and awakening in the world. As we also stated earlier, culture is the vehicle that will carry revival where it needs to go. However, in order to have a healthy culture that will support revival, we need to have healthy biblical, functional and practical structures in the Church—what I refer to as the "Quintessential Wineskin" model.

Quintessential Vision and Mission

We begin to develop this healthy structure in our churches when we recognize the importance of the full spectrum of the ministry of Jesus and commit to expressing every dimension of Jesus on the earth. This means understanding the foundational role of apostolic and prophetic leaders without neglecting the value of evangelists, pastors and teachers. It means appreciating that while not everyone is called to one of these five roles, everyone can be equipped and empowered to do ministry in each of these areas. It also means recognizing that because each person is uniquely wired and designed, he or she will be oriented toward one or two of these dimensions above the others.

Once we have the vision in place, our mission is to transform the church into a "destiny incubator" that will enable people to discover their unique design, gift orientation and God-given passions and dreams. As we develop this incubator, we need to institute clear pathways for people to develop in their destinies and provide them with incremental opportunities to help them grow and serve in their gifts and callings. We also need to raise up coaches and mentors and spiritual mothers and fathers who will guide emerging leaders step by step as they develop the character, knowledge and skills to serve the Lord according to their unique design.

In order for all this to happen, we must restructure the Church according to the five dimensions of the ministry of Jesus. We must make the critical transition from being a Pastoral Church to an Apostolic Resource Center. Although pastoral community is essential to the quintessential model, it can never be the dominant purpose of the Church—the Church must shift to the priority of "apostolic mission" for God's purposes to be fulfilled. As others have stated, we must move from being a community with a mission to a missional community. Only when we have successfully made this transition will the Church be able to break the pressures of consumerism and complacency and become the quintessential expression of Jesus on earth.

Implementing the Vision and Mission

So, how do we implement this model and restructure our churches around the five ministries of Jesus? In my opinion, it is best to rearrange these gifts in their developmental order, beginning with the new birth and growing through the other gifts into spiritual parenthood.

Believe

With this approach, we begin by incorporating the *evangelistic vision* to proclaim and demonstrate the gospel with boldness, supernatural power and practical service to those in need. Our mission becomes reaching the lost and equipping believers to share their faith with friends, family and co-workers in every aspect of life. We identify those individuals who demonstrate an evangelistic calling and train them to grow in greater effectiveness in their gifts. We also establish powerful ministries to channel people and resources to reach the unreached and enfold them into the Church. As we put these structures in place, a spiritual awakening begins to take place among the unreached.

Belong

Next, we incorporate the *pastoral vision* so we can care for the new believers and cultivate an atmosphere of love, acceptance and blessing in our churches. Our mission becomes helping believers grow in relational values and skills, including authenticity, accountability and conflict resolution. We identify those individuals who demonstrate a pastoral calling and train them to care for others in practical and spiritual ways. We also establish small groups and community events to facilitate greater connection and community in the congregation.

Become

Once the pastoral vision is in place, we adopt a *teaching vision* to create training opportunities at a personal, classroom and congregational level. Our mission becomes helping believers grow in their value and knowledge of the Word in a way that brings transformation to their hearts, minds and lifestyles. We identify those individuals who demonstrate a gift in teaching and train them to disciple new believers. We also establish teaching and training ministries and groups to facilitate greater growth in this area in the congregation.

Be Filled

Next, we incorporate the *prophetic vision* to enable believers to experience God's presence and power at work in their lives. Our mission becomes helping believers grow in the supernatural by teaching them how to connect with God, hear His voice, experience His power, and minister to others on His behalf. We identify those individuals who demonstrate a prophetic calling and then help them grow in their gifts and ministry skills. We also establish various kinds of ministries such as worship teams, prayer meetings, healing rooms and prophetic teams. As we do this, we encourage believers to engage in powerful worship and passionate prayer and have deep personal encounters with the Holy Spirit.

Be Strong

Finally, we incorporate the *apostolic vision* in order to mobilize every member to fulfill the Great Commission by serving God and serving others. Our mission is to provide the spiritual fathering and mothering to help believers discover who they are in Christ and grow in their gifts and callings. We identify those individuals who demonstrate a value for the mission of Jesus and train them to motivate and mobilize others for ministry. We also establish various kinds of equipping opportunities to train and release people into their callings and multiply ministers in the congregation.

In Closing

You and I are privileged to live in the most pivotal time in human history. We are living in a season forecasted by spiritual fathers, predicted by prophets and longed for by angels. We are truly on the cusp of what will certainly be the greatest harvest of souls in all of history. Our challenge is to prepare ourselves for what God is about to do by reviewing our strengths and weaknesses in the past and positioning ourselves for greater fruitfulness in the task before us.

The most important step we can take in preparing for this awakening is to develop a thriving culture of revival that is aligned with God's Word and God's heart. This revival culture will come about as we live out the vision, values and priorities of the kingdom of God. It will serve as a bridge for those who don't know the Lord and provide salvation solutions to help those with unmet Kingdom longings cross over into God's family.

As we grow in our understanding of the cultures of this world, we discover there are demonic blinders and hindrances that the enemy has sown into human culture (see 2 Cor. 4:3-4). At the same time, we discover there are heavenly keyholes that God has placed in human culture that may be opened by the keys of the Kingdom. As we match the keys of revival culture to the keyholes of the cultures of this world, we will unlock the hearts of multitudes, and millions of seeking souls will come into the family of God.

Revival culture prepares us to reach the unreached. It enables us to enfold new believers, equips us to raise up whole-hearted disciples, and trains us how to impact leaders in every area of ministry. Revival culture allows us to walk in the supernatural power of God so we can fulfill Jesus' promise that we will do even greater works than He did on this earth (see John 14:12). The culture of revival creates a foundation for the kinds of programs and personnel, or ministries and ministers that will create the wineskin of tomorrow.

As Bill Johnson and Banning Liebscher presented so powerfully in their chapters, God desires to bring a revival that will be sustained throughout the generations, and the key to that sustained revival will be intergenerational ministry. As we become spiritual fathers and mothers who create an atmosphere in which spiritual sons and daughters can be raised, we will witness this sustained revival. As our spiritual sons and daughters carry the flames of revival forward and become the fathers and mothers of the next generation, we will inherit a world that is as filled with the glory of God as the waters cover the sea.

Endnotes

Chapter 1: The Heart of Revival
1. *Merriam Webster Dictionary*, s.v. "culture." http://www.merriam-webster.com/dictionary/culture.

Chapter 2: The Big One
1. Winkie Pratney, *Revival: Principles to Change the World* (Pensacola, FL: Christian Life Books, 2002), p. 101-102,105-106.
2. "BBC TWO Reveals the Nation's Top 100 Greatest Britons of All Time," BBC, August 21, 2002. http://www.bbc.co.uk/pressoffice/pressreleases/stories/2002/08_august/21/100_britons.shtml.
3. Winkie Pratney, *Revival: Principles to Change the World* (Pensacola, FL: Christian Life Books, 2002), pp. 101-102,105-106.
4. Robert Liardon, *God's Generals—The Revivalists* (New Kensington, PA: Whitaker House, 2008), pp. 315-317.
5. Christian Literature Society for China, The China Mission Year Book (Shanghai, China: Christian Literature Society for China, 1911), pp. 281-282.
6. Lauren Green, "Christianity in China," FOX News, January 20, 2011. http://www.foxnews.com/world/2011/01/20/christianity-china/.
7. Rick Joyner, *The Power to Change the World* (Fort Mill, SC: MorningStar Publications, Inc., 2006), p. 35-36).
8. Ibid., pp. 94, 101-104; Winkie Pratney, *Revival: Principles to Change the World* (Pensacola, FL: Christian Life Books, 2002), p. 135.
9. "Global Peoples Summary," The Joshua Project. http://www.joshuaproject.net/.
10. Tommy Welchel, Dr. J. Edward Morris and Cindy McCowan, *They Told Me Their Stories* (Mustang, OK: Dare2Dream Books, 2006), pp. 106,128.
11. Smith Wigglesworth, letter to Lester Sumerall of South Bend, Indiana, 1945. http://www.friends ofgod.org/Prophecy/smith_wigglesworth_vision.html.
12. Ken Walker, "Whose Billion Is It?" *Ministry Today,* January 1, 2008. http://ministrytoday mag.com/index.php/ministry-outreach/evangelism/16475-whose-billion-is-it.
13. Bob Jones, "Heavenly Visions and One Billion Youth," AGM Conference, Washington, DC, June 2007. http://www.youtube.com/watch?v=i27Ut51rmYY
14. Paul Cain, Florida, 1999. www.paulcain.org/sandbox/newsite/pages/Stadiumvision/stadiumvision.html
15. Stacey Campbell, "Changing Times, Changing Season," January 2, 2007. http://www.cx tremeprophetic.com/archivesitem.php?art=413andc=0andid=11andst

Chapter 3: The Sleeping Giant
1. Bill Hybels, quoted in "Willow Creek Repents?" *Christianity Today*, October 18, 2007. http://www.outofur.com/archives/2007/10/willow_creek_re.html.
2. *Merriam Webster Dictionary,* s.v. "complacency." http://www.merriam-webster.com/dictionary/complacency.
3. The Barna Group, "A New Generation Expresses Its Skepticism and Frustration with Christianity," The Barna Update, September 24, 2007. http://www.barna.org/barna-update/article/16-teensnext-gen/94-a-new-generation-expresses-its-skepticism-and-frustration-with-christianity. For a deeper look at how the upcoming generation sees Christianity,

check out David Kinnaman's and Gabe Lyons' book *Unchristian: What a New Generation Really Thinks About Christianity... and Why It Matters* (Grand Rapids, MI: Baker Books, 2007).

Chapter 4: Paradigm Shift

1. Don Richardson, *Eternity in Their Hearts* (Ventura, CA: Regal Books, 1981).
2. Don Richardson, *Peace Child* (Ventura, CA: Regal Books, 1974).
3. John Dawson, *Taking Our Cities for God* (Lake Mary, FL: Charisma House, 2001).

Chapter 5: The New Jesus Movement

1. Ray Bakke, *The Urban Christian* (Downers Grove, IL: InterVasity Press, 1987).
2. S. Kent Parks, "What Happened to People Group Thinking?" The Joshua Project. http://www.joshuaproject.net/people-group-thinking.php.
3. Erik Qualman, "Over 50 Percent of the World's Population Is Under 30—Social Media on the Rise," *Socialnomics*, April 13, 2010. Percentage based on 2010 data of 3,548,760,268 people aged 0–29 and a total population of 6,830,586,985.
4. The Barna Research Group, "Evangelism Is Most Effective Among Kids," *Barna Update*, October 11, 2004. http://www.barna.org/FlexPage.aspx?Page=BarnaUpdateandBarna UpdateID=172.
5. Ray Bakke, *A Theology as Big as the City* (Downers Grove, IL: InterVarsity Press, 1997) p. 12.
6. Ron Luce, "The African Invasion," Teen Mania, June 25, 2008. http://www.ron-luce.com/the-african-invasion/.
7. A.W. Tozer, *Worship and Entertainment* (Camp Hill, PA: Wing Spread Publishers, 1997).

Chapter 6: Revival Culture and Family

1. Tim Stafford, "Miracles in Mozambique: How Mama Heidi Reaches the Abandoned," *Christianity Today*, May 18, 2012. http://www.christianitytoday.com/ct/2012/may/mira cles-in-mozambique.html?order=&start=1.

Chapter 8: Revival Culture and the Economy

1. Anup Shah, "Today, Around 21,000 Children Died Around the World," *Global Issues*, September 24, 2011. http://www.globalissues.org/article/715/today-21000-children-died-around-the-world.
2. Dan Tapscott and Anthony D. Williams, *Wikinomics* (New York: Portfolio Trade, 2010).
3. To explore this topic more deeply, I recommend Ché Ahn's book *The Grace of Giving: Unleashing the Power of a Generous Heart*, which provides an in-depth study of the power of giving and invites the reader into a generous lifestyle.

Chapter 10: Revival Culture and Spirituality

1. Thomas Cahill, *The Gifts of the Jews: How a Tribe of Desert Nomads Changed the Way Everyone Thinks and Feels* (New York: Anchor Books, 1998).
2. "The Four Spiritual Laws," Campus Crusade for Christ. http://www.campuscrusade.com/fourlawseng.htm.

Chapter 12: Discipleship and the Coming Harvest

1. I read this concept from Ted Haggard's book *Dog Training, Fly Fishing, and Sharing Christ in the Twenty-first Century*. My heart was stirred by one chapter in particular, "Intentional Discipleship," where he says, "True teaching, true Bible study, true Christian training happens in the context of real life."
2. E. M. Bounds, *Power Through Prayer* (Chicago: Moody, 1980).

Chapter 13: Spiritual Sonship in Sustained Revival

1. Throughout this chapter I will refer to spiritual "sonship," but note that this term applies to both men and women in the faith.
2. E. M. Bounds, *Power Through Prayer* (Chicago: Moody, 1980).

Resources and Bibliography

Ahn, Ché. *The Grace of Giving: Unleashing the Power of a Generous Heart.* Ventura, CA: Regal, 2013.

Bakke, Ray. *A Theology as Big as the City.* Downers Grove, IL: InterVarsity Press, 1997.

———. *The Urban Christian.* Downers Grove, IL: InterVarsity Press, 1987.

Barna Group, The. "A New Generation Expresses Its Skepticism and Frustration with Christianity." *The Barna Update,* September 24, 2007. http://www.barna.org/barna-update/article/16-teensnext-gen/94-a-new-generation-expresses-its-skepticism-and-frustration-with-christianity.

———. "Evangelism Is Most Effective Among Kids." *The Barna Update,* October 11, 2004. http://www.barna.org/FlexPage.aspx?Page=BarnaUpdateandBarnaUpdateID=172.

Bounds, E. M. *Power Through Prayer.* Chicago: Moody, 1980.

Brafman, Ori and Rod. A. Beckstrom. *The StarFish and the Spider.* New York: Penguin, 2006.

Cahill, Thomas. *The Gifts of the Jews: How a Tribe of Desert Nomads Changed the Way Everyone Thinks and Feels.* New York: Anchor Books, 1998.

Cain, Paul. Florida, 1999. www.paulcain.org/sandbox/newsite/pages/Stadiumvision/stadiumvision.html.

Campbell, Stacy. "Changing Times, Changing Season," January 2, 2007. http://www.extremeprophetic.com/archivesitem.php?art=413andc=0andid=11andst.

Campus Crusade for Christ. "The Four Spiritual Laws." http://www.campuscrusade.com/fourlawseng.htm.

Christian Literature Society for China (1911). *The China Mission Year Book*. Shanghai, China: Christian Literature Society for China., 1911.

Conner, Bobby. "The Kingdom Company Is Coming," September 10, 2008. http://www.elijahlist.com/words/display_word/6835.

Dawson, John. *Taking Our Cities for God*. Lake Mary, FL: Charisma House, 2001.

Galloway, Glen. "Reaching Out Through Underground Music." www.theundergroundrailroad.org/ministryhandbook/outreachmethods/underground-music.

Gladwell, Malcolm. *The Tipping Point: How Little Things Can Make a Big Difference*. New York: Back Bay Books, 2002.

Green, Lauren. "Christianity in China," FOX News, January 20, 2011. http://www.foxnews.com/world/2011/01/20/christianity-china/.

Haggard, Ted. *Dog Training, Fly Fishing, and Sharing Christ in the Twenty-first Century: Empowering Your Church to Build Community Through Shared Interests*. Nashville, TN: Thomas Nelson, 2008.

Hybels, Bill. Quoted in "Willow Creek Repents?" *Christianity Today*, October 18, 2007. http://www.outofur.com/archives/2007/10/willow_creek_re.html.

Jesus Freaks. "Church in a Hamburg Hip Hop Night Club." http://www.theundergroundrailroad.org/ministryhandbook/typesofministry/church-in-night-club.

Jones, Bob. "Heavenly Visions and One Billion Youth." AGM Conference, Washington, DC, June 2007. http://www.youtube.com/watch?v=i27Ut51rmYY.

Joyner, Rick. *The Power to Change the World*. Fort Mill, SC: MorningStar Publications, Inc., 2006.

Kinnaman, David and Gabe Lyons. *Unchristian: What a New Generation Really Thinks About Christianity . . . and Why It Matters*. Grand Rapids, MI: Baker Books, 2007.

Liardon, Robert. *God's Generals—The Revivalists*. New Kensington, PA: Whitaker House, 2008.

Luce, Ron. "The African Invasion." *Teen Mania*, June 25, 2008. http://www.ron-luce.com/the-african-invasion/.

Parks, S. Kent. "What Happened to People Group Thinking?" *The Joshua Project*. http://www.joshuaproject.net/people-group-thinking.php.

Pratney, Winkies. *Revival: Principles to Change the World*. Pensacola, FL: Christian Life Books, 2002.

Qualman, Erik Qualman. "Over 50 Percent of the World's Population Is Under 30—Social Media on the Rise." *Socialnomics*, April 13, 2010.

Richardson, Don. *Eternity in Their Hearts*. Ventura, CA: Regal Books, 1981.

——— . *Peace Child*. Ventura, CA: Regal Books, 1974.

Stafford, Tim. "Miracles in Mozambique: How Mama Heidi Reaches the Abandoned." *Christianity Today*, May 18, 2012. http://www.christianitytoday.com/ct/2012/may/miracles-in-mozambique.html?order=&start=1.

Tapscott, Dan and Anthony D. Williams. *Wikinomics*. New York: Portfolio Trade, 2010.

Tozer, A. W. *Worship and Entertainment*. Camp Hill, PA: Wing Spread Publishers, 1997.

Walker, Ken. "Whose Billion Is It?" *Ministry Today*, January 1, 2008. http://ministrytodaymag.com/index.php/ministry-outreach/evangelism/16475-whose-billion-is-it.

Wagner, C. Peter. *Apostles and Prophets: The Foundation of the Church*. Ventura, CA: Regal Books, 2000.

——— . *Apostles Today: Biblical Government for Biblical Power*. Ventura, CA: Regal Books, 2007.

Welchel, Tommy, Dr. J. Edward Morris and Cindy McCowan. *They Told Me Their Stories*. Mustang, OK: Dare2Dream Books, 2006.

Wigglesworth, Smith. "Letter to Lester Sumerall of South Bend, Indiana," 1945. http://www.friendsofgod.org/Prophecy/smith_wigglesworth_vision.html.

Wright, Fred and Sharon. *The World's Greatest Revivals*. Shippensburg, PA: Destiny Image Publishers, Inc., 2007.

Contact Michael Brodeur at

revivalculturebook@gmail.com
www.michaelbrodeur.com
www.destinyfinder.com

Jesus Culture
5090 Caterpillar Road
Redding, CA 96003
(530) 351-7555

www.jesusculture.com